THE CINEMA OF LATIN AMERICA

First published in Great Britain in 2003 by
Wallflower Press
4th Floor, 26 Shacklewell Lane, London, E8 2EZ
www.wallflowerpress.co.uk

A catalogue for this book is available from the British Library

ISBN 1-903364-83-3 (paperback)
ISBN 1-903364-84-1 (hardback)

Printed in Great Britain by Antony Rowe, Chippenham, Wiltshire

THE CINEMA OF
LATIN AMERICA

EDITED BY

ALBERTO ELENA & MARINA DÍAZ LÓPEZ

WALLFLOWER PRESS LONDON & NEW YORK

24 FRAMES is a major new series focusing on national and regional cinemas from around the world. Rather than offering a 'best of' selection, the feature films and documentaries selected in each volume serve to highlight the specific elements of that territory's cinema, elucidating the historical and industrial context of production, the key genres and modes of representation, and foregrounding the work of the most important directors and their exemplary films. In taking an explicitly text-centred approach, the titles in this list offer 24 diverse entry-points into each national and regional cinema, and thus contribute to the appreciation of the rich traditions of global cinema.

Series Editors: Yoram Allon & Ian Haydn Smith

FORTHCOMING TITLES IN THE **24 FRAMES** SERIES:

THE CINEMA OF JAPAN & KOREA *edited by Justin Bowyer*
THE CINEMA OF THE LOW COUNTRIES *edited by Ernest Mathijs*
THE CINEMA OF ITALY *edited by Giorgio Bertellini*
THE CINEMA OF CENTRAL EUROPE *edited by Peter Hames*
THE CINEMA OF SCANDINAVIA *edited by Tytti Soila*

CONTENTS

INTERNATIONAL EDITORIAL BOARD

NOTES ON CONTRIBUTORS

JULIE AMIOT is a Professor at the Université Lumière-Lyon II. A specialist in Spanish Studies and Cinema Studies, she is completing her doctoral dissertation on Mexican and Cuban melodrama. She has been a research associate at the Escuela Internacional de Cine y Televisión in San Antonio de los Baños and at the Centro de Investigaciones y Enseñanzas Cinematográficas of the Universidad de Guadalajara.

JOSÉ CARLOS AVELLAR is a film critic with numerous articles published in newspapers, journals and collective works (including *Le cinéma brésilien*, *Framing Latin America* and *Cinema Novo and Beyond*). He is also the author of several books on Latin American cinemas, such as *O cinema dilacerado* (1987), *O chão da palavra: cinema e literatura no Brasil* (1992), *A ponte clandestina: teorias de cinema na América Latina* (1996), *Deus e o diabo na terra do sol: a linha reta e o melaço de cana* (1997) and *Glauber Rocha* (2002). He was the Cultural Manager of Embrafilme (1995–97) and Director of the distribution company Riofilme (1994–2000). He is currently a member of the Editorial Board of the journal *Cinemais*.

RICARDO BEDOYA has been working as a film critic and as an university professor since 1973. He was a member of the Editorial Board of the journal *Hablemos de cine* and has published his articles in many Peruvian newspapers and magazines. Among his publications are the books *Cien años de cine en el Perú: una historia crítica* (1992; revised edition, 1995), *Entre fauces y colmillos: las películas de Francisco Lombardi* (1997) and *Un cine reencontrado: Diccionario ilustrado de las películas peruanas* (1998).

VICENTE J. BENET teaches History of Film at the Universidad Jaume I in Castellón de la Plana. He is also Managing Editor of *Archivos de la Filmoteca*.

IVANA BENTES is a film researcher and critic in visual arts, currently an Associate Professor of Audiovisual Language, History and Theory at the School of Communication and associate researcher at PACC (Advanced Programme of Contemporary Culture) of the Universidade

Federal de Rio de Janeiro. She is the author of the book *Joaquim Pedro de Andrade: a revolução intimista* (1996) and the editor of *Cartas ao mundo: Glauber Rocha* (1997). She is also the co-editor of the journal *Cinemais.*

NANCY BERTHIER is a Professor at the Department of Spanish Studies at the Université de Paris-IV (Sorbonne). A specialist in Hispanic cinemas, she is also the author of a number of books and articles about different aspects of contemporary Spanish and Cuban cinema, mainly related to the relationship between history and cinema, including *Le Franquisme et son image: cinéma et propagande* (1998).

MARINA DÍAZ LÓPEZ holds a PhD in History of Film and currently works at the Film Department of the Instituto Cervantes in Madrid. She is the Managing Editor of *Secuencias: Revista de Historia del Cine* and has published a number of papers on Latin American and Spanish cinema, and co-edited *Tierra en trance: el cine latinoamericano en cien películas* (1999).

MARVIN D'LUGO is author of two books on Spanish cinema – *The Films of Carlos Saura: The Practice of Seeing* (1991) and *Guide to the Cinema in Spain* (1997). He has also authored more than a hundred articles and reviews on Spanish and Latin American film topics including essays on contemporary Cuban, Argentine and Mexican film-makers.

ALBERTO ELENA teaches History of Film at the Universidad Autónoma de Madrid and is the Editor of *Secuencias: Revista de Historia del Cine.* He has extensively published on cinemas from the South and his publications include *El cine del Tercer Mundo: diccionario de realizadores* (1993), *Los cines periféricos (Africa, Oriente Medio, India)* (1999) and monographs on *Satyajit Ray* (1998) and *Abbas Kiarostami* (2002).

CLAUDIO ESPAÑA is a Professor both at the Universidad de Buenos Aires and at the Universidad del Cine, Buenos Aires. He has also worked as a film critic for different media and is the author and editor of numerous books on Argentine and Latin American cinema, including *Medio siglo de cine: Argentina Sono Films* (1984), *Luis César Amadori* (1993), *Cine argentino en democracia, 1983–1993* (1994) and *Cine argentino: industria y clasicismo, 1933–1956* (2000).

CARMEN ELISA GÓMEZ is an Associate Professor at the Universidad of Guadalajara. She is the author of the books *María Félix en imágenes* (2001) and *¿Verdad o ilusión? El cine fantástico y los géneros* (2002). She was awarded a Fullbright-García Robles scholarship to study her Masters and is currently preparing her doctorate at Ohio State University.

JUAN CARLOS IBÁÑEZ teaches at the Universidad Complutense in Madrid. A specialist in Luis Buñuel's work, he has published many articles about his relationship with Spanish culture and society in the 1930s.

CLARA KRIGER teaches at the Universidad de Buenos Aires, where she is also a researcher at the Institute of Scenic Arts and coordinator of the Tutorial Area of the Study Abroad Programme (COPA). She has contributed to a number of books, including *Cine argentino en democracia* (1994), *Cien años de cine* (1996), *Cine latinoamericano: diccionario de realizadores* (1997), *Nuestras actrices* (1998) and *Tierra en trance: el cine latinoamericano en cien películas* (1999).

CÉSAR MARANGHELLO has taught Argentine cinema at the Universidad de Buenos Aires and at the Instituto Nacional de Cine y Artes Audiovisuales (INCAA). He is the author of books such as *Hugo del Carril* (1993), *El cine argentino y su aporte a la identidad nacional* (1998) and *Artistas Argentinos Asociados: la epopeya trunca* (2002) and a contributor to *Historia del cine argentino* (1992), *Historia de los primeros años del cine en la Argentina, 1895–1910* (1996), *Fanny Navarro* (1997), *Cine argentino: industria y clasicismo, 1933–1956* (2000) and *El Grupo de los Cinco y sus contemporáneos* (2001).

ANA MARTÍN MORÁN teaches History of Film at the Universidad Antonio de Nebrija in Madrid. She is the editor of *El cine de los noventa: materiales para una historia* (2002) and is currently working on her PhD thesis on métissage in European cinemas.

MARIANO MESTMAN is a Lecturer of New Latin American Cinema and teaches Communication Theory at the Universidad de Buenos Aires. He is co-author of the book *Del Di Tella a Tucumán Arde: Vanguardia artística y política en el 68 argentino* (2000) and the author of a number of articles on political cinema in various jounals such as *New Cinemas* and *Cinemais*.

MARÍA LUISA ORTEGA is a researcher at the Institute of Educational Sciences of the Universidad Autónoma de Madrid, where she also heads the Audiovisual Resources Centre. An Associate Editor of *Secuencias. Revista de Historia del Cine*, she teaches and writes on scientific images, documentary cinema and visual representations in the social sciences.

DAVID OUBIÑA is a Professor both at the Universidad de Buenos Aires and at the Universidad del Cine, Buenos Aires, and has been a research fellow at New York University and the University of London. He is the author, among many other publications, of the books *El cine de Leonardo Favio* (1993) and *Filmología* (2000) and the editor of *El guión cinematográfico* (1997) and *El cine de Hugo Santiago* (2002).

MANUEL PALACIO is a Professor at the Universidad Carlos III and the Universidad Complutense, both in Madrid. A specialist in avant-garde cinema and in reception studies, he is the author, among other publications, of *Práctica fílmica y vanguardia artítica en España/The Avant-Garde Film in Spain* (1982) and several contributions to the *Antología crítica del cine español* (1997) and the editor of volumes V, VI and XII of the *Historia general del cine* (1995–98).

DIANA PALADINO is a Professor at the Universidad de Buenos Aires and the Universidad de Belgrano, Buenos Aires, as well as a researcher at the Institute of Scenic Arts (UBA). She is the author of *Itinerarios de celuloide* (2001) and has contributed to numerous collective works such as *Cine argentino en democracia, 1983–1993* (1994), *Los sueños de la memoria* (1995), *Cien años de cine* (1996), *Cine latinoamericano: diccionario de realizadores* (1997), *Tierra en trance: el cine latioamericano en cien películas* (1999) and *Encyclopedia of Contemporary Latin American and Caribbean Cultures* (2000).

JORGE RUFFINELLI teaches at the Department of Spanish and Portuguese of Stanford University. A specialist in Latin American literature, he is the editor of *Nuevo Texto Crítico* and has published thirteen books and more than five hundred articles, critical notes and reviews in journals throughout the world. During the 1990s his critical work has increasingly centered on Latin American cinema: his most recent book is *Patricio Guzmán* (2001) and he is currently completing an *Encyclopedia of Latin American Cinema.*

HELIODORO SAN MIGUEL holds a PhD in Philosophy and History of Science and currently teaches at the New School University in New York City. He has also studied cinema in the Graduate Film and TV Department at New York University and is one a contributor to *Tierra en trance: el cine latinoamericano en cien películas* (1999).

JULIA TUÑÓN is a researcher at the National Institute of Anthropology and History of the Universidad Nacional Autónoma de México, and has focused her work on the history of cinema and the history of women in Mexico. Her recent books are *Mujeres de luz y sombra en el cine mexicano: la construcción de una imagen, 1939–1952* (1998), *Mujeres en México: Recordando una historia* (1998; English edition, *Women in Mexico: A Past Unveiled*, 1999) and *Los rostros de un mito: Personajes femeninos en las películas de Emilio 'Indio' Fernández* (2000).

EDUARDO DE LA VEGA ALFARO is a Professor at the Centro de Investigaciones y Enseñanzas Cinematográficas of the Universidad de Guadalajara, Mexico. He is the author of twelve monographs on film-makers and actors, including *Del muro a la pantalla: S. M. Eisenstein y el arte pictórico mexicano* (1997) which was awarded the Luis Cardoza y Aragón National Prize of Art Critique, as well as of numerous articles and esssays.

JOÃO LUIZ VIEIRA teaches Film Language and Theory at the Film and Video Department of Universidade Federal Fluminense in Niterói, Rio de Janeiro, and holds a PhD in Cinema Studies from New York University. He has lectured extensively on Brazilian Cinema and taught in the US, England and Venezuela. His latest books include *Cinema Novo and Beyond* (1998) and *Câmera-Faca: o Cinema de Sérgio Bianchi* (2002).

BREIXO VIEJO obtained his Masters degree in Media Studies at the New School for Social Research, New York. He is the author of *Jim Jarmusch y el sueño de los justos* (2002) as well as numerous articles, and lectures on film history and aesthetics.

PREFACE

I remember it as if it were yesterday. The film begins. A dizzying sound of drumbeats invades the movie theatre. Pulsating bodies take the screen. Dozens, hundreds of people, mostly blacks and *mestizos*, are dancing. Everything is movement and ecstasy. All of a sudden, gunshots ring out. A man lies on the ground – a lifeless body. Surrounding him, the deafening music and the rhythm continue. The beat is frenzied. The camera travels from face to face in the crowd, until it stops at a young black woman. The frame freezes on her trance-lit face.

Thus begins *Memorias del subdesarrollo* (*Memories of Underdevelopment*) by Cuban director Tomás Gutiérrez Alea, and watching it was like a shock to me. The film navigated between different states – fiction and documentary, past and present, Africa and Europe. The dialectic narrative took the form of a collage, crafted with an uncommon conceptual and cinematographic rigour. Scenes from newsreels, historical fragments and magazine headlines mixed and collided. In *Memorias del subdesarrollo*, Alea proved that filmic precision and radical experimentation could go hand in hand. Nothing was random. Each image echoing in the following image, the whole greater than the sum of its parts.

Until then, having spent part of my childhood in Europe, I had a better knowledge of Italian Neorealism and the French New Wave than I did of the cinematic currents in Latin America. I admired Rossellini and Visconti and the early films of Godard and Truffaut – and with good reason. On taking the camera to the streets and showing the faces and lives of ordinary people, the neorealists and the directors of the *nouvelle vague* had fomented a true ethical and aesthetic revolution in films. But *Memorias del subdesarrollo* carried with it something more. A point of view that was vigorous, original and, more importantly, pertained directly to us, Latin Americans. It was like a reverse angle – one that seemed more resonant to me than that which was prevalent in other latitudes.

On returning to Brazil, while still an adolescent, I had the privilege of watching *Deus e o Diabo na Terra do Sol* (*Black God, White Devil*) by Glauber Rocha, together with a Brazilian psychoanalyst named Hélio Pelegrino. When the film was over, we sat there, ecstatic, overwhelmed by an emotion that is difficult to describe. Hélio turned to me and said: 'This film hits the heart of Brazilian-ity.'

And so it did. It was a dazzling experience. And the same thing happened when I discovered *Vidas secas* (*Barren Lives*) by Nelson Pereira dos Santos and *São Paulo S.A.*

by Luis Sergio Person – an extraordinary and sometimes overlooked film of the Brazilian Cinema Novo. Then came the revelation of *Limite*, the first and only film by 21-year-old director Mário Peixoto. This was a film of transcendent poetry and boundless imagination. Once again, I found myself in a state of shock, not only because of the film itself, which was made in 1931 and forgotten for many years, but also for the evidence it bore, that of our creative diversity.

I could speak of other Latin American films that caused a similar impact over the years, the same sensation of unveiling, but the list would probably be too long to fit in this short preface.

The most important thing is that this feeling remains alive. I was stunned to discover *Amores perros* (*Love's a Bitch*) by Alejandro González Iñárritu. Later came *Mundo grúa* (*Crane World*) by Pablo Trapero, another revelation, as well as *Bolivia* by Adrian Caetano and *La Ciénaga* (*The Swamp*) by Lucrecia Martel. In Brazil, the same could be said of the work of first-time directors Karim Ainouz and Laís Bodansky.

These films have renewed my faith in the narrative possibilities of the cinema made here in our continent. Yet, at the same time, they are in dialogue with a film past that was our own, with the roots of Latin American cinema. They are as harsh and essential in their form and content as the films made by the generations of the 1960s and 1970s. They are also different, since they portray another political and social moment.

Parenthetically, and paradoxically, I have never been able to view some of these films in Brazil. *Mundo grúa* and *Bolivia* have never been shown on the commercial circuit in my country. Today, young Latin American film-makers meet each other mainly at festivals. The bottleneck of distribution is a reality.

It is in this context that this book, *The Cinema of Latin America*, gains its full dimension. It allows not only for readers to discover films that deserve to be better known, but also allows us, who make films in the continent, to get to know each other better. And to ask ourselves the inevitable question: what is Latin American cinema today?

I believe that there is not just one Latin American cinema, just as there is no single Brazilian cinema. There are *cinemas*; made of sometimes contradictory currents that often collide, yet come together in a desire to portray our realities in an urgent and visceral manner. We make films that are, like the melting-pot that characterises our cultures, impure, imperfect and plural. It is this diversity that pulsates throughout this book, as it does through the bodies in the opening of *Memorias del subdesarrollo*.

Cinema is, first and foremost, the projection of a cultural identity which comes to life on the screen. It mirrors, or should mirror, this identity. But that is not all. It should also 'dream' it. Or make it flesh and blood, with all its contradictions. Unlike Europe, we are societies in which the question of identity has not yet crystallised. It is perhaps for this reason that we have such a need for cinema, so that we can see ourselves in the many conflicting mirrors that reflect us.

Walter Salles
October 2003

INTRODUCTION

> We cannot lie, we haven't learnt to do it. Being caught in our first lies, we provide a thousand explanations. As if we suddenly lost our faith in our reasons. Ignoring that, even when it is due to honesty or with honesty that we persist in choosing the ways of didactism, of behaviourism, of the lack of searching and experimenting spirit in drama crossroads, nevertheless it won't stop us from seeing, like Nazarín, how our just and honest intentions become terrible works. With this limitation of the horizons of poetic imagination, with such mistrust of the audiences, either *Memories of Underdevelopment* or *Black God, White Devil* would never have been even dreamt of. Yes, these are hard times. This is the confederacy of dunces. But underneath there's a non-stop struggle. A struggle for justice, for freedom, for life.
>
> – Orlando Rojas (1992)

This is certainly not the first anthology on Latin American cinema for readers, movie-goers and specialists. However, the task of offering a synthesis of its development, providing not only relevant information but also some necessary keys for its interpretation, is far from already accomplished. The atomisation of cinema studies in different Latin American countries, and therefore the lack of a truly continental span in most of them, is clearly what produces this phenomenon. But the remarkable advance of film historiography in Latin America in the last two decades and the renewed importance and international diffusion of films in this context recommend an approach that combines a globalising will with a popularising aim. While recognising the important contributions from diverse fronts in recent years, Latin American cinema is still in need of a guide that allows us better access to its major works and semi-hidden treasures. While modest in its format, the present anthology aims to be precisely that introductory tool.

The main criterion which has guided the organisation of this work has been the representativeness of the films under study and this is why, together with attention to less-known movies, we have thought it necessary to revisit some of the classics. Inevitably, considering the format and limitation of space, some drastic decisions had to be made. To begin with, as a good part of Latin American silent cinema has disappeared, and what is left awaits proper dissemination and re-assessment, this anthology focuses on talkies, attempting to find a balance among periods, countries, trends, etc. Further, this book aims to be an indicative anthology and not a ranking according to any artistic excellence. In our opinion, all the films gathered in it are well worth it, but other titles could have been included, such as *Ahí está el detalle* (*That's the Point*, Juan Bustillo Oro, Mexico, 1940), *El romance del Aniceto y la Francisca* (*The Romance of Aniceto and Francisca*, Leonardo Favio, Argentina, 1964), *Macunaíma* (Joaquim Pedro de Andrade, Brasil, 1969) and *Chircales* (*Brickmakers*, Marta Rodríguez and Jorge Silva, Colombia, 1968–72), to mention a few almost at random. In the same way, the vigorous commercial production of some countries may seem under-represented, but an appropiate consideration of this rich universe would undoubtedly demand a separate study. Without pretending to be exhaustive, this work should be an accessible and fertile way of approaching the thrilling history of Latin American cinema.

As old as the invention itself – the first film shows in the area took place in Rio de Janeiro on 8 July 1896, to be repeated in many other capitals before the end of that year – Latin American cinema would come to produce many significant achievements in its early history. To the *bela época* of Brazilian cinema (mainly 1908–12) we should add the profusion of documentaries and newsreels filmed during the Mexican Revolution, as well as other isolated initiatives that allowed hopes to flourish for a viable film industry in Latin America. However, the great offensive launched by Hollywood in the international marketplace coinciding with the First World War took this region as one of its main targets and would finally corner the market, leaving few chances for the distribution of local productions. This spelled the end of the dreams of the pioneers who became mere outsiders, even though some of them, such as Humberto Mauro in Brazil or José Agustín Ferreyra in Argentina, would manage to generate praiseworthy work even in such adverse circumstances. Others, like Mário Peixoto, author of the mythical *Limite* (*Limit*, Brazil, 1931), with little access to production resources as authentic independent film-makers, would never manage to develop a continuous career.

The cataclysmic effect of the arrival of talkies all over the world was also strongly felt in Latin America. In contrast to the Lumières' *cinématographe*, the technology of sound film was fairly complex and required heavy investments for adapting theatres to the new format. The US, which had turned Latin America into one of their best and most profitable external markets, attempted all available strategies to keep it. The Spanish versions shot in Hollywood (or in France at the Paramount Studios in Joinville), the subtitles, and finally the dubbing, were only some of the aces they had up their sleeve. The most modest local industries could not face the technological and economic challenge of sound film with the same firmness and determination as Hollywood, so North American hegemony in Latin American screens hardly altered. The introduction of dialogues and music nevertheless gave a new impulse to the main centres of cinema production (Brazil, Argentina and Mexico), resulting in a proliferation of *chanchadas* or musical comedies of carnival-like inspiration, tango films and the very popular *comedias rancheras*, a genre exported from Mexico to countries such as Peru, Colombia and Venezuela.

This was the origin of that *industrial mirage*, which Paulo Paranaguá has talked about, and which, at least in the case of Mexico, favoured by the success of some of its productions across the continent and by Franklin D. Roosevelt's Good Neighbour Policy, gave hints of becoming a reality. As a matter of fact, the 1940s were the *época de oro* (Golden Age) of Mexican cinema, able not only to create a powerful star system (Cantinflas, Dolores del Río, Jorge Negrete, María Félix *et al.*), but also to achieve certain international credibility thanks to Emilio 'Indio' Fernández's work. Argentina and Brazil had their own stars (Luis Sandrini and Niní Marshall in the first case; Carmen Miranda and Oscarito, in the second), but – except for Miranda, the *Brazilian Bombshell* who would soon be attracted by Hollywood – none of them crossed their national borders with much success, and those cinemas did not at the time find a figure comparable to 'Indio' Fernández.

One way or another, the three great local cinema industries managed to bear the brunt of Hollywood, and still find the energy to try and compete with the huge factory of dreams. The experience of the Companhia Cinematográfica Vera Cruz in 1950s Brazil should be interpreted as an attempt to offer products industrially comparable to those of Hollywood, but its complete failure effectively killed-off such aspirations – only *O Cangaceiro* (Lima Barreto, Brazil, 1953) generated profits and was paradoxically distributed abroad by Colombia, who also distributed the films of the Mexican comedian, Cantinflas. Along with a popular-rooted cinema, which with little exception was virtually unexportable, some film-makers nevertheless attempted new modes of expression, confronting a stagnant tradition with little acceptance abroad. Besides 'Our Lord Buñuel', as Glauber Rocha expressively called him, only the Argentine Torre Nilsson managed to attract international attention in the 1950s, even though his highly personal style, with its refined European-like character, was considered a model impossible to follow in either his own country or anywhere else in Latin America. But certain realist and socially inspired traditions began to take shape which found themselves in tune with some of the most innovative aesthetic movements coming from overseas.

If the influence of John Grierson and the British documentary school could be strongly felt in film-makers such as Bolivian Jorge Ruiz or Venezuelan Margot Benacerraf – creators of milestones such as *¡Vuelve, Sebastiana!* (*Come Back, Sebastiana!*, Bolivia, 1953) and *Araya* (Bolivia, 1959), respectively – it was Italian Neorealism which made a deeper impact on many directors of the region. Some of them, like Fernando Birri, Paulo César Saraceni, Julio García Espinosa and Tomás Gutiérrez Alea (among others) had studied cinema in Italy and it did not take them long to show the imprint this training left on them. In 1955, *El Mégano*, a short movie with clear Neorealist inspiration made by García Espinosa and Gutiérrez Alea – and forbidden by Batista's dictatorship – already heralded the new winds blowing in Latin American cinema. The very same year, Nelson Pereira dos Santos would shake the calm waters of Brazilian cinema with *Rio, 40 graus* (*Rio, 40 Degrees*, 1955) which propelled realist discourse further than his mentor, Alex Viany, was able to do in works such as *Agulha no palheiro* (*Needle in a Haystack*), shot only two years earlier. And finally, Fernando Birri was about to lay the foundations of the famous Santa Fe School, among the welcoming walls of the Universidad del Litoral, in Santa Fe.

Regardless of how far these and other initiatives reached across Latin America, the seeds of change and renewal were ready to sprout. A new generation of film-makers – attentive to what was happening in Europe, but who disagreed with the easy-going ways of their own national industries – was taking shape within the film-club movement found in many Latin American countries, the first specialised cinema magazines, and even the framework of a number of universities, though as yet without the possibility of standing behind the camera to realise their intentions. Soon the *new cinemas* would ripen.

An opening to the most innovatory international film movements and social and political concerns would hence characterise the blooming of the new Latin American cinemas in the 1960s. But if the first explosion came a few years before with Italian Neorealism, which still continued to exercise an influence beyond its moment, the *nouvelle vague* and the new European cinemas would logically galvanise the spirits of young Latin American film-makers. And of course, we should not forget the teachings of *cinéma vérité* and North

American direct cinema which were especially fruitful for the renewal of an important documentary tradition. But, together with works such as *Integração racial* (*Racial Integration*, Paulo César Saraceni, Brazil, 1964) or *A opinião pública* (*The Public Opinion*, Arnaldo Jabor, Brazil, 1967), brilliant as well as faithful exponents of this new set of ideas, feature films began to be influenced by the new methods and structures of documentary film-making, producing such emblematic titles as *La primera carga al machete* (*The First Machete Charge*, Manuel Octavio Gómez, Cuba, 1969) or the exemplary *De cierta manera* (*One Way or Another*, Sara Gómez, Cuba, 1974).

These Brazilian and Cuban examples are not there by chance: beyond any doubt, those countries would be the greatest powers – though, of course, not the only ones – of the aesthetic renewal in Latin American cinema during the 1960s. The Cuban Revolution brought the immediate creation of the ICAIC (Cuban Institute of Cinema), founded in 1959 to rule the destiny of a national cinema whose production had hardly taken off before that, apart from numerous co-productions with Mexico, with Cuba being used both as a backdrop and for its tropical exoticism. The debt which the main film-makers of this founding period, Julio García Espinosa and Tomás Gutiérrez Alea, owed to Italian Neorealism would translate not only into a general influence, but also into an invitation for the great scriptwriter Cesare Zavattini to work with the former, and for the cinematographer Otello Martelli – director of photography of classics such as *Paisà* (Roberto Rossellini, Italy, 1946) – to take part in the first movie by the latter. But they were not the only famous film-makers that visited Cuba at that time: Joris Ivens, Chris Marker, Agnès Varda and Mikhail Kalatozov also wanted to add their contribution to the revolutionary effort, diversifying the influences that the rising Cuban cinema was going to receive.

In fact, the 1960s took a different direction and the Cuban cinema reached its expressive adulthood in the second half of the decade, with approaches that did not correspond with those of cinematographic realism. *Las aventuras de Juan Quinquín* (*The Adventures of Juan Quinquin*, Julio García Espinosa, 1967), *Memorias del subdesarrollo* (*Memories of Underdevelopment*, Tomás Gutiérrez Alea, 1968), *Lucía* (Humberto Solás, 1968) and even *Now!* (Santiago Álvarez, 1965) were attached to other aesthetic coordinates where experimentation took precedence over inherited values. The very same effervescence began to bear fruit in Brazil in the same period.

Though it might be impossible – and probably useless – to try and give the precise date of the beginning of *cinema novo*, nevertheless three films made in 1963 are its magnificent coming-out in society: *Vidas secas* (*Barren Lives*, Nelson Pereira dos Santos), *Os fuzis* (*The Guns*, Ruy Guerra) and *Deus e o diabo na terra do sol* (*Black God, White Devil*, Glauber Rocha). While the first went even deeper in the realist tradition that its director had already explored, *Os fuzis* was more openly political and modern in its language, and Rocha created one of the most radically experimental and ideologically engaged movies in the history of Latin American cinema. Of course, none of these were appropriate credentials with which to face the coup d'état in 1964, but even in such hard circumstances *cinema novo* continued to develop and renew itself in the following years. Resisting the military dictatorship, the success of the *pornocharadas* (erotic comedies) or the inrush of the *udigudi* (a local variation for underground), Pereira dos Santos, Rocha, Diegues, Saraceni or Hirszman produced major new works for some years, while evolving new strategies. *Macunaíma* would become one of the popular successes of the time, though failing to surpass the enormous takings of *Dona Flor e seus dois maridos* (*Dona Flor and Her Two Husbands*, Bruno Barreto, 1976), which became the biggest box-office draw in the history of Brazilian cinema and second only to Steven Spielberg's *Jaws* (1975).

Rehabilitated by Walter Salles and other young film-makers in the last few years, after an agonising period in the wilderness of Brazilian cinema during the 1980s, in its day *cinema novo* had a great impact on a continental scale. Rooted in the reality and history of the country – frequently through the adaptation of some literary classics – this movement would satisfactorily blend the breakaway aspirations – at a political as well as aesthetic level – of what was beginning to be known as New Latin American Cinema, which celebrated its first forum in the Viña del Mar Festival, in Chile, held in March 1967. Along with Brazil, a major role was played by Cuba, through ICAIC and its support for troubled projects like Patricio Guzmán's *La batalla de Chile* (*The Battle of Chile*, 1978), and the Havana Film Festival, founded in 1979; but many other countries added to the energy of renewal. Even Argentina and Mexico, the biggest and most conservative cinema industries of Latin America, witnessed the blooming of a new generation of engaged film-makers – beyond their peculiarities and differences – along with this new continental project: Favio, Solanas, Leduc, Cazals and Ripstein, together with their Cuban and Brazilian colleagues, would contribute to raise New Latin American Cinema to the first row at international forums.

One of the most distinguishing features of this New Latin American Cinema was the valuable contribution of national cinema which were underdeveloped or even non-existent until then. Before the coup d'état in 1973, Chilean cinema gained artistic merit through the work of Miguel Littín, Patricio Guzmán, Aldo Francia and Raúl Ruiz's first films. Meanwhile in Bolivia, Jorge Sanjinés and the Ukamau Group finally created a national cinema beyond the pioneering efforts of Jorge Ruiz. Peru, Colombia and Venezuela, all countries with no film tradition outside mimetic efforts to develop a commercial cinema similar to that of the main producers in Argentina and Mexico, stood out with film-makers such as Francisco J. Lombardi, Marta Rodríguez or Román Chalbaud. In all, Latin American cinema experienced a great transformation, yet these were not the best or most ideal political and economic circumstances.

Though the spirit of New Latin American Cinema is still alive in the memory and work of a number of Latin American film-makers, the historic fate of that movement was sealed in the 1980s. The foundation of the Havana Film Festival, and the creation of the Escuela Internacional de Cine y Televisión (International Film and Television School) in San Antonio de los Baños, vouch for the permanent Cuban concern to keep the flag of an innovative and creative cinema flying high, but not even Cuba would find in the situation the means to promote renewal on a contintal scale – in spite of the praiseworthy labour of Julio García Espinosa, who took charge of ICAIC in the 1980s, ending a period of stagnation and crisis. With the economic collapse of the 1990s, its younger and most promising film-makers (Juan Carlos Tabío, Orlando Rojas, Fernando Pérez) had serious difficulties in pursuing their careers in a normal fashion. The fragmentation of the efforts would therefore be the keynote of a generalised survival process, albeit one with no lack of happy and unexpected surprises.

Also, survivors by definition were numerous exiles from different Latin American countries: Chile, of course, but also Argentina, Brazil or Bolivia, not to mention cases like Haiti. Some of them would eventually go back to their countries, but others would settle more or less permanently in Europe (such as Raúl Ruiz, Patricio Guzmán or Raoul Peck) or North America (Marilú Mallet). Additionally, names such as Edgardo Cozarinsky, Hugo Santiago or Alejandro Agresti would also, for different reasons, develop the greatest part of their careers in Europe, while in the 1990s Hollywood would develop a growing fascination with film-makers such as Luis Puenzo, Héctor Babenco, Alfonso Cuarón and Guillermo del Toro. The thorough hegemony of American cinema on the screens of Latin America, which suffer from a severe crisis of local film industries, would find its concomitant in the redefinition of the likes and preferences of young film-makers, who, not by chance, are often engaged in the renewal of popular genres and traditions, usually despised by new cinemas.

Still, the Hollywood competition is not the crucial factor of the drastic transformations of Latin American cinema that have taken place in the last two decades. At the roots of the situation, fossilised film industries, in some cases fragile or virtually non-existent, have been severely affected by a vigorous television industry which has become the most important manufacturer of images across the whole continent with its soap-operas, or *culebrones*. Thus at the end of the 1980s and the beginning of the 1990s, the best of the cinematic harvest collected in Latin American countries would come through co-productions with European institutions: films like *La deuda interna* (*The Internal Debt*, Miguel Pereira, Argentina/Great Britain, 1987), *La nación clandestina* (*The Clandestine Nation*, Jorge Sanjinés, Bolivia/Spain, 1989), *Danzón* (María Novaro, Mexico/Spain, 1991) or *Fresa y chocolate* (*Strawberry and Chocolate*, Tomás Gutiérrez Alea and Juan Carlos Tabío, Cuba/Mexico/Spain, 1994), would benefit from the financial provisions of different European broadcasting companies (especially the support offered during those years by Spanish state television, before abruptly withdrawing from the game). More recently, and due to success with critics and audiences on an international stage – the Academy Award given to *La historia oficial* (*The Official Story*, Luis Puenzo, Argentina, 1984) or commercial blockbusters such as *Como agua para chocolate* (*Like Water for Chocolate*, Alfonso Arau, Mexico, 1991) or *Central do Brasil* (*Central Station*, Walter Salles Jr, Brazil/France, 1997) – producers have put their money on this renewed breath of Latin American cinema, and up to now the trend seems to be continuing, although with uneven results.

Apart from these features – or other significant developments of the last two decades (like the birth of the Central American and Antillian film industries, or the inexhaustible goldmine of excellent documentary production, now including the work of native communities in countries like Brazil, Bolivia or Colombia) – if there is something that characterises recent developments at the heart of Latin American cinema, it is increasing government involvement in its financing. Even if this could undoubtedly lead to greater control or censorship, the price to pay seems a lesser evil if compared to the evident benefits. In practice, legislative measures to encourage film production as implemented in Bolivia (December 1991), Venezuela (September 1993) or Argentina (September 1994) have contributed decisively to the relaunch of these different national film industries. Nevertheless, none of the cases is as expressive in this regard as the Brazilian film production, a true Phoenix capable of rising from its own ashes.

The severe crisis of the 1980s – a period marked by a general economic recession, a spectacular increase in costs of production and the competition of television – ended in

March 1990 with President Collor de Mello dismantling Embrafilme, a partially privatised company linked to the Ministry of Culture and in charge of film distribution, which had been the last stronghold for the castaways of *cinema novo*. In 1990 just one Brazilian film would reach Brazilian theatres, even after being shown on television: Carlos Diegues' *Dias melhores virão* (*Better Days Ahead*). Only the foundation of institutions such as RioFilme, dependent on the Department of Culture of Rio de Janeiro, would allow a slight revitalisation from its starting point in 1993. The Law on Audiovisual Arts, promulgated the following year, would do the rest with its battery of tax incentives. Thus in 1995 the perspective for Brazilian cinema was very different from the way Collor de Mello had left it. Besides *Central do Brasil*, a great success all over the world, various titles by the Barreto family, daring films such as *Terra estrangeira* (*Foreign Land*, 1995) or *Meia noite* (*Midnight*, 1998) by Salles and his collaborator Daniela Thomas, or the surprising *Baile perfumado* (*Perfumed Dance*, Lirio Ferreira and Paulo Caldas, 1997) all predicted a hopeful future for a film industry that had managed to be literally reborn.

Whether the Brazilian pattern is followed or not – and with what results – by other Latin American film industries, or if in the end multinational co-productions give them back the international presence they once had, which seemed definitely lost, this is something we can only guess at. But the facts are clear for everyone to see: veterans such as Arturo Ripstein or Carlos Diegues, younger film-makers like Alfonso Cuarón (*Y tu mamá tambien/And Your Mother Too*, 2001), Alejandro Agresti (*Valentín*, 2002) or Fernando Pérez (*Suite Habana/Havana Suite*, 2003), and even beginners such as Alejandro González Iñárritu (*Amores perros/Love's a Bitch*), Lucrecia Martel (*La Ciénaga/The Swamp*, 2001) or Fernando Meirelles and Katia Lund (*Cidade de Deus/City of God*) show up again with full honours at international film festivals. Latin American cinema is still alive, if only because of the stubborn memory of its film-makers.

'Will Latin American cinema still exist in the year 2000?' wondered sociologist Néstor García Canclini almost ten years ago in a well-known and often-quoted article. Today we know it still does, but such certainty does not invalidate some of his other intuitions. García Canclini, for instance, pointed out that a growing privatisation of audiovisual consumption was happening at the expense of those traditional forms of entertainment that involved collective uses of urban spaces. Continuous closures of film theatres were going to be 'balanced' with the growing number of television sets and domestic VCRs, modifying both the consumer's habits and the funding of audiovisual supplies. But these new forms of consumption, far from motivating a large diversification or enhancement of supply, have just reinforced (through television programming and video distributors) the absolute hegemony of Hollywood. It is true that more images have been consumed within the privacy of the home, but it is still unclear whether this increase has benefited Latin American cinema at all.

The severe crises of Latin America's strongest film industries (or their endemic inability to consolidate themselves as such), together with the invariable and extremely high dependence on foreign funding, have characterised the course of Latin American film production during the last decades. But the announced revolution of digital video presages, here as elsewhere, crucial changes. Although this is not the place to focus on the several problems that such a perspective implies, nor the thorny aesthetic questions that the new medium presents, there is no doubt that the response of Latin American film-makers to digital video has been enthusiastic. Figures such as Ripstein and Hermosillo have used it in some of their latest films – which, fortuitously or not, are among the most daring Latin American pictures of the last few years. 'Will Latin American cinema still exist in the year 2010?' we could ask now. Let's bet it will.

The other main question is related to the concept itself of *Latin American cinema*, a theoretical supposition that is not exempt from the problematic perspectives that characterise the several national cinemas that co-exist in this conflictive era of globalisation. Although the question is not new at all, its pertinence and rebellious nature have been strongly revived due to the important debate on nationalism raised in the 1980s through the writings of Benedict Anderson, Ernest Gellner, Eric Hobsbawn, and many others. Far from being considered resolved, over the following years the debate permeated several areas of the Latin American cultural realm (including film production and film studies), renewing with extraordinary dynamism the already traditional question on *national* and (even more problematic) *regional cinemas*. Space disallows the opportunity to rehearse this debate in detail, but we would like to emphasise, paraphrasing Pierre Sorlin, the necessity of understanding the concept of *national* (or *regional*) *cinema* as 'the chain of relations and exchanges which develop in relation with films, in a territory delineated by its economic and juridical policy', rather than as a determined corpus of films supposedly idiosyncratic of a certain *national* specificity. In this sense, *national* or *regional* cinemas, far from being understood as fossilised and immutable entities, imply a changing and multifaceted dimension, whose essentially ambiguous and problematic nature is defined and characterised (through processes of reception, appropriation and reorganisation) by the audiences' different 'configurations of experience'.

In the case of Latin American cinema, this notion of tension and conflict can be applied in a very eloquent way. Thus, some authors have had good reason to maintain that every pretension of constructing the concept of *national* or *regional* cinema in a coherent, homogeneous or standardised form tends to sustain an essentialist vision that usually clashes with the recognition of difference. Simply speaking of *Latin American cinema* cannot avoid the important, existing differences between the diverse film traditions of the continent – those traditions that have developed disproportionately throughout the first century of cinema, generated highly dissimilar 'configurations of experience' and canonised local film-makers in a very unequal way. Even today, on the threshold of the twenty-first century, the extraordinary atomisation of the different *national* cinemas in Latin America (as well as of its own traditions of criticism and historiography) is particularly outstanding, and it is this very quality that the present book wants to evoke as much as possible.

At the same time, in a unique and decisive experience, Latin American cinema harboured in the 1960s and 1970s the beautiful utopia of becoming, using Zuzana M. Pick's words, a 'continental project'. Although the passing of time has revealed that it was doomed to failure, no self-respecting history can forget this prolific attempt. For that particular 'configuration of experience', inextricably linked to what was called *Nuevo Cine Latinoamericano*, generated its own myths, its own pantheon of renowned film-makers, and its own political and aesthetic commitment. This is not a simple episode of the past, but rather a continental utopia that has been kept alive, even through the most difficult times, in the work of several Latin American film-makers; in this era of globalisation from which cinema cannot escape, they are painstakingly committed to cinematic creation that does not renounce the expression of its own cultural roots. The different means through which this challenge will be channeled are, of course, unpredictable. But the ultimate goal of the exercise of living memory offered by a volume like this, which can only constitute a historical review, is to make a modest contribution to a 'reconfiguration of experience' from which future essays in cinematic creation and critical re-evaluation will emerge in the Latin American world.

Finally some minor questions about the organisation and elaboration of this volume require certain comments. First of all, as it should be in any collective work, we have tried to lend the utmost respect to the different viewpoints, styles and opinions of the contributors, even when the price to pay may be a certain heterogeneity in the different articles (which in our opinion is not necessarily a drawback). Working in Europe, the USA and, of course, different countries of Latin America, the different contributors do not only give different, complementary or even opposite viewpoints, but also represent different critical and historiographic options. Our greatest debt as editors is the one we have to all these collaborators, whose contribution in most of the cases exceeds the mere writing of the texts. Without their enthusiasm this work would have never seen the light. But, along with them, it seems fair to mention the collaboration of other friends who at different moments have contributed with their generous effort to this collection: our gratitude to Tina Malaney, Paulo Antonio Paranaguá, María Pérez Martín, Giulia Pratesi and María del Carmen Vieites, as well as to the Museo del Cine Pablo C. Ducrós Hicken in Buenos Aires and the Centro de Investigaciones y Enseñanzas Cinematográficas in Guadalajara for kindly providing us with stills of the Argentine and Mexican films included in this volume. And lastly, of course, to Walter Salles for his lucid and beautiful preface and to all those Latin American film-makers – mentioned in this book or not – who have fought and still fight that wonderful and silent struggle which Orlando Rojas talks about, and with which we began...

Alberto Elena and Marina Díaz López

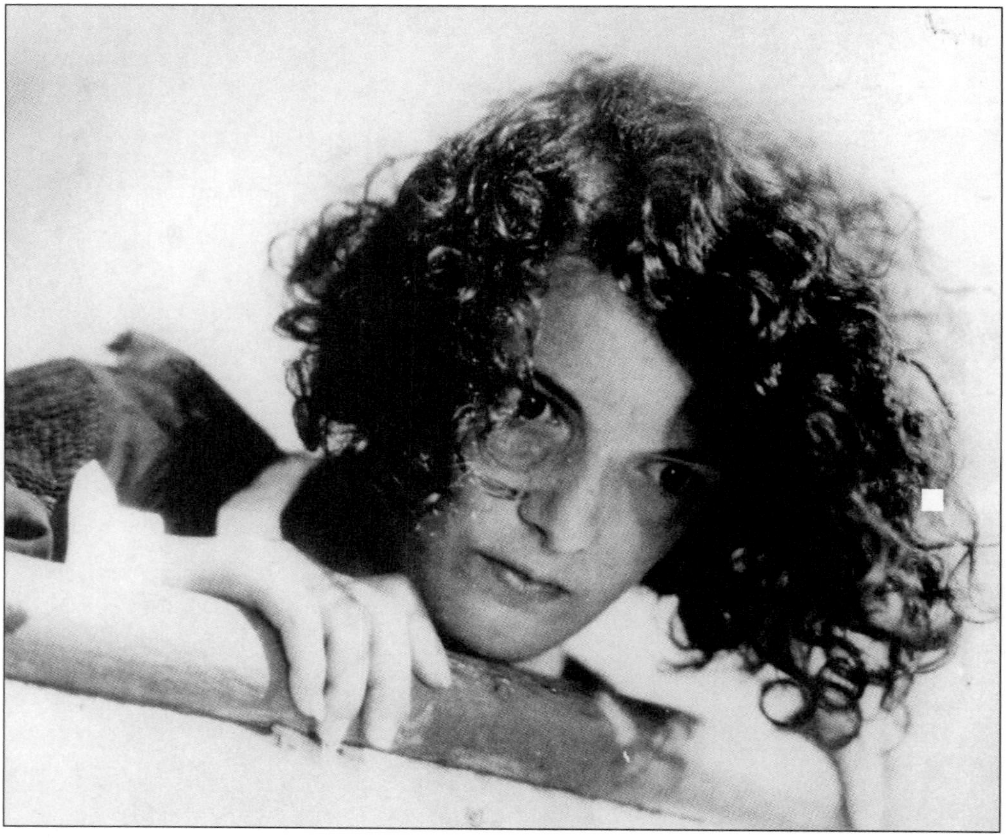

LIMITE LIMIT

01

MÁRIO PEIXOTO, BRAZIL, 1931

A woman looks at us. We see her face in close up, between cuffed hands. This is the first image. The second, the cuffed hands in close up. The third, a detail of the woman's eyes. The fourth, an expanse of sea, glittering beneath the fierce sunlight. Then once again, the eyes, staring directly at us. This is followed by a softer image: the face of the woman we saw in the first shot, now with her eyes closed. Then another woman, swaying gently on the edge of a boat, her back to the camera, looking out to sea. So begins the film: *Limite*.

Though, to be precise, an image is missing. There is another – the opening (and closing) image of the film: at the bottom of a blank, near-empty screen, vultures wheel about a cliff-top. There is also another image, which is integral to the film, yet does not appear within it. It is the image of a spectator, Saulo Pereira de Mello, who dedicated his life to the film; who preserved, studied and restored it, and who realised his dream as no other spectator ever has.

To see *Limite* today is to see the film through Saulo's eyes. Seventy years after the first screening and fifty after Saulo first saw it, it is impossible to separate the film from the myth that has grown up around it; to separate it from the spectator who never tired of repeating that 'no film is more beautiful, intense, poignant and powerful', and that the experience of seeing it is 'an unforgettable experience … an intense, transcendent pleasure because it is a work of art of enormous stature'.

Saulo's story begins in the early 1950s. A physics student with a vague interest in dating a literature student accepts an invitation from the would-be girlfriend to stay on campus and see a film due to be screened later that evening. Saulo remembers accepting the invitation more out of a desire to spend some time with the girl than because he wanted to watch a silent Brazilian movie. The prospective girlfriend remained exactly that but since that screening, Saulo – seduced by the images projected before him – spurned physics in order to dedicate himself to cinema. More specifically, silent cinema and the film that first aroused his passion for the medium. Not only did he see the film countless times, he kept the only existing nitrate copy at his home until he was able to make another negative. The restoration completed, he threw himself into studying the creative process behind the film.

Saulo has said that all his work on the film has been inspired by 'feelings experienced during its projection.' The session was one of those organised every year by Professor Plinio Sussekind Rocha at the National Faculty of Philosophy. One of the founders of the Chaplin Club, created in June 1928, the professor helped organise the first screening of *Limite*, in May 1931. It was never commercially exhibited and, after its premiere, was only shown on rare occasions. Saulo highlighted two of the most important screenings: January 1932, in the Eldorado Cinema, sponsored by *Bazar* magazine; July 1942, sponsored by Vinicius de Moraes – the then critic of Rio newspaper *A Manhã* – to show the film to Orson Welles, who was in Brazil making *It's All True*; and since then, once a year, every year, until 1959, at sessions laid on by Professor Rocha at the Salão Nobre at the National Faculty of Philosophy.

'Do you think there's a chance *Limite* might be lost? Is there anything you can do with this film?' This was asked in 1954 after a screening without the second reel, the nitrate print having deteriorated to the point where it could no longer be passed through a projector. Professor Rocha – at this time the sole guardian of the film – contacted Saulo and pleaded with him to help him save the film. The original negative had long since been lost and Edgar Brazil, the film's cinematographer, who had been responsible for preserving the only existing copy, had recently died. In 1959, when Professor Rocha tried, once more, to show the film at the National Faculty of Philosophy, it 'had to be projected without the first three sections: the chemical disintegration had begun'. After this, the film ceased to be shown and the battle to restore it began, a battle that would only be concluded twenty years later. The print was then kept at the National Faculty of Philosophy until 1966 when it was impounded by order of the Federal Police under the military dictatorship, together with *Mat* (*Mother*, 1926) by Vsevolod Pudovkin and Sergei Eisenstein's *Bronienosets Potemkin* (*The Battleship Potemkin*, 1926).

Released by the police, the film ended up in the hands of Saulo, who stepped up the fight against decomposition and hardly managed to raise funds for its restoration. At the end of the 1970s, a new negative was taken of the nitrate copy and the restoration was almost complete, 'but not quite, because it was not possible to save the section where the First Man helps the Second Woman, and so in the version in circulation today this section has been replaced by a caption'. Saulo then decided that in order to better understand the film, he should photograph 'the only nitrate copy still in existence, made under the supervision of Edgar Brazil'. He erected a special table in his apartment, with spools and a rough back-lit screen. He placed his camera in front of the table and photographed every scene of the film, frame by frame, taking many pictures of each scene to capture the internal movement of the image. This phase of the work took a little over three months and was later turned into a book: *Limite, filme de Mário Peixoto* (1979).

It was with one single image – the opening image of the film – of the face of a woman seen between cuffed hands, that the dream of *Limite* began. As Peixoto said in an interview recorded in 1983: 'The idea for *Limite* came about by chance. I was in Paris, having come over from England where I was studying, and I was passing by a newspaper stand when I saw a magazine with a photograph of a woman on the cover, with arms wrapped round her chest, handcuffed. A man's arms. And the magazine was called *Vu* [no. 74, 14 August 1929] … I carried on walking and I could not get this image out of my mind. And right after that, I saw this sea of fire and a woman clinging to the remnants of a sinking ship.'

The second image – the detail of the cuffed hands – grew out of the first; the third – the eyes – from the hands; the sea of flames, from out of the eyes; the eyes from out of the sea; the face of the woman with her eyes closed, from out of the wide open eyes; and the woman sitting on the edge of the boat, from out of the woman with her eyes closed. All these images are bound together in a series of fusions or visual links, that mirror how the idea for the film evolved in the mind of the director and how the film itself, as it emerges on the screen, must pass through the mind of the spectator. One image transforms into another through this extraordinary process of fusion. The eyes that emerge from the clinging hands sink into the sea of flames and return to the surface only to disappear and close in the face of the woman. Everything is designed to be seen, but seen by eyes that arise from between cuffed hands, and are consumed in a sea of flames. Everything, from the lines of composition to the texture of the image, reminds us that cinema does not open the eyes. On the contrary, it closes, narrows and limits them. Too little light – the murky darkness behind the face and the cuffed hands, focusing the eye on the foreground – and nothing else can be seen. Too much – the fierce sunlight sparkling on the waves – and the viewer is almost blinded and forced to close their eyes. A still shot, the focus is narrowed to one point: a section of measuring tape, cotton reel, scissors. An open shot and there is too much movement: the camera abandoning the woman on the rocks to career from one section of landscape to another, unable to settle on anything. The image conceals more than it reveals.

In a general sense, the cinema-goer regards the screen as a place without limits, because it expands in all directions. It is a dynamic space and one in immediate relation with what it finds beyond the limits of the frame; total objective vision. And the audience is used to experiencing this feeling, affirming that with photography and cinema we can see more and better. At the end of the 1920s, this feeling was acute. It seemed like a certainty. 'Photography is the possibility of seeing everyday facts, without any ambiguity,' said Laszlo Moholy-Nagy, defending the teaching of photography at the Bauhaus. 'In future', he claimed, 'illiteracy will mean not knowing how to take a photograph.' *Limite* exists at the epicentre of this juncture, as an immediate response to this moment, stating that in reality, cinema offers us a limited vision of the world. It causes us to see less, and less well. And this is its strength. Cinema, the film suggests, makes the visible invisible. It blurs and obscures. Everything in film begins with a cut, as if the cry 'Cut!' normally used to interrupt filming, here serves to begin the process; and the cry of 'Action!' to end it. The action belongs to the spectator.

It is true that at first, *Limite* appears to expand and not curb vision, because the camera moves with such freedom, constantly finding new angles and perspectives on things. One moment it is up on a lamppost watching a couple chatting on a street corner. The next moment it is on the ground, observing the same couple, with the lamppost transformed into a black cross silhouette, bisecting the strip of sky between man and woman. The camera clings to the heels of one character, then tilts to watch another moving to the end of the street. It strains to follow the gesture of a man lighting a cigarette or the way in which a woman turns the pages of a newspaper. It swoops from the ticket-office up to the bell of a railway station. It rises from the feet to the face of a man bending over to kiss the hand of a woman. It flies over the roofs of the city or over the sea. It races back to a trickle of water or the mouth of a man shouting at someone. It jumps from close-up to long shot, from the bright outdoors to a darkened room. And it is precisely these moments that cut, close, conceal and limit.

It 'limits' in the same way that Laszlo Moholy-Nagy's negatives of photos, his twisted perspectives of Berlin's streets and the fusions of his 'Multiple Portrait' limit. In the same way, the close-ups of leaves, flowers and cacti photographed by Albert Renger Patzsch, the face cut down the middle in Max Burchhardtz's 'Lotte eyes', and the way that the details of Man Ray's eyes and tears and his portraits of Luis Buñuel and Marcel Duchamp, limit. It can also be found in the dense shadows in Alexander Rodchenko's portraits of Esther Shub and Vladimir Maiakovski, or in Raoul Hausmann's studies of expressions. And the calm, still, ordered poses of the people photographed by August Sander, or the apparent disorderliness of Henri Cartier-Bresson's subjects, or the garden of the Eiffel Tower seen from above and Andre Kertesz's portrait of Eisenstein sitting on the ground, or even the blurred imprecision of Anton Stankowski's photographs of moving cars, all limit.

Peixoto claims that the idea for *Limite* came from a photograph he saw in Paris. But it could be argued that the film was inspired not by this one photograph, but by the whole of late 1920s European photography. Various schools were distancing themselves from what appeared to be the natural tendency of the photographic image: to record life as it is, to faithfully reproduce the world as it appears to be. Photography began to be conceived, let us say, not so much as a means of recording reality (life as we see it) but as a way of recording what goes on inside our heads (life as we dream it). With the film, Peixoto, like the photography of the time, 'tells a story that takes place within the mind'. In this sense, it is perhaps possible to argue that *Limite* is a cinematic adaptation of late 1920s European photography. Furthermore, it is perhaps possible to argue that even, in spite of its creator's conscious intentions, *Limite* is the fictional equivalent of Dziga Vertov's 1929 documentary, *Chelovek Kinoapparatom* (*Man With a Movie Camera*), in the way it does not so much record as interpret the world around it.

'*Limite* is not a narrative film', observed Saulo. The screenplay of *Limite*, he explained, was conceived 'as a collection of scenes. There was no plot or story to structure into a script. From the start, it was a series of shots or a series of visual poetic verses.' In the interview for the documentary *O Homem do morcego* (Rui Solberg, 1983), Peixoto explained that having glimpsed the image on the cover of *Vu* and having seen 'right after that' a sea of fire and a woman clinging to a fragment of a sinking ship, he wrote, almost automatically, the first draft of the script: 'at night, in a hotel, I scribbled down the opening scenes of the film, without knowing what I was doing. I did not arrange the scenes in any sort of chronological shooting order. I set them down and then sketched out some other scenes and, in the early hours, feeling sleepy, I stopped and put them away.'

But the screenplay itself was written in Brazil (probably, according to Saulo, in early 1930, three months after Peixoto's return, in October 1929), developed from the draft written in Paris ('written entirely in pencil, in one morning'). It is possible that Peixoto was encouraged to write this second script by his friends, Raul Schnoor and Brutus Pedreira. In a 1985 interview with Helena Salem, Peixoto explained how he had given Brutus 'some notes scribbled in Paris' to read, and how the latter had taken it upon himself to show them to Gonzaga, which resulted in his rewriting the whole script overnight. It is also likely that he had been driven to write by 'a kind of surge of enthusiasm' prompted by conversations about the favourable period through which Brazilian cinema was passing, inspired by a campaign being led at the time by the magazine *Cinearte*, the preparations for the foundation of the

Cinedia studios in Rio de Janeiro, and discussions of the films of Murnau and King Vidor in the newspaper *O Fan*, whose nine editions were published by the Chaplin Club between 1928 and 1930. It is possible that it was this 'surge of enthusiasm' that brought Peixoto to Europe, in June 1929, firstly to London, and then to Paris, to study cinema.

In 1937 Peixoto claimed that he had not intended to direct the film: 'I asked Adhemar Gonzaga to direct it. I have still got one of the original credits for the film where it reads, beneath the title: Direction – Luiz Gonzaga (as I thought he was called), so convinced was I that I needed to secure his services.' After reading the script, Gonzaga told Peixoto that 'that sort of thing could only work if directed by the author himself'. Peixoto claims that he stood there, transfixed, staring at Gonzaga. 'I, who had reserved for myself the pleasure of working as an actor on the film, suddenly elevated to this summit of responsibility!' Peixoto remembers Gonzaga encouraging him with a smile. 'That's what I'm telling you, Mário', and relates how it also occurred to him that Humberto Mauro could direct the film, 'my idea, as I remember, inspired by what I had seen of him in *Brasa dormida*. But by this time, a second film was already emerging from his camera [*Labios sem beijos*].'

In May 1930, in Mangaratiba, they started filming, with the crew billeted on a farm belonging to Mário's uncle, Victor Breves, the then mayor of the city. They used four cameras in the film, of which one was a very old hand-cranked model. All wooden props were made by Edgar Brazil. The shoot lasted until the end of January 1931, and took place in a friendly atmosphere. Mário, as well as directing, took a cameo role – the man in the cemetery; Edgar Brazil appeared as an extra – sleeping in the cinema with a toothpick in his mouth; Rui Costa, the assistant director, also played an extra – one of the laughing spectators in the cinema; and Brutus Pedreira, as well as playing one of the main characters – the cinema pianist – took charge of the soundtrack (which consisted of popular 78 gramophone records) and on several occasions was responsible for the synchronising of the projections.

Completed in early 1931, *Limite* failed to secure a commercial screening. And so it was that on Sunday 17 May, 1931, at 10:30 in the morning, *Limite* was shown at a private session for members and guests of the Chaplin Club. In the programme-cum-ticket, the introduction began with a resumé of what the spectators could expect to see: 'The meeting of three lives, destroyed by life in the confines of a ship lost at sea. Two women and a man, three destinies that life, having repeatedly limited their desires and options, brings together in the most limited space of all. Everything is limit.'

It goes on to say that the camera 'flees with the characters towards the natural world, it crosses seas and skies, it chases clouds, it flies with the birds, it runs with men possessed, it follows the swaying branches of trees that seem to be responding to the despairing call of nature'. Furthermore, 'even in the limitlessness of nature, everything is limit'. It claimed that the director had tried to make 'a film that was pure cinema, in which the images spoke for themselves, through their rhythm' and that 'everything in the film is rhythmic. That it is the rhythm in every situation which defines its "limitation"; that it is the rhythm that, throughout the film, determines the idea and limits the meaning of each event.' It concludes with the claim that 'It is rhythm which defines limitation; it is rhythm which defines *Limite*.'

The screening was 'something incredible', according to Mário Peixoto in his interview with Helena Salem. Numerous articles appeared in the press, but Saulo did not find any reference, in any of the published texts, to 'the success as far as the initiated were concerned' or the enthusiasm that the film was to inspire in him twenty years later: 'The state of perfection to which a humbly born and popular art managed to attain, caused only rejection.' The film would only be shown again one year later, at a private screening sponsored by the magazine *Bazar*, but the response was no better. Writing in *O Globo*, on 11 January 1932, Brazil Gerson said that he was certain that the majority of the people present at the screening 'did not like it and I know that if the general public had seen it, they would not have liked it either', because 'it was a film for obsessives, made from a wholly subjective position, to explore certain philosophical ideas – like, for example, the idea that we exist with limited freedom within a limitless universe, that, ultimately, there are limits even within this limitlessness'.

Ten years later, another special screening was organised by Vinicius de Moraes to show the film to Orson Welles. 'We do not know what Welles thought', observed Saulo, 'but the date is important: it marked the reuniting of Mário with Professor Plinio Sussekind Rocha. From that moment, *Limite* would be exhibited regularly at the National Faculty of Philosophy.' The date is also important because, from May to August 1942, Vinicius pursued an argument about this screening in his column in the newspaper *A Manhã*. In it, he spoke of the superiority of silent cinema – 'the art borne of the Image, an original medium of boundless poetry and art, the means of total expression in its transmissive power and its emotional capacity' – over sound cinema. It is still important because, intentionally or not, all this contributed to reinforce the myth of *Limite* as a misunderstood film, condemned to obscurity because it 'is a work of art for art's sake'. The myth, if essential in creating the conditions which would guarantee the preservation of the film, if calculated to emphasise the uniqueness of *Limite* in the context of Brazilian film-making, in no way contributed to the better understanding and enjoyment of the film. When, one year before the screening organised by the poet Vinicius, the novelist, José Lins de Rego, wrote that the whole thing appeared to be a 'lot of literary nonsense' or an 'unmentionable illness' (in the newspaper *O Globo*, 6 May 1941), he was reacting more to the myth than to the film, which he had not seen or shown any interest in seeing.

And, in the same way, it is to the myth that Glauber Rocha is reacting when he says in his *Revisão crítica do cinema brazileiro* (1963), 'Art for art's sake, pure cinema, films that are only beautiful in appearance, in the subjectivity of their bourgeois sentiments are not interesting.' Glauber, talking of the urgent need 'to salvage this Mona Lisa of our cinema', said that 'having read and heard everything about the film, I've never seen *Limite* and I do not know if it will ever be possible [to see it] … The Brazilian copy, which lots of people have seen, has been impounded by Saulo who is battling frantically against its decomposition.' Though he had not seen the film, he was familiar with reviews such as those he reproduced in his book that were attributed to Eric Pommer, Pudovkin, Eisenstein and Eduard Tisse. These had been written after a supposed screening in London, in 1931, and published in *The Tatler* and *The Sphere*. Two years after Glauber's book, the magazine *Arquitetura* (no. 38, August 1965) published a text attributed to Eisenstein but written, in fact, shortly before its publication, by Mário Peixoto (who may have been the author of the other passages previously mentioned).

As with the other three essays that Mário wrote on the cinema, 'this piece of writing expressed, in some way, Mário Peixoto's hope of making his second film, *A alma segundo salustre*', explained Saulo. 'Mário attributed the article to Eisenstein and invented various stories to justify the appearance – without the original – of the article.' There he defined *Limite* as a kind of movement frozen in the air, 'a great cry. It does not dare (or want) to anayse. It is what it is; and this is how it will remain.' He concluded by saying that 'in twenty years time, I am sure, it will have as much resonance, as many authentically cinematic elements as it does now; poetic and bitter at the same time – born with deep roots – traumatically thrust into adulthood, as if it had never known infancy'. This last phrase seems to express something of what was imposed on the film by the context in which it emerged, and what it imposed on itself as a condition of its existence.

Mário Peixoto died, without making another film, in February 1992, at the age of 84. Only one subsequent project was attempted, back in 1931, and this, *Onde a terra acaba*, remained uncompleted. The various other frustrated efforts which followed appear to have resulted, at least in part – albeit in very small part – from Peixoto's desire to remain cloistered within his own limitations.

Few films have succeeded in affecting a small group of spectators so profoundly and turned into a myth, created in accordance with the same laws imposed by the film; those of a film which contains something of the musician, with the anguished chords of a synthetic and pure cinematic language; something of the painter, with its luminous pain; a poetic transposition of despair and impossibility, the product of a trance attainable only in a state of solitude – according to what Peixoto tells us.

Every film – as Tomás Gutiérrez Alea argued in his *Dialéctica del espectador* (1982) – creates its own spectator, and addresses itself, primarily, to this privileged spectator, to whom, without neglecting the others, it pays particular attention in the hope of provoking a creative gesture that will feed it anew. In this respect, *Limite* is no different from other films that have attempted to find their own privileged spectator. But no other film has managed so successfully to create and define its own spectator, no other has provoked the sort of passionate response that led Saulo Pereira de Mello to insinuate himself into every frame of film and to remain there, invisible but eternally grafted onto the fabric of the film.

At the start of the film, when the eyes emerge from within the manacled hands to sink into the sea of flames, before returning to the surface and disappearing into the face of the woman, what we actually see in those eyes are the eyes of Saulo. He is there behind the staring eyes, attentive, making sure that we are watching the film as it was made and meant to be seen.

José Carlos Avellar

REFERENCES

Amâncio, T. (1998) *Estudos sobre 'Limite' de Mário Peixoto* [CD-Rom]. Niterói/Rio de Janeiro: Universidade Federal Fluminense/RioFilme.

Castro, E. (2001) *Jogos de armar: a vida do solitário Mário Peixoto, o cineasta de Limite*. Rio de Janeiro: Lacerda.

Melo, S.P. de (1996) *Limite*. Rio de Janeiro: Rocco.

_____ (ed.) (2000) *Mário Peixoto: escritos sobre cinema*. Rio de Janeiro: Aeroplano.

Peixoto, M. (1996) *Limite, scenario original*. Rio de Janeiro: Sette Letras.

_____ (2001) *Poemas de permeio com o mar*. Rio de Janeiro: Aeroplano.

Peixoto, M, & Melo, S.P. de (2001) *Outono, o jardim petrificado*. Rio de Janeiro: Aeroplano.

ALLÁ EN EL RANCHO GRANDE OVER THERE ON THE BIG RANCH

02

FERNANDO DE FUENTES, MEXICO, 1936

1931 was a key year in the history of Mexican cinema. The great Russian film-maker Sergei Eisenstein was traveling throughout the country, shooting scenes for his ultimately frustrated project, *¡Que viva México!* Toward the end of the year, shooting began on *Santa*, a feature-length film that came to embody the struggle to develop the first Mexican talkie. Elements of sound had been incorporated into several films produced in the preceding year, including *Dios y ley* (*God and Law*) by Guillermo 'Indio' Calles, *El águila y el nopal* (*The Eagle and the Pricky Pear*) by Miguel Contreras Torres, and *Más fuerte que el deber* (*Stronger Than Duty*) by Raphael J. Sevilla. While these films used occasional sound effects, *Santa*, directed by the Spaniard Antonio Moreno, was the first to be filmed with synchronised sound. The movie enjoyed considerable box-office success upon its March 1932 release. The second film version of Federico Gamboa's naturalistic novel (the first, shot in 1918, was of course silent), *Santa* provided the basis for the development of a Mexican national cinema. All attempts to establish a film industry in Mexico during the silent era had proved fruitless, in large part due to the constant and overwhelming invasion of movies coming out of France, Italy, Germany and the United States. In 1917, following a slowdown in the Mexican Revolution, several producers and financiers planned to build the foundations of film industry that would in time satisfy local demand as well as export to the world images of a modern Mexico, very different to the racial and derogatory views of the country and its people being produced by Hollywood. Such negative propaganda was the continuation of a series of confrontations between the two countries, which had calmed down in the nineteenth century and broke out again following the commencement of the Revolution.

The series of Spanish-language films emanating from Hollywood did have a considerable effect on the advent of sound in Mexican cinema. US movie moguls intended to maintain their clear dominance of the Spanish and Latin American markets. To this end, between 1929 and 1931 alone, the self-proclaimed Mecca of Cinema produced somewhere around 82 feature films and 67 shorts for the Spanish-speaking market. During the same period, Mexico City movie theatres exhibited 963 films made in the United States, amounting to 89 per cent of all the movies premiering there during those three years. Regardless of Hollywood's lead, in the early 1930s the panorama began a rapid change. Between 1932 and 1935, Mexican cinema surged ahead to transform itself into an industry capable of fulfilling the demands of the vast film market, represented by Latin America and parts of the United States inhabited, then as now, by growing nuclei of Spanish-speaking emigrants. Film production in Mexico gained further momentum when Hollywood realised that its 'Hispanic' movies were not as profitable as they had hoped. In 1932 the number of Hollywood movies shot in Spanish diminished greatly. That year saw five features made, with 11 in 1933, 14 in 1934, and 14 in 1935. Meanwhile, the same period saw the production of an average 22 features a year in Mexico.

In its desire to capture the Spanish-speaking market, the incipient Mexican sound cinema started to explore a variety of styles and themes. With the exception of a few successful films such as *Juárez y Maximiliano* (*Juárez and Maximiliano*), *Monja, casada, virgen y mártir* (*Married Nun, Martyr Virgin*), *Luponini de Chicago* (*Luponini of Chicago*), and *Chucho el Roto,* which captured the public imagination both in Mexico and abroad, the majority of the films of this era were commercial failures. Juan Orol, the father of Mexican melodrama, finally led the way to big box-office success with *Madre querida* (*Beloved Mother*, 1935), which not only reaped impressive financial rewards but also gave birth to the sub-genre of the 'exalted mother'. Soon savvy Mexican producers dedicated themselves to the exploration of the melodrama in all its forms. But in spite of their first artistic and cinematic successes, Mexico's primitive sound films were not capable in terms of either quantity or quality of creating a true movie industry. Competing not only with the 'Hispanic' films from Hollywood but also against film-makers in Argentina and Spain, who were by that time using commercial strategies similar to those employed by Mexican film producers, made capturing the market a formidable obstacle.

The situation caused pioneer historian José María Sánchez García to state that 1936 was 'the year of the great crisis', when it was feared the national cinema would disappear because of the lack of support of Spanish-speaking people, both in Mexico and abroad. Numerous production companies, once flourishing, had to abandon camp, and there stood only a few private, poorly-funded production houses who existed mainly on the hope that times would improve. Then came the movie that saved the industry from imminent ruin and proved that Mexico is capable of producing quality cinema. That movie was *Allá en el Rancho Grande*. Aside from some exaggerated claims (with the exception of the Compañía Nacional Productora de Películas, which between 1931 and 1936 had financed *Santa* and six other films, there still did not exist in Mexico 'flourishing' companies, nor could one speak yet of a national film industry), Sánchez García was right to single out the case of *Allá en el Rancho Grande*, a film based on the story *Cruz*, by writer Luz Guzmán Aguilera de Arellano, as being a turning point. Director Fernando de Fuentes started filming on 3 August 1936 in the Mexico Films studios and on location in the countryside around Rosario, near the town of Tlalnepantla.

The production of *Cruz* finally fell upon the shoulders of Antonio Díaz Lombardo, who had some previous experience with the medium. In 1935, with the American Paul H. Bush, Lombardo had financed *María Elena*, a tropical film directed by Raphael J. Sevilla. It is probable, then, that the real promoters of the idea to bring to the screen Guzmán Aguilera's story had been as much Díaz Lombardo as Guz Águila and that, at some point, the former had decided that Fernando de Fuentes would replace Sevilla as the director of the movie. It was a logical decision in view of the fact that de Fuentes, his career beginning shortly before the dawn of sound cinema, had gained fame as one of the best and most capable of Mexican film directors.

Born on 13 December 1894 in the port of Veracruz, the son of a bank employee, Fernando de Fuentes Carrau studied engineering for a time, before transferring to the humanities department at Tulane University, New Orleans. Returning to Mexico, he briefly held the position of assistant secretary to General Venustiano Carranza, leader of the 'constitutional' faction who, after overthrowing the reactionary government of Victoriano Huerta and quashing the popular army of Francisco Villa and Emiliano Zapata, installed a new political and social order in Mexico. In 1917, with his passion for the arts undiminished by his political activity, de Fuentes won a poetry contest run by the daily newspapers *Excélsior* and *El Universo*. Two years later, the newly-wed artist moved to Washington, D.C. to work in the Mexican Embassy.

Returning to Mexico City, de Fuentes lent his hand to political journalism before embarking on a career as a film exhibitor in 1925. He initially took charge of a chain of theatres known as Circuito Máximo before becoming responsible for the Cine Olimpia, one of the most technically impressive and important theatres of the era. As sound became increasingly popular, he initiated Spanish subtitling for movies shown in the Cine Olimpia. Thoroughly seduced by the moving images coming out of the United States, de Fuentes became one of their most ardent supporters. He was soon contacted by a Hollywood producer to collaborate in the production of 'Hispanic' films. His move there was ultimately canceled due to the decline in production for the Spanish-speaking market. Instead, de Fuentes took advantage of his good relations among the Mexican film community and was offered the position of assistant director on *Santa*. This experience led to collaborations on two other movies financed in 1932 by the Compañía Nacional Productora de Películas: *Águilas frente al sol* (*Eagles Facing the Sun*) directed by Antonio Moreno, and *Una vida por otra* (*A Life for Another*), by John H. Auer, a Hungarian who arrived in Mexico by way of Hollywood. In the first of these de Fuentes acted as editor, and in the second he held the title 'Dialogue Director'.

These posts were sufficient to land de Fuentes a 1932 contract with the Compañía Nacional Productora de Películas to direct *El anónimo* (*The Anonymous One*), a melodrama penned by him and based on a little-known French play. Thanks to newspaper coverage appearing after the film's premiere, *El anónimo* can be seen, despite its conventional theme, to have served to reveal the creative potential of its director. This potential was clearly demonstrated by the fact that of the 22 feature films produced in Mexico in 1933, de Fuentes directed four of them. More important than quantity was the quality of these movies, which profiled the director as a key figure of the new Mexican sound era. His *El prisionero trece* (*Prisoner Number Thirteen*), *La calandria* (*The Lark*), *El tigre de Yautepec* (*The Yautepec Tiger*) and *El compadre Mendoza* (*Godfather Mendoza*) were all exceptional works of the early sound period.

The films that followed only served to confirm de Fuentes' control over narrative cinema. *El fantasma del convento* (*The Convent Ghost*, 1934), *Cruz Diablo* (1934), *La familia Dressel* (*The Dressel Family,* 1935) and above all *¡Vámonos con Pancho Villa!* (*Let's Go with Pancho Villa!*, 1935), an excellent adaptation from the novel of the same name by Rafael F. Muñoz, are authentic classics in their respective genres. The same can be said of *Las mujeres mandan* (*Women Command*, 1936), a sharp satire against the provincial and conservative values of the time.

When he was chosen to direct *Allá en el Rancho Grande*, de Fuentes was approaching the pinnacle of his career. He would muster all of his facilities to maintain his lead at the vanguard of a cinema that still was struggling to focus on the formulas that would change the industry. Once signed on to direct his eleventh feature film in four years, de Fuentes began to think in terms of casting which would adequately meet his objectives. His by now well developed intuition for the cinema led him to acquire the services of Tito Guízar, a young singer who had lived for several years in the United States and who had become well known for singing Mexican folk songs on New York radio. Moreover, Guízar had some Hollywood film experience, having appeared briefly in *Bajo la luz de las pampas* (*Under the Pampas Moon*, 1935), a Fox film directed by James Tinling in which he sang just one song. Guízar also stared in a 'Hispanic' short titled *Milagroso Hollywood* (*Wonder Hollywoood*), directed by Allen Watt for Royal Films, owned by the Argentinian Raúl Gurruchaga. It was Guízar who suggested that the original title of de Fuentes' film be changed to *Allá en el Rancho Grande*, the name of one his career's most successful theme songs.

Along with Tito Guízar and the composer Lorenzo Barcelata, de Fuentes brought to his project Cuban actor René Cardona who also had experience in the 'Hispanic' cinema of Hollywood. Between 1929 and 1931 he had appeared in such films as *Sombras habaneras* (*Shadows of Havana*), *Del mismo barro* (*Out of the Same Clay*), *Cuando el amor ríe* (*When Love Laughs*), and *Carne de cabaret* (*Destined for Cabaret*). Young Esther Fernández only had experience as an extra and, in the film *El baúl macabro* (*Macabre Trunk*), second lead. The comic Carlos López 'Chaflán' had previously worked with de Fuentes in *El compadre Mendoza*, *Cruz Diablo*, *La familia Dressel*, *¡Vámonos con Pancho Villa!* and *Las mujeres mandan*. Emma Roldán, who counted among her roles the outstanding part of the deaf-mute servant in *El compadre Mendoza*, and Dolores Camarillo, who had also worked in the film version of Rafael F. Muñoz's novel, rounded out the cast. In the all-important role of cinematographer, the director chose Gabriel Figueroa who had made his debut as a still photographer and moved on to lighting and camera work in *¡Vámonos con Pancho Villa!*, *María Elena*, and a few other films. He had taken a Hollywood course from Gregg Toland, who would later gain fame for lensing Orson Welles' masterwork, *Citizen Kane* (1941).

Completed at start of September 1936, the film – whose cost was estimated at 100,000 pesos – was slated for its premiere in many of the Mexico City's 39 movie theatres. *Allá en el Rancho Grande* was not, however, an isolated phenomenon in 1936. Both prior to and following de Fuentes' film, two others were produced which celebrated Mexico's musical folklore, *Cielito lindo* (*My Sweetheart*), directed by Roberto O'Quigley and Roberto Gavaldón, and *¡Ora Ponciano!* (*Now Ponciano!*) by Gabriel Soria. Taking into account the existing socio-political environment in the country, one could surmise that the production of these three films was not a complete coincidence. Each forms part of the reaction, consciously or not, that some social sectors held toward the intense and controversial process of dividing up the land in the Agrarian Reform Act implemented this same year by the government of Lazaro Cárdenas del Rio. But before analysing the factors that came together to create the colossal and unexpected success of *Allá en el Rancho Grande*, it is helpful to look at an outline of the film itself.

Jalisco, Mexico. 1922. Little Felipe, only son of Don Rosendo, owner of the prosperous Rancho Grande estate, is growing up alongside the orphans José Francisco and Eulalia, living in care of their godparents, washwoman Ángela and lazy alcoholic Florentino. These last two characters, living in a common-law relationship, have had to take in little Cruz, who had been adopted by Marcelina, the deceased mother of José Francisco and Eulalia.

The action then moves forward to 1936. Don Rosendo is dead and Felipe has inherited the Rancho Grande, naming José Francisco his second-in-command. José Francisco competes with his friend Martín for the love of beautiful but asthmatic Cruz, who has been the object of exploitation and bad treatment at the hands of Ángela. Cruz secretly loves José Francisco, who together with Martín goes with Felipe to serenade his bride-to-be Margarita, who lives in a nearby town. Celebrating at a cockfight in the town square, José Francisco is hurt when struck by a bullet a rival cockfighter meant for Felipe. Thanks to the care given him by Cruz and a blood donation from Felipe, José Francisco makes a speedy recovery. With Eulalia's pledge to wed Nabor, majordomo of the Rancho Chico estate, Ángela offers Cruz's virginity to Felipe in return for the money needed to complete the wedding plans. Through trickery, Ángela lures Cruz to the hacienda. Left alone with Felipe, the girl suffers an attack of asthma and faints. Felipe lets her go when he learns she is the girlfriend of José Francisco, but the watchmen Emeterio and Gabino see them leaving together.

José Francisco returns triumphant from a horse race held at Rancho Chico, which has won him the money he needs to marry Cruz. During his celebrations, Emeterio and Gabino start some tongue wagging about the supposed relationship between Cruz and the boss. José Francisco hears the rumours from Martín, singing verses in the cantina. José Francisco goes in search of Cruz and when he cannot find her, sets out to kill Felipe. Felipe convinces José Francisco that nothing had occurred between him and Cruz. José Francisco, who was considering leaving the Rancho Grande, decides to stay on living there. Florentino forces Ángela to beg forgiveness from Cruz. All ends happily in a multiple wedding. José Francisco marries Cruz, as does Felipe and Margarita, Nabor and Eulalia, and Florentino and Ángela.

The story takes place in the state of Chihuahua, in a zone rich in ranch and hacienda folklore, justifying the use of songs and dances including 'El jarabe tapatío', interpreted by Emilio 'Indio' Fernández and Olga Falcón. A few of the novel's ideas were reversed or deleted, possibly to avoid the censorship of the era. The death of Marcelina, victim of a difficult birth, was transformed into the agony of a fatal disease; the intended rape of Cruz by Felipe, which the author describes with a wealth of details ('He began to kiss her eyes, her mouth, her throat, her chest, madly ripping off her blouse to expose a small breast'), was reduced in the movie to a few gyrations. While the novel ends tragically, with José Francisco and Cruz preferring to flee to avoid the gossip and Cruz dying on the mountainous cliffs, the film ends with the jubilant celebration of four simultaneous weddings. All the while the title music soars in the background, for the third and final time.

According to Jorge Ayala Blanco, de Fuentes' film 'is the free and humorous version of the theatre play by Joaquín Dicenta' and its evolution can at least be traced to 'the parodies of Spanish drama produced at the beginnings of the twentieth century'. Also perceptible in the film is another influence of the Spanish stage, 'a respect for the one-act comedies popular in Madrid and for light opera. Regarding the first, the "ranch comedy" incorporates a taste for the humorous situation, the trifling complication, for superficial heat, for the entangling webs that result from misunderstandings, for the arbitrary resolution of sentimental conflicts and a verbal wit ... With light opera, the ranch comedy shares three fundamental characteristics: the assurance of people jealous of their intimacy, the singers of popular songs who lend incentive, and the uplifting explosions of happy music.'

Another literary influence on de Fuentes' film is that of the *teatro mexicano de revista* of the 1920s. Derived from the *tonadilla*, which in turn has roots going back to the time of Spain's colonialism, this genre, mixing social satire with popular music, enjoyed great success among urban audiences with works like *El país de la metralla*, *México en cinta*, *La tierra de los volcanes*, *México lindo*, *Del rancho a la capital*, *La india bonita*, *Cielito lindo*, *Esta es mi tierra*, and others. Antonio Guzmán Aguilera, who had authored several generically similar works (*La huerta de Don Adolfo*, *Chaplin candidato*, *Elecciones presidenciales*) brought some of the characteristics of *Revisionist Theatre* to the script of *Allá en el Rancho Grande*, especially in the characters and dialogues given to Carlos López 'Chaflán' and Emma Roldán. The influence of this style can also be felt in the satirical stereotyping of foreigners, both Spanish (Hernán Vera, as a shopkeeper) and Gringo (Clifford Carr, who bets on cockfights).

De Fuentes' film also has narrative and aesthetic antecedents in silent films such as *El caporal* (*The Foreman*, Miguel Contreras Torres, 1921), *En la hacienda* (*At the Hacienda*, Ernesto Vollrath, 1921, from the novel by Carlos Federico Kegel), *La parcela* (*A Plot of Land*, Ernesto Vollrath, 1921, based on the novel by José López Portillo y Rojas) and *Del rancho a la capital* (*From Ranch to Town*, Eduardo Urriola, 1926) as well as the travel rushes shot by Eisenstein and his cameraman Eduard Tissé for *Maguey*, one of the six episodes that were going to make up the fascinating dramatic structure of *¡Que viva México!*

Finally, *Allá en el Rancho Grande* embodies thematic and folkloric elements that can be evidenced in several of the Hispanic films of Hollywood, such as *Allá en el Bajío* (*Over There on the Bajío*, Arcady Boytler, 1929), *Charros, gauchos, y manolas* (*Charros, Gauchos and*

Manolas, Xavier Cugat, 1930), and *Serenata mexicana* (*Mexican Serenade*, director unknown, 1930). The same is seen in the Mexican sound films that had started to experiment with the use of music and ambient sound, as well as the Spanish film *Nobleza baturra* (*Aragonese Nobility*, Florián Rey, 1935) with Imperio Argentina, which constituted a study of the rural customs of Aragon. *Nobleza baturra* updated two previous films, both of which enjoyed great success in their respective countries of origin, *Nobleza gaucha* (*Gaucho Nobility*, 1915), an Argentine film by Humberto Cairo, and the silent version of the film by Florián Rey, filmed in 1925 by Juan Vilá Vilamala. As for the rest, some pictorial influences on de Fuentes' film can also be traced back to travelogues and documentaries of customs cultivated in the nineteenth century by artists such as José María Velasco, Luis Coto, Eugenio Landesio and Ernesto Icaza, 'the cowboy painter of cowboys'. The influence also extended to the photography of Hugo Brehme, Luis Márquez and Roberto Turnbull.

With respect to its songs, *Allá en el Rancho Grande* draws from the musical folklore that could be found in the small towns of Jalisco, the area the *mariachi* tradition originated from, as well as an ample repertoire of *ranchera* and bucolic ballads; genres that enjoyed great popularity thanks to their success on radio and in record sales. They also generated a number of composers and singers, including Silvestre Vargas, Ignacio Fernández Esperón, Tata Nacho, Emilio D. Uranga, Silvano Ramos, Ernesto Cortázar, Agustín Ramírez, Jesús 'Chucho' Monge, Lucha Reyes, Alfonso Esparza Oteo, Mario Talavera, Jorge del Moral, and of course Lorenzo Barcelata and Tito Guízar. With its innovative use of folklore and popular music, de Fuentes' film presented the Mexican national identity in a positive light, whilst also reflecting positively on all of Latin America which, of course, resembled México in social composition and culture.

The principle merit of *Allá en el Rancho Grande* consists, then, in having synthesized all of its various cultural roots. The solid narrative, the professionalism, even the good taste of de Fuentes permitted that this amalgam of styles, although quite disparate, arrive at a point of equilibrium. The film never descends into the excesses often seen in the Mexican cinema of the era. The elements are constructed in such a way that the public is able to strongly identify with the characters and situations presented on the screen, always a key to popular success and a strong box-office. After its premiere in Mexico City, *Allá en el Rancho Grande* began its successful run in all but a few Latin American countries, in addition to Spain and the United States. At the end of December 1936, the picture had grossed 400,000 pesos, four times its initial cost. Upon its arrival in New York, the film attracted acclaim from some of the world's most prominent critics.

The reaction to the extraordinary commercial triumph of de Fuentes' film was unexpected. In 1937 Mexican cinema produced a record 38 feature films, in which more than half repeated the formula, in one way or another, of *Allá en el Rancho Grande*. The director himself took advantage of this trend to produce two more folkloric pictures that year: *Bajo el cielo de México* (*Under the Mexican Sky*) and *La Zandunga*, starring Lupe Vélez (fresh from her notable career in Hollywood). With so many films being produced, Mexico moved into the vanguard of Spanish-speaking cinema and consolidated its preeminence in the open market, thanks in large part to *Allá en el Rancho Grande*. In a process that appeared irreversible, the next year saw 58 films produced, marking the beginning of what would become, with minor setbacks, the most important cultural industry in Latin America. Although it would never overshadow Hollywood, the Mexican film industry continued to satisfy, at least in the 1940s and 1950s, a large part of the market's demand throughout Latin America and, to a lesser extent, in Europe and Asia.

The importance of *Allá en el Rancho Grande*, therefore, should not be underestimated. Arriving at a difficult time in the history of Mexican cinema, the film provided the impetus necessary to start up the national film industry. It was the first internationally acclaimed result of the Mexican mandate to construct a cinema that would project to the rest of the world an image of the country that was in large part authentic and which, at the same time, would strike a balance between the internal market and the overwhelming quantity of films arriving from Hollywood.

Eduardo de la Vega Alfaro

REFERENCES

Ayala Blanco, J. (1968) *La aventura del cine mexicano*. México: Era.

García Riera, E. (1984) *Fernando de Fuentes*. México: Cineteca Nacional.

____ (1998) *Breve historia del cine mexicano. Primer siglo, 1897–1997*. Guadalajara: Mapa/Conaculta/IMCINE/Canal 22.

Vega Alfaro, E. de la (1991) *La industria cinematográfica mexicana: perfil histórico-social*. Guadalajara: Universidad de Guadalajara.

Viñas, M. (1987) *Historia del cine mexicano*. México: Universidad Nacional Autónoma de México/UNESCO.

BESOS BRUJOS ENCHANTING KISSES

03

JOSÉ AGUSTÍN FERREYRA, ARGENTINA, 1937

The story starts *in medias res*. A successful singer, Marga Lucena, abandons her career to marry Alberto Pisano, heir of an aristocrat city family. In order to separate them, the young man's cousin deceives Marga by saying that she is expecting his baby. Believing her, Marga runs away to a distant province, taking a job as a singer in a theatre-bar of dubious reputation, in order to disappear from her lover's life. After her debut before an audience of lustful men, the greedy bar owner auctions a kiss from the singer without her consent. The winner is Don Sebastián, a solitary and crude landowner, enchanted by the young lady and her songs. Kissed against her will Marga suffers an outburst of hysteria: 'You want my kisses? My kisses! Have my kisses!' she yells through her tears whilst violently kissing the man. Obsessed by the Marga, Sebastián has her kidnapped and hides her in a cottage deep in a tropical forest, hoping to gain her love. When Alberto tries to enter the forest to rescue her, he is bitten by a snake and would have died had Sebastián not saved him. After some confusion between the lovers, the film ends with Marga and Alberto reunited.

The structure of the film can be divided into three parts; the love affair between Marga and Alberto, undermined by his cousin's deceit; Marga's life in the bar and her subsequent kidnapping by Sebastián; and finally Marga's attempted rescue by Alberto. The first part has all the trappings of a popular style of melodrama, defined by the inter-class love between Marga and Alberto. In the Argentinian cinema of the 1930s and 1940s, the structural difference between classes was not measured in terms of power (rich high-class opposed to poor low-class), but according to the social relationships and status that each class established. In this sense, the tango singer, no matter how successful or rich she was, was always considered part of a lower cast. In some cases the 'artists' were treated as prostitutes. In *Besos brujos*, the class difference is defined by Alberto's mother: 'It's time for you to leave that lady and return home, where people of your own rank are waiting for you with their arms wide open.' In a desperate attempt to appeal to class loyalty, she reproaches him, asking 'What would your father say about this!' This incarnation of the *pater* ruling in the mother was not new in José Agustín Ferreyra's films. It recalled his silent movie *Perdón, viejita* (*Forgive Me, Mother*,

1927), in which the mother punishes or forgives according to patriarchal rules and criteria. *Los muchachos de antes no usaban gomina* (*Boys in the Past Didn't Use Hair Gel,* Manuel Romero, 1937), *Gente bien* (*Beautiful People*, Manuel Romero, 1939), *Puerta cerrada* (*Closed Door*, Luis Saslavsky, 1939) and *Pobre mi madre querida* (*Poor My Beloved Mother*, Homero Manzi and Ralph Pappier, 1948) also followed this line to a certain extent.

A second melodramatic conflict takes place at the end of the first part, when Alberto's cousin lies to Marga: 'Soon I'll be his mother's baby … That's why I came to beg you to leave him. I know you are good and will do so.' Betrayed and heartbroken, the singer gives up the man she loves and disappears. However, instead of focusing on Alberto's despair and search for the women he loves (except for a few scenes), or on the pain that this resignation creates for Marga, the plot takes off in other, less expected, directions.

The second part of the story opens in a different setting of the theatre-bar, with the action beginning with the kiss auction and ending after the kidnapping. Though the film opens with close-ups of Marga in a distinguished city theatre, responding to the applause of her audience – who are never seen – there is the suggestion of respectability. The scene in the theatre-bar begins with a shot of the singer moving through tables occupied by less salubrious clientele. The desire on their faces is threatening. The kidnapping is proof of the presence of this danger.

The final part takes place in the tropical forest. In this landscape the centre of the conflict shifts from inter-class love affairs to one-sided love. Sebastián, similar to the troubled characters played by Terence Stamp (*The Collector*, William Wyler, 1966) and Antonio Banderas (*¡Átame!* [*Tie Me Up, Tie Me Down*], Pedro Almodóvar, 1986), patiently and respectfully waits to conquer the love of the lady he has kidnapped:

Marga: How long are you thinking of having me here?
Sebastián: Until you are convinced that I am a good man.
Marga: It's not by goodness that you can have a woman.
Sebastián: With what is it then?
Marga: With love! With love!

When Marga asks, 'But are you thinking of keeping me prisoner here?', Sebastián's reply is direct, 'Until you are tamed.' The allusion to Shakespeare's *The Taming of the Shrew* within the exotic environment of the tropical forest (exuberant vegetation, wild animals, tropical climate, up-country horizons) contrasts well with the erotic game between victim and abducter. The initial avoidance of eye contact, followed by brief glances and Sebastián spying Marga while she is bathing in the lake, later progresses to his carrying her in his arms up to the cottage, her body barely covered by a blanket.

A change takes place in this final part, when Alberto arrives. The love triangle of the beginning, Marga-Alberto-cousin, becomes Marga-Alberto-Sebastián. Both triangles feature a one-sided love interest. Even this relationship is unexpectedly unbalanced when, towards the end of the film, Marga feigns love for Sebastian in order to obtain the antidote for the snakebite, in the process breaking Alberto's heart. The resolution to this mistake comes when Alberto is fully healed and discovers through a tango sung by Marga that she had lied to save him: 'Lie, lie said my lips/kept in my heart the pure truth/I only did it fearing to lose you/fearing death and loneliness.' Realising his lover's sacrifice he decides to fight for her. Sebastián finally relents in one of the most unexpected and impulsive acts of repentance in the history of Argentinian Cinema.

Besos brujos is part of a popular and mythical Argentinian cinematic trilogy known as *opera tanguera* (tango opera) which combines melodrama and musical, employing the songs as a part of the plot. The idea was not original. The films made by the legendary Carlos Gardel for Paramount between 1931 and 1935 followed a similar pattern. It was a simple and successful low-budget formula, since the films were almost exclusively popularised by the use of songs and their star singer-actor. Alfredo Murúa, a sound technician, who in 1936 founded the record company SIDE (Sociedad Impresora de Discos Electrofónicos), realised that in order to guarantee the success of his new studio, he needed to start with a big hit. His answer was to produce a musical melodrama in the Gardelian style, starring the popular radio and theatre tango singer and actress, Libertad Lamarque.

Following Murúa's offer, Lamarque abandoned her hectic touring schedule, instead devoting her time to building a screen career. Excited by the project, the actress invested her money and time, involving herself in many aspects of the production. Confident of how her screen image should be presented, she rejected the original plot written by acclaimed scriptwriter, José González Castillo, because, as she explained in her memoirs, 'the idea did not suit my personality, as I had to go to jail for stabbing a man in the back with a pair of scissors'. Other writers were sought after to give Lamarque a project that would suit her needs. These were the early days of sound in Argentinian cinema, with a lack of competent scriptwriters and most playwrights considered the art beneath them. Lamarque finally came up with a storyline herself which would become the first film of the trilogy, *Ayúdame a vivir* (*Help Me to Live*, 1936). To direct it, Murúa first called Mario Soffici, who had worked with Lamarque in *El alma del bandoneón* (*The Soul of Bandoneon,* 1935). Classical and moderate, Soffici was not interested in making a film in which the character breaks into singing during an action scene. The contract was given instead to José Agustín Ferreyra, a film-maker of vast experience in silent films and a willingness to experiment with the rules of the romantic melodrama. He immediately took up the task as if it was his own idea, not only directing the whole trilogy but using the template for other productions. As with *Besos brujos*, the co-star in the first film was Floren Delbene, a leading actor from the silent period, which went some way to accounting for his declamatory performances.

The same technical team that made *Ayúdame a vivir*, worked on *Besos brujos*. By that time Lamarque was a star, the first of Argentinian cinema and perhaps even Latin America. As for Ferreyra, responsible for many movies since 1915, he finally achieved major recognition. *Besos brujos* earned more money at the box-office than its predecessor. The trilogy ended with *La ley que olvidaron* (*The Law They Forgot*, 1938), a tear-jerking melodrama that set the mould of the maternal role that Lamarque would play for much of her film career.

The model presented by the *tango opera* trilogy prompted the creation of another type of story: a more cosmopolitan film, not necessarily anchored to the stage or the 'arrabal tanguero', the slums where tango was created. Incorporating the convention that under any circumstance the star could sing instead of talk, whether they were a young, aristocratic student at the end of a religious education (*Ayúdame a vivir*), a servant and adoptive mother (*La ley que olvidaron*) or a tango singer (*Besos brujos*), it was no longer necessary to justify each song on stage. With this, the thematic possibilities of these films increased. *Besos brujos* was alone in featuring a song sung in front of an audience ('Quiéreme'). The remaining songs appear arbitrarily within the film. In this regard, some reviews of the time aptly remarked that 'We had never seen a movie in which the songs would be blended so naturally and without constrictions, as part of the plot' (*Sintonía Magazine,* 1937). *El Argentino*, in reviewing *Besos brujos* remarked that 'Libertad Lamarque makes her best work for the screen and is expressive singing several songs that at times are forced into the rhythm and action of the movie'.

It is worth noting the importance and function of each song within the film. The first one, as previously mentioned, is the only song that is narratively justified by her being a singer. 'Look at me, kiss me/give me the honey of your mouth', sings Marga at the theatre-bar. This bolero, even without the narrative effect of the other songs, is the vehicle that moves the action forward, arousing the desires of the men and resulting in the kiss auction. The second song ('Ansias – Como el pajarito') is exactly the opposite. More an inner monologue or a lyrical expression of pain in the isolation of the forest (Marga, alone, sings while she is bathing in the lake and in the background we hear music from a harp). The lyrics of the song speak of her captivity and express her wish for freedom: 'I want to break free from this slavery/I live prisoner of my youth/I want to break free from this loneliness and return to the lights of my city … get out of this hell, get out of this bore, that makes me mourn.'

The third song is the central theme that lends its title to the movie. Locked in the cottage, Marga argues with Sebastián and when he goes over to console her, she answers abruptly with 'Besos brujos', a tango that works as an explicative dialogue and passes from the imperative tone ('Leave me, I don't want you to kiss me/it's your fault that I am living the torture of my pain/Leave me, I don't want you to touch me/those hands hurt me/they hurt and burn me') to reach a begging tone ('Let me go my way/I am asking your conscience, I can't love you'), and ends up blaming herself ('I don't want my witch-spelled mouth/to bring more hopelessness/in my soul, in my life/enchanting kisses, ah … if I could tear this curse from my lips'). Once the song is over, an orchestral version links this scene to the next. Meditatively, Sebastián ventures into the forest, accompanied by this music. Simultaneously, Alberto also journeys into the forest, which borders a lake. His image reflected in the water merges with that of Marga, who is sewing her dress on the opposite side. This variation of the musical motif of *Besos brujos* unifies and strengthens the dramatic intensity of the action, with a crescendo of wind instruments that play as a snake silently approaches Alberto.

The fourth song is played at the end of the film when Alberto, believing he has been rejected in favour of Sebastián is ready to return to civilisation and Marga reveals, through the song 'Tu vida es mi vida', that she still loves him and the story ends on a happy note. As with the films of Carlos Gardel, the Argentinian and Latin American public of the 1930s demanded on many occasions that the film be replayed so they could listen to the main songs. Today, these scenes offer a similar function, often used in video clips as examples of the style of tango of the period.

With the exception of a few clichéd moments, *Besos brujos* resists the passing of time and film styles. Elegant tracking shots and creative fade-ins, indicating ellipsis between scenes (a kiss of Marga and Alberto takes them from a restaurant to the apartment; during the kidnap a man's hand suffocates Marga's yell, blending this sound effect with the whistle of a locomotive in the following scene) or highlighting out simultaneity (in a walk, the servant at Alberto's home is replaced by another servant in the Hotel Provincia) have benefited the film. It is also helped by the impressive art-deco interiors designed by Juan Manuel Concado, reminiscent of the RKO movies during the same period, as well as the expressionistic lighting by Gumer Barreiros, with its heavy shadow-light. In terms of the narrative, Ferreyra proved himself to be an articulate director. Careful composition of images, fluid camera movement and impressive exterior-set sequences (they were actually filmed in the studio) underline his skill and recall his training on silent movies. The impressive technical achievements and the naturalness of certain scenes, such as the one at the restaurant or the wedding gown sequence, compensate for the pompous dialogue, particularly Alberto's, though they are unable to hide some shoddy editing.

Besos brujos is based on the novel of the same title written by Enrique García Velloso for the magazine *La novela semanal* in 1922. It is a naturalistic 'soapy' novel with strong melodramatic strokes, whose main character is the beautiful and fragile French prostitute, Juliette, a woman who drives men crazy with her kisses. 'One of my kisses is tantamount to signing a deal of eternal feeling. My kisses are cold, but carry a poison so fatal for me, that I give them with contempt, such as those that anxiously receive them … I've always had the disgrace to awaken mad-driven passions', she explains resignedly. Except the hypnotic power of the kisses and the kidnapping (although the central part is reduced to what the Argentinian cinema of the time could show), all resemblance between both works ends. The robust Marga was neither fragile nor a whore, partly the result of the mores of the society at that time, and an acknowledgement by the fledgling star system that it would do Lamarque's career no good to portray her as a prostitue. In Garcia Velloso's story, no one goes to save her but there is a witness who, in spite of his fascination for the woman, avoids kissing her. 'My coldness, my serenity, my withheld sensual desire were determined by the superstitious fear of those enchanting kisses from that admirable mouth, from those enchanting lips?', he states. In the film, the action is simplified, characters and settings disappear, conflicts are shortened, transgressions as well as the melodramatic intensity at the end of the story are smoothed, whereas in the original text the prostitute is punished with gangrene, the resulting amputation and finally, death. It is important to mention the necrophilic quotation with which the narrator standing before the dead woman closes his story: 'the thin lips, in the anxiety of breathing, unveiled beautiful teeth … The mouth of the enchanting kisses! I felt the need of kissing her, and now without fear of the spell, I placed my mouth on hers, for a long kiss.' Sordid spaces, some pathetic situations and class determinism are diluted in the film. Marga is kidnapped by a landowner who is in love with her, with the intention of conquering her love. In the novel, Juliette leads a dissipated life, with the dangers that this carries; a lover who beats her, a madam who sells her for money and the owner of an factory who kidnaps and harasses her. In the film, certain psychological notes with which Garcia Velloso criticizes the oligarchy ('the high-class Argentinian is proud, self-confident, arbitrary, informal, jealous, not out of passion but of vanity. In other countries, men have interest for spiritual life, philosophy and … More admiration for women') simply disappeared.

Curiously enough, the scriptwriter George Axelrod faced similar difficulties with the adaptation of Truman Capote's *Breakfast at Tiffany's* (Blake Edwards, 1961). It featured a prostitute of high standing whose profession was made deliberately ambiguous to benefit the film's star (Audrey Hepburn). As for the narrative techniques, this adaptation, as well as Ferreyra's, transformed the anonymous narrator of the novels into a fervent lover of the heroines. Another common element in both adaptations is the contrast between the protecting city (Buenos Aires and New York) with the enigmatic and unknown tropical forest, whose spirit is, in both cases, represented by a wild man. At the premiere of *Besos brujos*, few recalled García Velloso's original story. Nonetheless, on 28 June 1937 the author sent a letter to a major national newspaper in which he stated: 'After having attended a private screening of the film, I believe that this version artistically and literally demerits the nexus of the action and its language, the argument and dialogues I wrote. For this reason I am forced to declare that I repudiate this version, for the sake of my modest labour and the respect for beauty and grace.' As time passed, the film was seen as a Latin American classic. Conversely, the novel has been forgotten.

Despite the critics, who underlined the artificial character of the film, audiences were fascinated by the musical formula. The success spread swiftly to other countries, including Mexico, Colombia, Venezuela and Cuba, taking with it the fashion for Buenos Aires talk, its accent and, above all, its tango. In this sense, SIDE's tango trilogy opened the way for Argentinian cinema in the huge Latin American market. Unfortunately for the studios, inspite of the big success, only a small share of the profits from the exploitation of the films would return to them, due to their carelessness in the establishment of a commercial circuit. Distributors and theatres would run the films *in aeternum* indiscriminately, and profitless for SIDE. As a result, like many other small studios, SIDE filed for bankruptcy only a few years after the film's release, finally being absorbed by a new expanding company, Estudios San Miguel. Another reason for SIDE's bankruptcy was the unavoidable loss of Libertad

Lamarque. After becoming *the* star of the moment, Lamarque jumped from Murúa's modest studio to the major Argentina Sono Film. By doing so, she moved from Ferreyra's old-fashioned aesthetic world to that of the more contemporary film-maker, Luis César Amadori. Her first high-budget production, *Madreselva* (*Honeysuckle*, 1938), was also a romantic melodrama. The film displays a solid narrative structure and a concern for its visual style, thanks to the work of artist Raul Soldi's scenery, John Alton's accomplished photography, and Amadori's mature direction. The result was the development of a more sophisticated side of Lamarque's persona. The new company took advantage of her quality and popularity, a formula that directors such as Luis Saslavsky, Mario Soffici and Carlos Borcosque helped to foster in future films. Because of this, Lamarque's films began to appeal to a more cultivated and pretentious audience – the urban middle class. The actress lost weight, gained a more youthful image, extended her repertoire (including arias of operas and Argentinian folk music) and left behind the colloquial traits of previous films. If *Besos brujos* was another step upwards for the star, for Ferreyra, it marked his highest achievement and beginning of his artistic decline. For Calki (Raimundo Calcagno) – the respected film critic of the newspaper *El Mundo* – 'it was the best work in all his career'. He followed it with just seven films, each as modest and imperfect in quality and artistic pretensions. After leaving SIDE, he became his own producer, repeating the mistakes of his earlier films. His vision of Buenos Aires in the 1940s had changed little from how he saw the city in the 1920s, a difference Ferreyra failed to notice and which made his films increasingly irrelevant. Alone and old-fashioned, in his biographer Jorge Miguel Couselo's words, 'his time had passed, although his example and vision would live on'.

Despite the enormous success of this trilogy, the narrative discourse of *tango opera* inspired few sequels. With a carefree approach, kitsch elements, a certain pathos and occasionally unintended humour, *Besos brujos* was nonetheless one of the freshest early sound films made in Argentina, a feat achieved by the unique symbiosis of Libertad Lamarque, José Agustín Ferreyra and Alfredo Murúa.

César Maranghello and Diana Paladino

REFERENCES

Couselo, J. M (2001) *'El Negro Ferreyra': un cine por instinto*. Buenos Aires: Altamira.
Di Nubila, D. (1959) *Historia del cine argentino, vol. 1*. Buenos Aires: Cruz de Malta.

García Velloso, E. (1922) 'Besos brujos', in *La novela semanal*, 225 (Buenos Aires: 6 March).
Maranghello, C. (1999) 'Besos brujos', in A. Elena & M. Díaz López (eds) *Tierra en trance: el cine latinoamericano en cien peliculas*. Madrid Alianza, 44–8.
Paladino, D. (1999) 'Libertad Lamarque: la reina de la lágrima', in A. Elena & P. A. Paranaguá (eds) *Mitologías latinoamericanas*, special issue of *Archivos de la Filmoteca*, 31, 60–75.

MARÍA CANDELARIA

04

EMILIO FERNÁNDEZ, MEXICO, 1943

The Mexican director, Emilio Fernández, nicknamed 'El Indio', finished his third film, *María Candelaria*, in 1943. It would become one of director's best films and would serve as a cinematic paradigm in his country. Shown in a number of foreign countries, it was seen to consolidate a stereotype of Mexico and Mexicanness.

The film opens with a prologue in which a famous painter is interviewed by a reporter who presses the artist to reveal a painting he jealously guards. It is the portrait of a beautiful indigenous woman. On showing it, the painter recounts the misfortune that years before befell María Candelaria, a young girl of 'pure Mexican race … with all the beauty of ancient princesses'. The flashback that follows becomes the main body of the film. The painter's reference to the portrait is also a reference to the act of looking and, even if we as spectators actually never see its content, we get to know the story behind the work thanks to the film. Whisked suddenly from the artist's dour studio, we find ourselves in the flowery landscape of Xochimilco, where slender trees throw thin shadows onto sunlit water, and where the various characters of the film seem to form part of the natural landscape. It is 1909, the eve of the Mexican Revolution, when the region was inhabited almost exclusively by indigenous people whose existence was dependant on the produce of flowers and vegetables in the *chinampas*, the fertile islands of the lake-covered area they live in.

The film tells the story of two people in love in Xochimilco. The use of the flashback, which offers a stark contrast between the sombre tones of the artist's studio and the explosion of light and colour in the main story, lends an ethereal, timeless and lyrical tone to the narrative, presenting it as a mythical tale. The flashback also introduces a distance between the spectator and the indigenous characters whose story is being told. The voice that speaks for the characters is that of a white, 'cultivated' man; his telling an act of voyeurism, the gaze of art and of the artist, which constructs and interprets the 'other'. It is the painter who identifies the innocence and dignity with which Emilio Fernández wanted to represent the Mexican Aborigines. He is the mediator between us and the characters in the story. By highlighting the importance of his gaze, he alludes to the gaze of the spectator watching the film.

The film is a melodrama and in accordance with that genre's conventions, Fernández presents human problems without possible solutions; the predominance of fortune (good or bad) which fulfills the dictates of destiny and of an unhappy end. Lorenzo Rafael and María Candelaria want to get married so they try to raise a piglet to earn some money. Rejected by the community because her mother was 'a street woman' killed by people of her own kind, María receives no support other than her boyfriend's. She also suffers the attacks of everyone in the town; Lupe, her rival for the young man's love; Don Damián, the mestizo owner of the store who, sporting traditional *charro* dress, exploits local indigenous people and who, rejected in his sexual approaches towards María, kills the piglet and refuses to buy Lorenzo's vegetables. Having thus forced the collapse of the lovers' future, Damián also refuses to give the couple the quinine sent by the government to fight a malaria epidemic that later leads to María's illness. Lorenzo steals the medicine, as well as a dress that María was to wear at her wedding. In desperation, she seeks the support of the priest and the painter, the latter eager to paint her portrait after having been struck by her beauty when he passed her in the market one morning. These characters, along with the doctor who tries to heal her, are the only ones who come to help the couple in their despair. Nevertheless, all of their attempts to help the couple and save María fail.

The climax is provoked by the painter's final work. Presented with María Candelaria's refusal to pose in the nude, the painter completes the portrait of the girl with the body of another woman. The painting is seen by the entire town, which leads to the couple's fatal end. María is pursued by an irrational and bloodthirsty mob and is stoned to death, the victim of the mass, while her boyfriend is kept in prison. Lorenzo finally escapes, in order to carry her lifeless body, now bathed in flowers, through Xochimilco's canal of the dead, in a sombre ceremony.

Fernández claimed that he wrote the first version of the plot on 13 napkins. Sitting in a restaurant, he was suffering a night of anxiety because he did not have the money to buy a birthday present for Dolores del Río with whom he was then involved in an intense romance. In a previous script the film was entitled *Xochimilco* and the protagonist was called María del Refugio. She was not outcast by the community, but was instead loved and admired by all. The film's conflict revolved around the jealous disposition of Lorenzo Rafael and his rejection of outsiders, an element that only partially appeared in the final version of the script. Ultimately, it was the townsfolk's hatred towards María's mother that results in the ensuing tragedy. As such, *María Candelaria* dramatizes the woman's situation, making her goodness more evident and her sacrifice more absurd. The mythical issue of an original sin that is inherited, regardless of one's own conduct, is thus re-emphasized. The central issue is that of the couple pursued by a community to which, nonetheless, they belong. They face the dilemma between defending their own individuality and dignity, and being seen as the community's scapegoats.

This theme would become one of Fernández's obsessions and is similarly portrayed in *Janitzio* (Carlos Navarro, 1934) in which he himself played the protagonist. In 1948, he filmed *Maclovia*, a remake of *Janitzio*, although produced with more resources. He also changed the ending, in which the protagonist (played by María Félix) is able to escape before being stoned to death. An antecedent to these films is *Tabu*, made in 1930 by F. W. Murnau, which focuses on the same topic. The German director explored the Polynesian islands in order to find 'good savages' and a remote and idyllic setting that would serve as the backdrop to his exotic tale. In *Tabu*, the couple is similarly pursued by their own community, with the woman being the main target for victimisation by the mob. The story is narrated with rich and lyrical symbolism that even today stands out as a remarkably subtle work. It is clear that Fernández assimilated this film into the development of his own project.

In every one of his films, Fernández articulately expressed the problems that concerned him: indigenousness, nationalism, agrarianism and the need for a lay education. All these issues and the conflicts they embody are presented didactically and at great length. The themes are organized around romantic stories of failed love. The love relationship is never questioned, as if it were a model of perfection. The problems always come from outside the relationship. In accordance with the author's own way of thinking, the hero provides and cares for the woman's needs while she obeys him submissively, even comforting him when he is low. This structure is observed in *María Candelaria*. Fernández first expressed his obsessions in 1941 with his debut, *La isla de la pasión* (*Passion Island*), also known as *Clipperton*. Yet it is in *María Candelaria* that these issues are organised with the strength and poetry that enabled the director to fully express his aesthetic concerns, notably helped by Gabriel Figueroa's photography.

Fernández was impressed by some of the rushes filmed between 1930 and 1932 by Eduard Tissé for Eisenstein's unfinished film *¡Que viva Mexico!* The ethical and aesthetic principles of the Soviet film-maker became a template for Fernández. He was also influenced by certain films from Hollywood, particularly the work of John Ford. Fernández wanted to blend both styles in order to create his own, and it was from these different influences that he founded the so-called 'Escuela Mexicana' (Mexican School). These were years of nationalist feeling in Mexico and artists and intellectuals celebrated everything that was Mexican. They valued the country's indigenous elements and its popular culture. Due to its character as an art for the masses, Fernández considered that cinema was similar to mural painting. Muralists depicted on the walls of public buildings the social problems the population complained about, aiming to create a political consciousness on which class struggle could be based. In this sense, the influence of Eisenstein on Fernández's work and ideology is evident. To both, the cinema acquires the character of an instrument of revolution.

Eisentein's influence is also evident in Fernández's visual style. *María Candelaria* highlighted the beauty of landscape, which Gabriel Figueroa successfully portrays through the flora and fauna of Xochimilco, the great clouds made more dramatic through the use of filters, experimentation with deep focus and dramatic low- and high-angle shots, and the use of diagonal axis, to produce mesmerizing images. The landscape is accentuated through the use of light and shadow in order to capture the brilliant sun of Mexico's central plateau. Effects created by flaming torches carried by the mad crowds, were a favourite of Fernández's. The stiffness of human figures, as if they were part of the landscape, and the priest-like faces of Indians also fit into Fernández's aesthetic schema, as well as the use of pre-Hispanic monuments and colonial churches, whose beauty and solemnity is enhanced by an atmospheric score.

Fernández was also interested in presenting rituals and artifacts of the cultures he portrayed. Xochimilco's local traditions are presented in the film, such as the blessing of animals in the church's atrium, a scene crucial to the plot, where the couple brings their piglet decorated with ribbons. There are scenes of a popular local market, and vendors and workers are filmed as they parade through the streets. The people's devotion to the Virgin of Guadalupe is also presented, as are the rituals of the healer who competes with the doctor to cure María. We are provided with a repertoire of all that is considered typical of Mexican indigenous culture, and Fernández shows the world in which this culture exists: the water- and foliage-covered landscape of Xochimilco.

These aesthetic choices point to an experimental genre that nonetheless aspires to commercial success. The Mexican film industry would shine throughout the 1940s and its popularity would last until the early 1950s. The producer Agustín Fink, of Films Mundiales, was a supporter of a certain type of 'quality' cinema and from 1943 he became an associate and champion of Fernández, with whom he created *Flor silvestre* (*Wild Flower*). Fink supplied Fernández with the means to group a production team who could bring to the screen his vision while maintaining a level of harmony during filming. Fernández and cinematographer Gabriel Figueroa worked together on many occasions, sharing a similar approach to the material. Writer Mauricio Magdaleno, with whom Fernández wrote *María Candelaria*, provided welcome support, while Gloria Schoemann proved to be an effective editor on a number of Fernández's films, including *María Candelaria.*

This exceptional team, along with the stars Fernández hired, were key to his success. Dolores del Río, who had recently returned from the United States where she had achieved a significant level of success, and Pedro Armendáriz had previously worked with Fernández on *Flor Silvestre*, in 1943. After *María Candelaria*, Del Río and Armendáriz would star in many of Fernández's most memorable films. However, in accordance with Eisensteinian aesthetics, Fernández also used native actors, like the indigenous people of Xochimilco. Even so, these characters remain background figures. Fernández's enthusiasm for authenticity is limited by classic film conventions and his desire to make the film a success. The clothing worn by the leads was the work of the most famous of Mexican designers of that time, Armando Valdés Peza, hired to highlight the beauty of the film's star. In this way, Fernández's films and especially *María Candelaria* exist somewhere between Eisenstein's ideals and the requirements of a Hollywood drama.

The picture enjoyed the benefits of an effective publicity campaign. From the moment filming began, in August 1943, film magazines recorded its 'indigenist' bent and the way in which it represented the 'authentic' Mexico. Nonetheless, it was sharply criticized by some intellectuals because of its play with the truth. Diego Rivera, the famous muralist, considered the film 'un mamarracho' (a piece of trash), which irritated Fernández immensely. It is worth noting that in one of the first versions of the script the character of the painter was precisely Diego Rivera, but in the final version his name is never mentioned.

At the film's premiere, attended by the native actors of Xochimilco along with its stars, various opinions were aired. There were some hecklers who expressed their disdain for the film. However, the Soviet Ambassador for Mexico ardently defended the film, apparently going so far as to impose his opinion on others. Newspaper critics treated the picture reasonably well. It was shown commercially for four weeks in early 1944. In the United States it was shown in Spanish in 1944 and in a dubbed version in 1946, entitled *Portrait of Maria*. In the same year, the Cannes Film Festival offered an excellent opportunity to publicise the film on the world stage, and it joined a number of films representing an increasingly vibrant Mexican cinema. To the surprise of Mexicans, various critics such as Georges Sadoul enjoyed the film which, along with ten other films, was awarded *ex-aequo* the Palme d'Or. Gabriel Figueroa also won a prize for his outstanding photography.

After this success, Emilio Fernández was considered Mexico's 'quality film' director. His work was exported throughout much of the world and was nominated for many prizes at international film festivals. In 1947, *María Candelaria* won three prizes at the Locarno Film Festival in Switzerland for acting – by both leads – and cinematography. Paradoxically, a film that was intended as a genuine expression of Mexicanness acquired a place of prestige outside of its true home. Following this success, even though *María Candelaria* was not the first Mexican picture to receive a prize, the Mexican film industry would produce one type of film for the domestic market and another for export, with an imagery that has reinforced certain characteristics of Mexican stereotypes, the world over.

The indigenist politics of that time centered upon the re-evaluation of Mexico's indigenous cultures but, in contradiction, also aspired to those peoples' assimilation of modern values and demanded that they renounce their own cultural codes. Fernández participated in many of these contradictions. *María Candelaria* lovingly expresses the dignity and innocence of its protagonists, but at the same time it places their adversaries in a collectivity that is also indigenous and as merciless as the natural world of which it is part; bloodthirsty and lacking the possibility of redemption. This populace is not equivalent to the people that forms it, but is an irrational and ferocious mob. Not even the priest can put a stop to the hatred manifested toward María Candelaria, heir of a mythic sin.

The film shows Mexican indigenous culture in great detail. Women speak Nahuatl when they get angry and both María and Lorenzo share a love of land and animals. However, the stereotypes are never far away. The protagonists are submissive when faced with injustice and they appear incapable of transforming their destiny. María's only acts of rebelliousness occur when she fights with Lupe, her rival, and when she reprimands the Virgin of Guadalupe for not protecting her. Yet these events last only an instant and never achieve any level of reflection. The social exclusion of María Candelaria is enormous, because she is a woman and because she is indigenous, but also because she is excluded from her own community, accentuating her problem. When the young man suggests that they should emigrate in order to bring about a change in their luck, she responds negatively, claiming that 'strangers are worse'. The possibility of starting another life is illusory. The best option appears to be inertia. They are noble and innocent, but their resources are minimal against misfortune and their future is closed. What kind of indigenism are we talking about when only hatred and irrationality can be found among members of the same community, and solidarity is all but void? The mestizo, embodied by Don Damián, plays the villain, unleashing misfortune, but actually never producing it himself. The culturally Westernised, modern characters (the painter, the priest and the doctor) are powerless when faced with the fury of the indigenous mob. In this way, the contradictions remain unresolved and the film becomes an ambiguous defense of the abstract indigenous person.

Nonetheless, *María Candelaria* is also the expression of a fundamental human problem of universal order – the struggle against adversity. Its characters appear stranded between the possibility of living their own lives and fulfilling the desire to become part of a rigid and homogenous collectivity. The group appears more like a natural force than a form of social organisation, to which they nonetheless belong. At the heart of the film, the struggle that Lorenzo and María confront, is the choice between being independent, autonomous individuals, according to the modern conceptualisation, or being part of the beautiful yet ferocious landscape of Xochimilco. Their choice is between freedom and destiny. This issue became a true obsession for Fernández and he presented the conundrum in many of his films. In *María Candelaria* it is expressed in a lyrical and moving way; in an anecdote which attempts to be in defense of indigenous people, giving the film an exotic and picturesque tone. At the same time, the film raises fundamental themes that still exist within Mexican culture and as such, it explains why it occupies such an important place in the history of Mexican cinema.

Julia Tuñón

REFERENCES

Fernández, A. (1986) *El Indio Fernández. Vida y mito*. México: Panorama.

García Riera, E. (1987) *Emilio Fernández*. Guadalajara: Universidad de Guadalajara.

Reyes Nevares, B. (1974) *Trece directores del cine mexicano*. México: Secretaría de Educación Pública. (English edition, *The Mexican Cinema. Interviews with Thirteen Directors*. Albuquerque: University of New Mexico Press, 1976).

Taibo, P. I. (1986) *El Indio Fernández: el cine por mis pistolas*. México: Joaquín Mortiz/Planeta.

Tuñón, J. (1988) *En su propio espejo. Entrevista con Emilio 'El Indio' Fernández*. México: Universidad Autónoma Metropolitana-Iztapalapa.

____ (2000) *Los rostros de un mito. Personajes femeninos en las películas de Emilio 'Indio' Fernández*. México: Consejo Nacional para la Cultura y las Artes/Instituto Mexicano de Cinematografía.

LOS OLVIDADOS THE YOUNG AND THE DAMNED

05

LUIS BUÑUEL, MEXICO, 1950

> ... si la madre España cae – digo, es un decir – salid, niños del mundo, id a buscarla...!
>
> – César Vallejo

In 1994, with the commemorations of the centenary of cinema drawing near, the Mexican magazine *Somos* invited a select group of critics, historians and professionals, including Jorge Ayala Blanco, Nelson Carro, Carlos Monsiváis, Tomás Pérez Turrent, Eduardo de la Vega Alfaro, Gustavo García and Gabriel Figueroa, to nominate the hundred best films from the history of Mexican cinema. *¡Vámonos con Pancho Villa!* (*Let's Go with Pancho Villa!*, 1935), by Fernando de Fuentes was rated the best. In second place was Luis Buñuel's *Los olvidados* (1950). In spite of the considerations and arguments that could arise from the contemporary habit of organising rankings or similar mechanisms of 'selective reduction', to use the words of Pedro Salinas, one could safely say that *Los olvidados* has reached the present day as a masterpiece and is in an optimum position to be considered as one of the finest achievements in the history of Mexican cinema. But on the road to its current acclaim amongst critical circles, the film experienced a great deal of negativity. Its initial reception was not as favourable as one could infer by reading the list published by *Somos*. The film was so harsh and innovative, so critical and daring in its statements that during its first screenings, spectators openly aired their indignation towards the features of Mexican identity activated by Buñuel. *Los olvidados* attempted to expose the problem of infantile and juvenile delinquency in the poorest districts in Mexico City, and did so by committing, as never before in Latin American cinema, to a verisimilitude in the telling of its story.

Buñuel did not hesitate to deploy three far-reaching strategies in his film: one was artistic and would ensure the renovation of cinematographic expression (the film as an instrument of poetry); one ideological and political, which gave his story a body of social protest that was strictly revolutionary (a critique to the left of the Neorealist movement as the surrealists in the 1930s had done with the social realism from the Soviet Union); and one cultural, which enabled the assembly of former strategies within the emergence of new processes of identity (the achievement of a film that injected the values of Western culture into the traditional moulds of an emergent America). His ability to integrate these objectives explains why *Los olvidados* holds such a privileged position in Mexican cinema today. The tremendous influence of its imagination on the social cinema that began to develop in Latin America from the mid-1950s envisaged a new approach to identity through the merging of realism and poetry.

At the end of the film's opening credits, one can read the following notice: 'This film is based in its entirety on real life events and all the characters are real people'. Following it is a list of the names of the public institutions involved in ensuring the story's authenticity. The idea of notifying the audience about how grounded in reality the film is does not end here, but continues with the documentary prologue which opens the film. A montage of images of sumptuous and magnificent buildings in New York, Paris and London file past, with a voice-over informing us about the existence of poverty-stricken homes in these cities, 'which house undernourished children, with no hygiene or schooling, the breeding ground of future delinquents'. Mexico City, the narrator concludes, 'is not an exception to this universal rule'. Thus, the framework for the fiction is established and the film begins with the return of cruel Jaibo, leader of a street gang, following his recent escape from a reformatory.

All the children and youths in his gang live on the verge of poverty and experience feelings of abandonment; a mixture of paternal loss and maternal neglect. When the father figure timidly appears, the same father figure that has abandoned Pedro or Ojitos, he does so in a condition of absolute decrepitude. Meche's weak grandfather or Julián's alcoholic father exemplify this environment of parental neglect. The mothers, although present, can hardly attend to their offspring. Pedro's mother, far from attempting to interpret the gestures of his rebellion, mercilessly rejects him in the name of moral principle, while Meche's mother lies prostrate in a bed. In the midst of this infernal situation, tragedy soon presents itself. Jaibo uses Pedro to punish Julián, whom he accuses of having reported him to the authorities. The murder of Julián by Jaibo forces Pedro to reconsider his future, but the ruthless delinquent will resort to any measures to get his way. On one occasion he is the cause of Pedro's internment on a farm for infant re-education and later, when the reformatory's director gives Pedro an opportunity to prove himself, Jaibo steals money from him, landing Pedro in trouble again.

As a result of the humiliations and beatings suffered when reckoning with the former gang leader, Pedro takes revenge by publicly accusing Jaibo of murder. That night Jaibo finds

Pedro in Meche's stable and beats him to death, the same as he did with Julián. Finally, thanks to the information volunteered by a blind old man, one of Jaibo's many victims, the police close in on him and shoot him as he attempts to escape. Over the close-up of his agonised face, are superimposed images of his delirium, whilst the soundtrack plays the imaginary and absent voice of his mother: 'I am alone, alone! – the same as always my son, the same as always. Now go to sleep and don't think. Go to sleep me'son, go to sleep!'

The cruelty of the film attracted the rancour of members of the film crew, including the dialogue writer Jesús Camacho. Pedro de Urdimalas, another colleague of Buñuel's, preferred not to appear in the credits of a film that he believed to be untruthful and 'wretched'. After the film's premiere, influential members of the Mexican film business and intellectual circles accused Buñuel of betraying the country that had granted him refuge, and of painting a false picture of Mexico's displaced. The film only screened for four days in the capital's cinemas before being withdrawn. When everything indicated that there would be a repetition of what happened with *Las Hurdes/Tierra sin pan* (*Land Without Bread*) and *Los olvidados* ran the risk of becoming another of Buñuel's damned films, some of his faithful enthusiasts, including Octavio Paz, were able to present it in competion at the Cannes Film Festival, where it won the top prize. The film's spectacular success in Europe helped to calm the atmosphere in Mexico and at the same time dilute much of the deep rooted prejudice against it. The public began to reassess the challenging narrative and artistic devices used by the Spanish film-maker and *Los olvidados* began to be recognised, at last, as something very special.

The fact that *Los olvidados*, the first art film that Buñuel would embark on in exile and after 17 years of advertising and commercials, could be seen as the film that represented Mexican cinema, and that was valued for being genuinely Mexican, does not take into account the personal and political position of the person who made it. How can we explain how such a Mexican film was made by a crew populated by Spaniards (Luis Buñuel, Max Aub, Juan Larrea, Luis Gustavo Pittaluga and Luis Alcoriza) who all maintained and demonstrated intense feelings of being affiliated to the recently inaugurated Spanish Republican exiled community ('transterrados' as they were called by the philosopher José Gaos, who included himself in this group)? In order to answer this question one could examine a few details surrounding the film's creation.

In the late 1940s, the Spanish poet and essayist Juan Larrea met with Buñuel most Sundays to converse and exchange ideas. These discussions engendered ideas and work that would be of tremendous influence on Buñuel's later productions, such as the script based on the novel

Larrea had written in 1927, *Ilegible hijo de flauta*. Indeed, Víctor Fuentes has said that 'visual themes and ideas in the script and the breath that embodied the words of the introduction found their way into Buñuel's Mexican films, not only leaving an unmistakable mark on them, but reappearing as the reality of Mexican life and culture'. 'We can say', Fuentes added, 'that *Los olvidados,* in its basic conception is the *Ilegible* … Mexicanised, or that on the pathway from the script of *Ilegible* … to the production of *Los olvidados,* Buñuel found the style that would dominate in his Mexican films and which he would develop from *Los olvidados* to *Simón del desierto*, including his great achievements *Él*, *Nazarín* and *El angel exterminador.*'

When and how did Buñuel begin to choose this alternative? 'I was not at all interested in Latin America and always said to my friends: "If ever I disappear, look for me anywhere in the world except there"', is how the Spanish film-maker opened the chapter of his memoirs that covered his life in Mexico. He was not exaggerating. There is evidence that his move to the continent had little to do with any previous affinity with the country, but was more a result of the film-maker's need of an income. From 1943 Buñuel had been the object of serious accusations and was unjustly reported on by former friends who were up to date with his political activities; initially by the painter Salvador Dalí, then later by Gustavo Durán, a republican retired from the army. As a result, his presence in North America was less than welcome. As things were, the Spanish film-maker found his career was at a dead end and was inclined to accept the opportunities that he was offered from Mexico. On his arrival in the Mexican capital he prepared his return to a film studio with *Gran Casino* (*Great Casino*, 1946) a musical produced by Óscar Dancigers and featuring Libertad Lamarque and Jorge Negrete. It was in this close-knit world that Buñuel encountered a heavily populated and culturally active Spanish community.

One of the most remarkable republican exiles in Mexico was Juan Larrea, who stood out because of his energetic pro-Latin American militancy. The admiration that Buñuel showed towards Larrea proved longstanding and steadfast, originating through a number of shared interests. The publication of some poems written by Larrea, arranged by his friend Gerardo Diego, was enough to attract the attention of the literary circles in Madrid. His rapid ascent as a poet of note was extraordinary. During one of his trips to Spain, César Vallejo discovered to his surprise the prestige his friend enjoyed, and even told Larrea himself as much in a letter: 'the Spanish elite show great admiration towards [you] and have, above all, an almost religious respect for your work'. It was not in vain that Buñuel referred to him in his memoirs as 'one of the greatest Spanish poets'.

At the end of the 1920s, after going through a profound personal crisis, Larrea decided to abandon poetry and focus his interests on essay writing and the study of archaeology and Pre-Columbine art. In 1930 he travelled with his wife to Peru, where he stayed until the following year, and there he accumulated a valuable collection of Inca works of art that he would finally donate to the Spanish Republican government. His friendship with prominent personalities such as José Bergamín, president of the Anti-Fascist Intellectual Alliance or Pablo Picasso, placed him as one of the key personalities, together with Buñuel, in a position to promote cultural projects and art forms internationally, in defence of the Spanish Republic. At the beginning of 1938 Larrea constituted the Aid Committee for Spanish Refugees and the Board of Spanish Culture, through which Louis Aragon and Pablo Neruda collaborated in the task of obtaining immigration visas to America for the intellectuals going into exile. On his arrival in Mexico, in 1940, he edited a short-lived magazine, *España Peregrina*, which became the basis of his next publishing project, *Cuadernos Americanos.* In 1943 he published *Rendición de Espíritu*, with *Surrealismo entre viejo y nuevo mundo* appearing the following year.

Since his arrival on the American continent, Larrea had systematized in his books and articles a powerful theory about the symbolic place that Mexico, the New Spain, occupied in the history of humanity and consequently in universal contemporary culture. Through the practice of humanism, Larrea prophesied, humanity would recover its true spiritual raison d'etre, and would so enable a new Golden Age to arrive as a contemporary paradise lost. Influenced by the teleological interpretations of Judeo-Hellenist-Christian thought and the work of Rimbaud, Darío, Huidobro and Vallejo, Larrea understood that history was moving towards a new type of world and human being, towards a new form of reality that would be spiritual, harmonious and free from social inequality, the advent of which would be announced by a devastating catastrophe (the Second World War).

Some events related to the *Camino de Santiago*, and the medieval cult to *Finisterrae,* the essence of Western European identity, emerged as key episodes in Larrea's discussions; and even more so when, in 1944, professor Ramón Martínez López disclosed some clues concerning work undertaken to identify the remains that were worshiped in the Cathedral in Santiago de Compostela, found under the central nave during excavations occurring towards the end of the nineteenth century. The research suggested that they belonged to the heretic Priscillian and his martyred companions. In later studies, Larrea defined Priscillian as an 'ascetic, intensely devoted holy man [who] in no way attempted to deviate from the

Christian faith but wished to prolong it to its natural consequences which are those of the spirit'. His persecution and execution by the materialistic Roman Church, a tool in the hands of the fourth-century political powers, became a landmark in the decimation of Christian Humanism. 'If there is truth in the supplantation of Priscillian by Santiago' Larrea affirmed, 'the discovery at this particular time is the equivalent of an effective substantiation of the trunk thesis of "Rendición de Espíritu".'

In the article 'Introducción a un Nuevo Mundo' (Introduction to a New World), published in the first issue of the magazine *España Peregrina* (1940), one could read some of Larrea's strongest convictions set forth with impeccable clarity and which attracted Buñuel's attention and that of other distinguished intellectuals in exile. He stated that 'It is the responsibility of Spain, the Spanish people, the sacrificed, to enable, by handing over their Truth, the access to this world of true civilisation, to be its effective and indispensable harbinger.' This is not the place, as the reader can no doubt sense, in which to expand on the life and work of Larrea. It is sufficient to note how his proximity to Buñuel, during the first four years of residence in Mexico, would determine not only the thought and later work of the Spanish film-maker, but also, decisively, his change of attitude towards the existence and events, within infinite nuances, of the complex and fascinating reality of Mexico.

Once refined, the mystic-prophetic spirit of the images and the themes upheld by Larrea became influential over many Spanish Republican exiles, as well as outstanding Latin-American poets that had first-hand experience of the Spanish tragedy, such as Octavio Paz or Pablo Neruda. Buñuel found himself particularly susceptible to Larrea's writings. The concept of religion became something more complex than a simple strategy of domination by the powerful. At the same time, the film-maker was soon convinced of being immersed in a complex society of enormous cultural resources, capable of transforming his contradictions into a promising scenario of ideological and political renovation that could be vigorously encouraged throughout the rest of Latin America and even the world.

Mexico was no longer a country of folklore and picturesque revolutions, condemned to failure due to their populist nature – as the first scene of *Ensayo de un crimen* (*Essay of a Crime*, 1995) recalls – or the mythical space in which the eternal characters Cervantes, Calderón or Galdós can come to life. 'Some of the films by Luis Buñuel – *L'age d'or, Los olvidados* – not ceasing to be films', Octavio Paz wrote, 'take us to other regions of the spirit: certain engravings by Goya, a poem by Quevedo or Péret, a passage from Sade, an *esperpento* by Valle Inclán, one page from Gómez de la Serna ... These films can be enjoyed and valued as cinema and also as something belonging to a broader and freer universe of such works, precious amongst many, their object being both to reveal human reality to us and also suggest a means to surpass it.'

The image of Mexico and the imaginative mechanisms of reflection suggested by Larrea appealed to the visionary spirit of the avant garde, which Buñuel was so fond of, and established an adequate umbrella that separated them from the *costumbrista* formalism in vogue at the time, the origins of which can found in the mural paintings of Rivera, Orozco and Siqueiros, or the photography of Edward Weston, Tina Modotti or Manuel Álvarez Bravo, who was present during the shooting of the unfinished *¡Que viva México!* in 1933 and who taught the camera operator Gabriel Figueroa. Inspired by Vallejo, Larrea presented an image of Mexico that related to the tragedy in Spain and its cultural tradition, veering away from the commonly used stereotypes so despised by Buñuel ('I am horrified by Mexican hats!'). However, it is not a question of finding connections between the visions of either author, but of understanding how Larrea's cosmovision became the key that enabled the Spanish film-maker to access a previously unknown intellectual and cultural territory, that enabled him to articulate new features of the Mexican identity – and that of the rest of Latin America – more attuned to the social and political realities of the time.

From these diverse influences came the inspiration for *Los olvidados*. 'We were going through hard times', Buñuel remembered. 'Well, above all Larrea ... I still had something left over from *El gran calavera* (*The Big Reveller*, 1949). We laughed a lot. More than he admits. He was ready to do anything in order to earn some money, and it occurred to us to do the worst type of melodrama, about a little bragger: *Su huerfanito, jefe*. We enjoyed collecting bits and pieces, one worse than another, copying from here and there, as if it were a film by Peter Lorre.'

The box-office success of *El gran calavera,* the second film Buñuel directed in Mexico, encouraged the producer Oscar Dancigers to keep an old promise – to produce a film with artistic pretensions with which the Spanish film-maker could demonstrate his particular talent for surrealism and the absurd that was so evident in *Un chien andalou* (1929) and *Las Hurdes/Tierra sin pan* (1933). Buñuel, who had already seen how Dancigers rejected the experimentalism of *Ilegible hijo de flauta* suggested something seemingly more commercial, *¡Mi huerfanito, jefe!*, the story of a poor boy, a lottery seller, who becomes wealthy due to an unexpected turn of fortune – the last lottery ticket that he had been unable to sell in spite of his efforts, wins the first prize.

Though dismissed by many as one of Buñuel's anecdotes, the film-maker himself attributes the initial idea for *Los olvidados* to this in an interview with Tomás Pérez Turrent and José de la Colina. 'I proposed [*¡Mi huerfanito, jefe!*] to Dancigers … "Not bad" Dancigers said to me, "but it's a bit of a feuilleton. Let's do something rather more serious. A story about the poor children in Mexico".' If we eliminate Buñuel's tendency towards irony and self parody, one could reasonably conclude that the producer simply implied that a dramatic structure, without puns or ambiguities, would be received with more enthusiasm by the general public than a burlesque and anti-sentimental piece. For Dancigers, the option of child tragedy appearing in the story on poverty, but constructed as a social drama, would reduce the risks in national and international circuits of exhibition and might also obtain acceptable returns at the box-office, given the success of Italian Neorealism worldwide.

Such observation, worthy of an experienced producer aware of the interaction between cinema and spectator, as Buñuel himself was, triggered alternative forms of creativity and obliged the Spanish film-maker to reflect on the true scope of the opportunity he was being offered. In effect, why not take a risk and insert the transgressive capacity of experimental cinema within the conventional stream of fiction? The project of adapting *Wuthering Heights* or *Las cuevas del Vaticano* in the early 1930s had constituted the first attempt of confronting this challenge. Years later, during his North American travels, removed from artistic or literary ideas, he developed, unsuccessfully, some ideas for the Hollywood film industry; sketches for gags, scenes and even whole scripts, like *La novia de medianoche* in collaboration with the professor of literature and writer from Galicia, José Rubia Barcia. 'This return to your old self with *Los olvidados*', Max Aub came to ask Buñuel, 'did it happen a little by chance or because you were searching for yourself since you got to Mexico?' 'No, no. I wasn't looking for anything', Buñuel answered, 'I thought it was impossible. I thought I would never make a personal film again. I thought I was finished.'

Even though it is true that Buñuel had not deliberately planned the project that would lead to *Los olvidados*, we should, on the other hand, reject the idea that the film came about by chance. When returning to Dancigers' suggestion, which was based on the initial figure of a poor boy, a lottery seller, Buñuel realised that the circumstances encouraged him not to approach fiction through literature but rather through the simple recording of life; through a genre, the documentary, which he so impeccably had come to master in his dual role of film-maker and supervisor of propaganda documentaries, first for the Spanish Republican embassy in Paris and then in New York's Museum of Modern Art. In light of Dancigers' proposition, the new idea, once converted into the project of *Los olvidados*, became both a fascinating challenge and one of the most decisive milestones in Luis Buñuel's professional career.

Juan Carlos Ibáñez and Manuel Palacio

REFERENCES

Aub, M. (1985) *Conversaciones con Buñuel*. Madrid: Aguilar.

Buñuel, L. (1982) *Mi último suspiro*. Barcelona: Plaza y Janés.

García Riera, E. (1969–78) *Historia documental del cine mexicano*, 9 vols. México: Era (Revised and expanded edition, 18 vols., Guadalajara/México, Universidad de Guadalajara/Gobierno de Jalisco/Consejo Nacional para la Cultura y las Artes/Instituto Mexicano de Cinematografía, 1993–97).

Pérez Turrent, T. & Colina, J. de la (1993) *Buñuel por Buñuel*. Madrid: Plot.

Sánchez Vidal, A. (1988) *Buñuel, Lorca, Dalí: el enigma sin fin*. Barcelona: Planeta.

O CANGACEIRO

06

LIMA BARRETO, BRAZIL, 1953

> Not the myth of a past people, but the story-telling of the people to come.
>
> – Gilles Deleuze, *The Time-Image* (1985)

In March 1968, the magazine of Brazil's Instituto Nacional do Cinema (National Film Institute), *Revista Film Cultura*, published a list of the ten best motion pictures in the history of Brazilian cinema. At that time nobody was surprised by the fact that Lima Barreto's *O Cangaceiro* was voted the top film. The movie, produced by the prestigious studio Vera Cruz of São Paulo, had achieved overwhelming success both in Brazil and abroad due to its artistic achievements and to the international distribution by Columbia Pictures. Doubly awarded at the 1953 Cannes Film Festival and premiered in 22 countries, *O Cangaceiro*'s influence spread beyond Brazilian borders, but not always in a fortuitous way. For some years the film was seen to present a stereotypical image of Brazil only comparable to the one exposed later in *Orphée noir* (*Black Orpheus*, 1958) directed by the French film-maker Marcel Camus.

In March 1999, more than 30 years after that first survey, the *Folha de São Paulo* consulted 24 critics and scholars of Brazilian cinema and published a new top-ten list. It included films as diverse as Mário Peixoto's *Limite*, (*Limit*, 1931), Glauber Rocha's *Deus e o diabo na terra do sol* (*Black God, White Devil*, 1964) and Hector Babenco's *Pixote, a lei do mais fraco* (*Pixote*, 1980). However, Lima Barreto's film was not included. Why? Had the critics lost their memory? Or did the 'artistic achievements' of *O Cangaceiro* fail to survive the passage of time?

This essay analyses *O Cangaceiro* as a cultural and ideological phenomenon through the study of its aesthetic and thematic qualities. It also intends to explain the reasons for its original success and its current position. Beyond the personal attack of some film-makers of the *cinema novo* – particularly Glauber Rocha – and beyond the superficial reconciliation that certain film critics, such as Ana M. López have recently shown, it is preferable to understand the film as a regressive work that preserves reality as a 'depoliticised image'. Since the film, in its own way, presents a particular idea of the past, it is appropriate to focus on how

O Cangaceiro reconstructs an episode of Brazil's history in order to analyse its aesthetic and thematic qualities.

O Cangaceiro is often described as a story of love and death, but this dramatic aspect is just one part of the plot. The tragic romance between the bandit Teodoro and the teacher Olívia hides a potentially more interesting second story about the armed struggle of a *cangaceiros* band commanded by the captain Galdino Ferreira. The primary narrative – the love story – reflects personal and passionate forces, while the second – the *cangaceiro* story – has a communal and historical character. If we understand that the *cangaceiro* of the film's title is Teodoro (the 'good bandit' who sacrifices his life for Olívia, a young lady kidnapped by the captain during an assault on a town), we clearly give priority to the romantic and dramatic elements of the plot. But if, on the other hand, we understand that the true *cangaceiro* is the evil Galdino, then we are emphasising the historical dimension of the film, because the love story yields to the depiction of the *cangaço*, the popular armed movement that rose up in the northeast of Brazil between the 1880s and the 1930s. Due to the effective portrayal of Galdino and the idiosyncratic performance of the actor Milton Ribeiro, most viewers still link the bandit of the title to the mean captain; in other words, they understand the movie in historical rather than in emotional terms. Although both narrative lines are effectively combined, it is evident that if we are today still interested in Lima Barreto's film, it is because of its particular representation of the figure of the *cangaceiro*, and not because of the trivial love adventures of Teodoro and Olívia.

The *cangaceiros* emerged from the *sertão*, the vast region in the northeast of Brazil, during periods of economic crisis and severe droughts, over the last years of the nineteenth century. They were bandits who attacked towns in order to avoid slavery and starvation. In constant revolt against big landowners and agents of the various central governments, the *cangaceiros* became cult figures of Brazilian folk tales, due to their courage, strong mysticism, and violent opposition to any kind of social injustice. The *literatura de cordel* and other famous texts, such as *Os sertões* by Euclides da Cunha (1902), characterized in detail the main features of this figure that was used repeatedly in the Brazilian cinema of the 1930s and 1940s. With *O Cangaceiro*, Lima Barreto (1906–82), a former journalist and award-winning director of documentaries, internationalised the genre that only achieved its true poetic dimension in the following decade when the film-makers of the *cinema novo* revisited Brazil's history and made several films about the *cangaço* movement. Vera Cruz studios described Barreto's film as 'a sum of fiction and the reality of the Northeast, a kind of great mural of the *sertaneja* life of those famous highwaymen bands that drifted around certain regions of Brazil some time ago'.

In a moment of national economic growth, Vera Cruz was founded as a replica of the American studios. Both the structure and the management of the company imitated the production form established in Hollywood. In the postwar period São Paulo became, paradoxically, 'the locomotive of Brazil' and 'the city that grows most in the world'. As Antonio Moreno has pointed out, the city began the 1950s 'with prosperity; with a modern industrial know how; and with a working class that, due to the waves of both rural and foreign immigrants, doubled in less than ten years'. Politician Getúlio Vargas' ascent to power for a second time produced the birth of a *nouveau riche* class with a thirst for patronage, an interest in internationalism, and a desire to invest in different cultural institutions and artistic expressions. The Museo de Arte de São Paulo (MASP), the Museo de Arte Moderno, the Teatro Brasileiro da Comédia and the Cinemateca Brasileira were established in the city during those years.

In this context of economic growth Franco Zampari and Francisco Matarazzo Sobrinho, two members of São Paulo's wealthy bourgeoisie, founded the Companhia Cinematográfica de Vera Cruz in São Bernardo do Campo. The main goal of the company was to produce films with international quality that, at the same time, dealt with issues of 'national relevance'. In its five years of life, Vera Cruz produced several documentaries and 18 feature films, most of them melodramas, like *Tico-Tico no Fubá* (Adolfo Celi, 1952), *Apassionata* (*Passionate*, Fernando de Barros and Adolfo Celi, 1952), and *Sinhá Moça* (*Young Lady*, Tom Payne, 1953). In all cases, neither the aesthetic of these films nor the treatment of the issues responded to the complicated reality of Brazil. Alex Viany wrote in his 1959 *Introdução ao cinema brasileiro* that in Vera Cruz there 'scarcely existed any preoccupation for observing the Brazilian character'. This lack of interest to communicate *with* Brazilians *about* Brazilians, together with the non-existence of economic infrastructure and, over all, with the absence of channels of distribution, forced the studio into bankruptcy in 1954, the same year that Getúlio Vargas committed suicide in Rio de Janeiro.

In a Third World country economically dominated by American multinationals, the company's slogan, 'From the Plateau de Piratininga to the Screens of the World!', reflected Vera Cruz's ideological imitation of the increasingly globalised Hollywood studios. Vera Cruz's version of Brazil and its history outraged intellectuals and left many indifferent. In 1963 Glauber Rocha wrote in *Revisão crítica do cinema brasileiro*, 'In Brazil, where a capitalist structure is consolidated in the contradictions of the agrarian and metropolitan underworld, cinema has been a disastrous alliance between immature authors and amateur capitalists.' Among all the movies produced by Vera Cruz only *O Cangaceiro* obtained both critical and financial success. However, the high box-office takings were not enough to save the company from liquidation, because the international distribution rights for the film had been sold to Columbia Pictures for approximately $15,000. The American company took advantage of the film's success at Cannes and, with a new ending and under the title of *The Bandits*, distributed it worldwide as if it were a film produced in their studios. This successful appropriation by Columbia was possible because the film was already embedded with stylistic features that made it commercially exportable. The aesthetic and ideological canons of Vera Cruz systematically reproduced the common characteristics of the American film industry in a process that could be called 'self-colonisation'. In the case of *O Cangaceiro*, the result of trying to reconstruct a native historical past with foreign methods of representation produced, despite the stylistic achievements, a pastiche work. Hence the difficulty of understanding the film as a 'mural' of the life in the *sertão* or as a reconstruction of the historical phenomenon of the *cangaço*.

Glauber Rocha criticized the film for this reason: 'Without having heard about the *cangaço* fiction and without having understood the meaning of Northeast popular stories, Lima Barreto created a conventional and psychologically basic adventure drama illustrated by mystical figures with leather hats, silver stars, and comic cruelties. The *cangaço*, as a phenomenom of mystic, anarchic revolt born from the Northeastern *latifundio* system and worsened by droughts, was not represented.' Lima Barreto borrowed typical elements from the *cangaço* fiction to create a feature film à la Hollywood and not to portray the greatness and misery of the armed movement. From the three tasks that Heliodoro San Miguel has linked to the new Latin American cinemas (the adoption of Italian Neorealism's narrative models, the rejection of conventional American films and the commitment to leftist politics), it is evident that *O Cangaceiro* fulfills none. Lima Barreto himself would later say that, in his opinion, Italian Neorealism was born lifeless. Although the boom of new Latin American cinemas would take some years to happen, diverse films like Herbert Kline's *The Forgotten Village* (1941), Luis Buñuel's *Los olvidados* (*The Young and the Damned*, 1950), or Nelson Pereira dos Santos' *Rio, 40 graus* (*Rio, 40 Degrees*, 1955) already adopted aspects of these three tasks. But Barreto, of course, was not interested in producing a film of that kind.

The elements of pastiche that Rocha criticized in *O Cangaceiro* are identified in different aspects of the film. First, the genre that the film inaugurates, 'the Northeastern', is a

Western *sui generis*. It replaces the lonesome cowboy with the violent *cangaceiro*, but keeps the main features of the Hollywood style (linear narrative, the description of the protagonists through supporting characters, and a certain Manichaeism in the exposition of moral action and values). Secondly, Barreto's conventional though undeniably meticulous *mise-en-scène* is photographed in the manner of Gabriel Figueroa, but edited in the cutting room as if it were a silent Soviet film. The locations and the languages are inauthentic because São Paulo's high plains pretend to be the rugged *sertão* (the film was shot in Vargem Grande do Sul, in the interior of São Paulo) and the *mineiro* and *gaucho* accents replace the original Northeastern dialect. Finally, the Murnau-like expressionism and frequently lyrical style is adapted by Lima Barreto to the nationalistic imperatives of Vera Cruz, with the constant use of popular music and the insidious presence of Brazilian flora and fauna. These hybrid alterations were probably the reasons why Glauber Rocha talked about the 'detestable principle of imitation' and described *O Cangaceiro* as 'a monster that drove the country crazy'.

However, critics like Ana M. López have recently seen this pastiche as a positive feature of the film. In her thought-provoking article 'The São Paulo Connection: The Companhia Cinematográfica Vera Cruz and *O Cangaceiro*', she points out that 'rather than disjointed foreign borrowings, the deployment of these elements produces a coherent 'narrative and representational space'. López suggests that the film's hybridity is 'transformative', instead of 'imitative', and that the new visual representation 'transplanted a series of thematic and stylistic elements into an "other" audiovisual and historic context in which their function and effects were reinscribed'. This concept of an emancipatory alterity proves to be convincing because the film, although presenting some progressive ideas, is ultimately regressive.

It is true that, at the beginning of the movie, when the band violently attacks the town, the villainous *cangaceiro* Galdino frees the birds from the cages and punishes one member of the gang for having killed one goat unfairly. And it is also true that after the assault Teodoro decides to reject violence and liberate the prisoner. In the best tradition of *cangaço* literature, neither character differentiates between good and evil, perhaps because their action is both liberating and repressive at the same time. This absence of Manichaeism, characteristic of many modern films, disappears as the story moves forward and one cannot judge *O Cangaceiro* for its admittedly fascinating first twenty minutes. From then on, Barreto does not characterize the *cangaceiro* as a *guerrillero* that fights for his survival in a violent region besieged by droughts and poverty but as a figure who lives beyond his historical context, as a positive or negative hero whose link to the land seems magical and supernatural (when dying with mud in his hands, Teodoro exclaims, 'Look, look, the soil of my *sertão*!'). The division between good and evil in the group of *cangaceiros* becomes more and more radical, and with this radicalisation the film displays racist elements. Robert Stam has discovered in the film that color-coded moral schema, reminiscent of 'conquest fiction' and the American western, which 'correlates darkness with villainy and pits a cruel mulatto antagonist against a white actor-hero'. The description of women is even more disturbing. Olívia, white and docile, civilises the illiterate children in the school, while Maria Cláudia, *mestiza* and wild, makes sexual advances on Teodoro in the middle of the night, her natural habitat. Moreover, the sequence in which the brave Teodoro saves Olívia from an attacking leopard explicitly presents the woman as a defenseless being unable to survive in the hard conditions of the *sertão* and in constant need of the male, particularly his violent nature.

As a whole, *O Cangaceiro* emphasizes the individual adventure by dismissing social conflict. It puts the notions of will and destiny (sentences like 'it is *impossible* to escape' or 'every sinner knows his time has come' are repeatedly used) before those of social reality and alienation; and it eventually combines the elements of blood, sacrifice and nation in the manner of the most suspicious propaganda films. Glauber Rocha even declared that the ideology of the film, due to the omnipresence of myth as ultimate truth and natural regulator, was 'typically fascist': 'In his book *Le Cinéma Italien* the film critic and director Carlo Lizzani says that the success of *Cabiria* during the golden age of the Italian silent cinema contributed to the nationalistic exaltation and disseminated a pre-fascist ideology inspired by D'Annunzio. *O Cangaceiro* had, in lesser proportion, a similar effect on the masses.'

López points out that *O Cangaceiro*, because it participates in an 'elusive "impregnation" with Brazilian reality ... powerfully reinscribed the myth into the national cultural imaginary'. However, this attempt at replacing history with myth is precisely the most regressive feature of the film. In his 1970 text 'Le mythe aujourd'hui', Roland Barthes wrote that one of the most pernicious processes in the narration of history is to turn preterite facts into myths. The French philosopher considered that the writing of the past often recurred to the mythic speech that transforms history into nature and meaning into form. Mythic expression, according to Barthes, continually changed the products of history into static essential types, and preserved reality as a 'depoliticised' image. The figure of the *cangaceiro* presented by Lima Barreto with long shots and instrumental music is undoubtedly similar to one of those myths that impose a 'universal order which has fixated once and for all the hierarchy of possessions'. Linked to the land from the beginning of the film ('here I was born, here I live, and here I will die no matter what', says Teodoro), the bandit appears doomed by a supernatural force that emanates from the *sertão*'s mysteries. Fire, dance, guns, nocturnal animals, all are mystical components that Barreto uses to hide the dynamic, non-reconciled historical reality of the vast Brazilian Northeast. Thus *O Cangaceiro* does not tell the story of the real people of Brazil, but the myth of a past people who, in fact, never existed.

It is difficult to agree with López when she writes that 'it was perhaps Vera Cruz and its films – rather than the *cinema novo* – that left the most lasting legacy upon Brazilian media production'. It is especially difficult if we understand that the true legacy of any culture is formed by its poetic expressions and not by its culture industry. If mythic speech is, as Barthes wrote, 'a prohibition for man against inventing himself', then *O Cangaceiro*, because of its insistence on transforming characters, story and history into static types, denies the emancipatory tendencies of an authentic cinema. It would be only some years later, with the birth of the *cinema novo*, that films would reconstruct the past as a dynamic reality and not as a reified image. It would be only the strange and revolutionary *cangaceiro* of Glauber Rocha's *Deus e o diabo na terra do sol* who would talk directly to the camera about 'the story-telling of the people to come'.

Breixo Viejo

REFERENCES

Barreto, L. (1984) *O Cangaceiro.* Fortaleza: Universidade Federal do Ceará/CAPES.

Galvao, M. R. (1981) *Burguesia e cinema: o caso Vera Cruz.* Rio de Janeiro: Civilização Brasileira.

Moreno, A. (1994) *Cinema brasileiro: história e relaçoes com o Estado.* Niteroi: EDUFF.

López, A. M. (1998) 'The São Paulo Connection: The Companhia Cinematográfica Vera Cruz and *O Cangaceiro*', in *Nuevo Texto Crítico,* 21–2, 127–54.

Rocha, G. (1963) *Revisão crítica do cinema brasileiro,* Rio de Janeiro: Civilizaçao Brasileira.

Stam, R. (1997) 'Vera Cruz: Hollywood in the Tropics, 1949–1954', in R. Stam (ed.) *Tropical Multiculturalism: A Comparative History of Race in Brazilian Cinema and Culture.* Durham, NC: Duke University Press.

Viany, A. (1959) *Introdução ao cinema brasileiro.* Rio de Janeiro: Instituto Nacional do Livro.

RIO, 40 GRAUS RIO, 40 DEGREES

07

NELSON PEREIRA DOS SANTOS, BRAZIL, 1955

Rio, 40 graus marked the start of Nelson Pereira dos Santos' directing career, one that spanned over 40 years of Brazilian cinema, encompassing 17 feature films as a director, numerous shorts and documentaries, and several other movies as producer and editor. The father of modern cinema in Brazil and probably the most important film-maker in this country's history, he was both a precursor to and a pivotal member of the *cinema novo*, making *Vidas secas* (*Barren Lives*, 1962), one of the movement's masterpieces. Later in his life he would navigate through other intellectual currents such as *Antropofagia* (Anthropophagy) and *Tropicalismo* (Tropicalism), leaving his mark on all of them, while at the same time keeping a very personal and independent vision already present in his first film.

Rio, 40 graus is the earliest manifestation of Pereira dos Santos' rich and individualistic personality. Pereira dos Santos came from a middle-class family and his love for the movies started as a child, when his parents used to take him for weekend matinées. Later, as a law student in his native São Paulo, he became a member of the Communist Party of Brazil (PCB). In October 1949, he had the opportunity to travel to Paris with the painters Luís Ventura and Otávio Araujo, where they were received by the leading Brazilian artists and intellectuals exiled in the French capital. Pereira dos Santos stayed there for two months, and this period, albeit brief, proved to be decisive for his film career. The future director was introduced to Henri Langlois and became a constant visitor of the French Cinémathèque. It was here that he was exposed to the Italian Neorealist films, and came into contact with the ideas and writings of Cesare Zavattini, who impressed him deeply. He was also influenced by the documentary style of John Grierson and Joris Ivens, whose leftist humanism left a powerful mark on him. Neorealist principles and documentary approach would later inspire the whole process of the production of *Rio, 40 graus*.

For personal reasons Pereira dos Santos had to return to Brazil (to marry his girlfriend Laurita who was expecting their first child, and because he was called into military service), but his passion for cinema and his determination to become a film-maker were already ignited. He soon became a regular member of the *cine-club* circles of São Paulo, and had an active participation in the Congresso Paulista do Cinema (São Paulo Congress of Cinema) celebrated in 1951, and in the first two Congressos Nacionales do Cinema Brasileiro (National Congresses of Brazilian Cinema) that took place in 1952 and 1953. In those conferences, aimed to debate the future of Brazilian cinema, young left-wing intellectuals like Pereira dos Santos advocated the production of national films that would portray the culture and social realities of the people of Brazil, from the poverty of the *favelas* to the drought of the *sertão*, and in this way attempt to improve their living conditions by raising awareness of their situation. These same ideals were defended in his articles in *Fundamentos,* a leftist magazine for which Pereira dos Santos began writing after his return from Paris.

The main target of their discontent with Brazil's current cinema was the style of the movies made by the Companhia Cinematográfica Vera Cruz. This company was an ambitious project created in 1949 to produce commercially viable movies replicating the Hollywood studio system, blended with aspects of a high European style. The Vera Cruz company even hired foreign technicians, most of them from Europe. Its movies, for the most part, had no roots in Brazilian culture, nor did they have any pretentions to authenticity, ignoring the country's national, historical and social themes. Politically progressive intellectuals and aspiring film-makers like Pereira dos Santos were not opposed in principle to corporations like the Vera Cruz. On the contrary, they even defended the need for state intervention and public support of the country's film industry and the obligation to show a quota of Brazilian films in movie theatres. What they contested was the direction taken by that industry. Within a few years Vera Cruz went bankrupt. Its only real box-office success was one of its last movies, *O Cangaceiro*, ironically the most Brazilian film of all, and the one that practically created a domestic genre.

Since the Vera Cruz company was synonymous with the technically impressive movies and the commercial narrative patterns identified with Hollywood, rejecting it required the search for an alternative model. This called for a film-making style devoid of the ties of an industrially crafted cinema in favor of an aesthetics of urgency and poverty in which technique was secondary to content. And here is where Italian Neorealism filled the gap. Like other Latin American countries, the adoption of Neorealist tenets was formal, and not based on mere imitation. The themes were purely Brazilian, but Neorealism provided a method and a tool to depict and denounce the different social conditions of the country. It also opened the doors for the possibility of making low budget artisan films that could be made in the streets without professional actors, and that could address popular themes and social problems, making clear their authors' political inclinations and intentions.

It was in this highly charged ideological and cultural context that Pereira dos Santos embarked on the production of *Rio, 40 graus*. After returning from Paris, he had made two short propaganda movies for the Communist Party, and later worked as assistant director in three feature films. Among themm was *Agulha no palheiro* (*Needle in the Haystack*, 1952), a movie directed by film critic Alex Viany that introduced some critical social elements inside the popular *chanchadas*, and where some influence of Neorealism could already be felt. But this movie proved to be crucial for other reasons. During the shooting Pereira dos Santos met Hélio Silva, who later became the director of photography on *Rio, 40 graus*, as well as on many of his subsequent movies. Working on *Agulha no palheiro* also required his moving to Rio de Janeiro, which was considered a step back by the leftist cultural circles of São Paulo. However, it was in this new city that Pereira dos Santos found the inspiration and the freedom to make *Rio, 40 graus*. From then on Rio would always be his base.

Rio, 40 graus suffered problems even before it went into production. The preparation and subsequent shooting was a complicated and prolonged process, plagued by endless financial, technical and personal conflicts. Pereira dos Santos was at this time a recent law graduate in his mid-twenties, married with two children, and writing for magazines and newspapers to provide his family with a living. He wrote the script between the last months of 1953 and the beginning of 1954. However, he could not find a producer that would invest in a story many considered unfit for the big screen. The Communist Party did not support him either, although Pereira dos Santos was a very active political member. Still tangled up in the strict Stalinist political guidelines of the period, the Party found that the movie was not faithful to Socialist Realism. Pereira dos Santos was even removed from the Cultural Commission of the Party and, although he would always remain a supportive member, he maintained a certain distance, especially in matters related to personal creativity. Despite these setbacks, and determined to make *Rio, 40 graus*, Pereira dos Santos created a cooperative in which participants would contribute with work or money to the production of the film. The cooperative was named Equipe Moacyr Fenelon (Moacyr Fenelon Team), in honor of the founder of the Atlántida film company. Even the camera was borrowed from Humberto Mauro, the great Brazilian film pioneer who was at that time the director of the INCE, the National Institute of Educational Cinema. The final budget of the movie was less than two million cruzeiros, a very modest amount for the period.

Under these circumstances, the making of the film proved to be extremely stressful. Pereira dos Santos started filming in Maracanã in March 1954, but in just a few days had to stop due to technical and financial difficulties that delayed the production for three months. When they began again in July, the entire crew moved into the same apartment (a feature that would happen again in many of Pereira dos Santos' films), living in such dire conditions that, at times, verged on borderline poverty. Another time-consuming activity for many of the crew members was their political commitments. In those agitated years of Brazil's history, all of them, including Pereira dos Santos, actively participated in the presidential campaign of Juscelino Kubitschek. As a result, *Rio, 40 graus* took one year to complete, but with less than a hundred actual days of filming. Immediately afterwards, Pereira dos Santos came up with the idea of making a trilogy on the conditions of life in Rio de Janeiro. His second movie, *Rio Zona Norte* (*Rio North Zone*, 1957) depicted the city's poor neighborhoods. The third project, *Rio Zona Sul* (*Rio South Zone*), focusing on the prosperous areas, remained unfilmed. Instead, he produced the excellent *O grande momento* (*The Great Moment*, 1958) directed by Roberto Santos, who had also worked on *Rio, 40 graus*. Following a similar pattern, the movie takes place in one day in the Bras neighborhood of São Paulo, where Pereira dos Santos had spent his childhood.

Just prior to the release of *Rio, 40 graus*, the Chief of the Department of Public Security, Colonel Geraldo de Menezes Cortes, accused the film of degrading Rio's image. He argued that the movie offered a distorted view of the city, where nobody seemed to work (forgetting that the action takes place on a Sunday), and that in Rio the temperature never reached 40° celsius. Made in a period of great political turbulence when it felt like a military coup d'état could happen at any moment, *Rio, 40 graus* was deemed too controversial, resulting in it being banned by the authorities. Laurita, Pereira dos Santos' wife, left for São Paulo with a copy of the movie so that it could be saved. The same leftist intellectuals who previously showed little or no support for the film, including politicians and journalists of major newspapers, now orchestrated a huge campaign that reached international proportions. The coup ultimately did not take place, Kubitschek was elected president, and the film was finally authorized on 31 December. It opened commercially in March 1956. The publicity generated by the scandal provoked long lines during the first few weeks, but they soon disappeared, and the movie was a relative commercial failure. It took more than two years to recover the amount originally invested. According to Pereira dos Santos' own account to his biographer Helena Salem, the public thought that nudity was the reason for banning the film, and were disappointed with what they finally saw.

Rio, 40 graus was for the most part ignored by the people that were its inspiration and should have been its audience. Here resides the most inescapable contradiction of this movie. As was the case with the ensuing *cinema novo*, and contrary to what happened in other countries like Cuba, these films had very limited popular success. Later in his career Pereira dos Santos would acknowledge this, and try to approach more popular themes that could appeal to larger audiences, such as *O amuleto de Ogum* (*The Amulet of Ogum*, 1974). In the mid-1990s, when he was asked by the British Film Institute to make a movie to commemorate the first century of motion pictures, instead of making the expected documentary on the *cinema novo*, Pereira dos Santos chose to direct a fiction film, *Cinema de lágrimas* (*Cinema of Tears*, 1995). This film, so far his last, was devoted to the Mexican melodramas of the 1930s and 1940s; an example of popular cinema that touched people in a much deeper way than most socially conscious movies did.

Rio, 40 graus earned wide national critical acclaim, receiving an excellent reception in intellectual circles, and a warm response in foreign countries. The French critic André Bazin considered that despite some defects, the film should be seen in Europe. It was shown at the Karlovy Vary Film Festival, where Pereira dos Santos was awarded the Best Young Director prize. Ironically, the production of the film coincided with the collapse of the Vera Cruz company, defining the years from 1953 to 1955 as a major turning point in the history of Brazilian cinema. *Rio, 40 graus* became the symbol of this transformation in which the only previous referents were the regional cinemas of the silent period, *Limite* (*Limit*, 1931), Mário Peixoto's avant-garde work, and the films of Humberto Mauro, specially *Ganga bruta* (1933). Pereira dos Santos himself told Helena Salem that they thought they were 'starting from zero' and that even when Humberto Mauro lent them the camera, he had only seen Mauro's last film, and was not aware of the true meaning of his work. Glauber Rocha considered that Peixoto, Mauro, and Pereira dos Santos were the antecedents of the authentic Brazilian cinema, and that *Rio, 40 graus* represented the coming of age of a cultural and political consciousness whose products would crystallise in the 1960s with the emergence of the *cinema novo*; *Rio, 40 graus*' aesthetics of poverty prefigure their 'aesthetics of hunger'.

But labeling this film as just an antecedent of the *cinema novo* does not do it justice. *Rio, 40 graus*, the resulting work of a personal and social struggle, was a seminal film in many other ways, and it would radically affect the way movies were made in Brazil and Latin America in the coming years. Starting with the inventive cooperative method of production, although this was more a consequence of the situation rather than an option, the film was revolutionary. Over the years, its significance in the history of Brazilian cinema has been steadily growing, and it is still today, along with *Vidas secas* and *Memórias do cárcere* (*Prison Memories*, 1983), one of Pereira dos Santos' most influential works.

Rio, 40 graus is a seemingly simple black-and-white movie that in an unassuming and concise style shows the street life of Rio de Janeiro, centering around the people of the *morro* of Cabuçu, a very poor neighborhood of *favelas*, where many of the real inhabitants worked as actors in the film. The title refers not only to the warm climate, but also to the overheated social environment. Depicting people in a realistic manner, and showing the conditions of urban life, mostly working class, the camera follows the happenings of five black *manisero* kids from Cabuçu that sell their peanuts all over the city, from the stadium of Maracanã to the Pão de Açucar.

Pereira dos Santos' graphic portrait of Rio de Janeiro reveals a powerful and instinctive director with a taxonomist's eye for small meaningful details, a perceptive mind for social relations, and a humanist heart with his characters. From the *favelas* of Cabuçu to the beaches of Copacabana, and from troubled soldiers to rich landowners turned politicians, the people of Rio are the focus of Pereira dos Santos' analysis, and it is to them that this film is dedicated. The film's characters have everyday problems. Some seem small, like a child losing his little lizard. Others bigger, like the young girl and the soldier discussing her pregnancy and marriage. But the director takes all of them as seriously as their protagonists do, showing genuine sympathy, while at the same time avoiding excessive sentimentalism and unnecessary drama. From football to samba, and from Corcovado to Quinta de la Boa Vista, the life of the city is depicted as slices of that complex reality that is Brazil, building on contrasts and social inequalities of class, gender and race.

One of the most original features of this film, and one of its main achievements, was to point the camera towards the poorest urban classes of a major city, ignored for the most part by the previous Brazilian cinema. *Rio, 40 graus* portrays their marginal and oppressed condition, and exposes the people of Rio in all their diversity and multiracial complexity, exploring the subtle interactions between skin color and social status. The black population is shown without stereotypes, without a hint of the typical patronising attitude all too frequent in earlier films. It is not a coincidence that one of the sambas they sing at the end of the movie refers to the end of slavery. Women are also characterised as complex and strong characters. Some carry the household responsibility on their shoulders, and others are independent in their relationships. Beyond class, race and age, all of the women, even those suffering the consequences of being framed in a male dominated society, are depicted as unusually active and determined, many times taking the initiative in resolving problems.

Rio, 40 graus also addresses the role of football, a topic very poorly treated in Brazilian cinema considering its tremendous social impact. It works as a microcosm of social interactions: power struggles, manipulation of the press, an escape for the masses from the problems of everyday life, and men as market commodities. In a period when football players did not have the same economic status as they have today, the retiring idol complains to the new star, 'one day we will not be merchandise', describing an exploitative situation that will be taken to the extreme in *Vidas secas*, where the family decides to move to the city so as 'not to be animals'. Although the film has few moments of hope, it shows the dreams and illusions of its protagonists, displaying a festive side that conveys some optimism and a positive outlook. This is best exemplified by the ending, in which the samba school of Portela visits one in Cabuçu, and the camera flies high above the hills, metaphorically taking the 'voice of *morro*' (the title of the film's musical theme), all over Rio de Janeiro.

The film is not preachy or moralizing in its social critique and political commentary. Its analysis surfaces naturally as a consequence of the stark depiction of the situation, and not as an elaborate ideological discourse by the director, nor is it rhetorically voiced by any of his characters. It comes across as a sort of critical realism in which the discourse is not external to the contents, and where the spectators need to elaborate their own conclusions by looking at the reality that is unveiled in front of their eyes. But not everything works smoothly in the movie, and at times it is obviously simplistic. Some characters are rather one-dimensional caricatures, especially those from the upper classes. A number of situations are resolved by unconvincing gestures, like the dispute between Miro and Alberto regarding Alice, that is quickly settled and forgotten when they recognised each other as supportive comrades in a violent strike that took place the previous month.

Yet it was not just a ground-breaking film for its subject matter; its structure is equally innovative. The film does not have a traditional story line, or any semblance of linear narrative, but is more of a collage; a collection of snapshots taken on any given Sunday on the streets of the then Brazilian capital. It has its share of faults, being technically imperfect at times, but in other moments concealing a refined and complex formalism. Pereira dos Santos' approach to the stories and characters defines a style in which the use of ellipses and transitions are major cinematic tools. The director sets the circumstances, the characters and the tone of the scene to make the spectator aware of the situation. But when the source of the conflict and the object of the conversation are exposed, he arrests our expectations by taking us to another area of the city with different problems. The succession of sequences takes place in two ways. Sometimes they just flow gracefully between characters and scenes, connected by any small element that can serve as a link. The shoes of someone walking fast with the intention of spoiling a party lead us to the harmonious movement of the feet of samba dancers. A car passing by in the background of the main characters is then naturally followed by the camera to transport us to a new location. Other times transitions take place by violent juxtapositions, many of which are anticlimactic, like the *montage* between the child's deadly accident and the enthusiasm over Foguinho's goal in Maracanã. Even the soundtrack of the film becomes a significant element to facilitate those transitions and punctuate the narrative, initiating a defining feature of Pereira dos Santos' style (it is worth remembering the obsessive sound of the carriage in *Vidas secas*). The noise of traffic, people screaming at the football stadium, the sounds of the radio, the catchy theme written by Zé Keti, they all contribute to enrich the story and blend, smoothly or sharply, seemingly disconnected elements.

This functional use of editing in Pereira dos Santos' hands has the same goals as it did in the Soviet classics. He does not employ suspense, nor does he resort to any other narrative means to grab the public's attention. His intention is to provoke a rational response, to generate an idea in the spectator's mind, and not to produce an easy emotional identification. He avoids this through anticlimactic transitions and resolutions of conflicts that break the viewer's expectations, as presented in conventional narratives. What Pereira dos Santos aimed for was to make us aware of the multiple layers of reality and their complex interconnections. Life and death, poverty and wealth, power and weakness, joy and sorrow, all happening together, inescapably linked, impossible to dissociate, and separated by a very thin line.

Through its depiction of urban realities and its unusual cinematic structure, *Rio, 40 graus* exposed a previously concealed and powerful image of Rio de Janeiro, quite different from the stereotype of vibrant carnivals and colorful postcards. It irked the authorities who banned it, but opened the eyes of many young film-makers who found in its style their inspiration. Pereira dos Santos' first work had the same impact that Buñuel's *Los olvidados* (*The Young and the Damned*, 1950) did in Mexico, and offered a new way to make movies, which later became a well travelled road for all the main figures and currents inside the New Latin American Cinema. The paramount features behind this movement are all present and deeply interwoven in *Rio, 40 graus*; the rejection of the mainstream Hollywood-type commercial narrative; the adaptation of the Italian Neorealist style to the diverse realities of the Latin American countries; the leftist political commitment of their practitioners; and the affirmation of the film-maker as an *auteur* with, in Rocha's words, 'an idea in his head and a camera in his hand'. The camera of a director attentive to the dynamic and ever-changing nature of reality. The camera of an artist that anticipates trends, explores new paths, and searches for innovations in film language, while at the same time sharing an intrinsic humanistic approach, and keeping his faith in cinema as a tool to understand, explain and, maybe, even transform reality. Nelson Pereira dos Santos, with *Rio, 40 graus*, intended a radical departure from the past, signaling the birth of modern Brazilian cinema, whose powerful echoes still reverberate today.

Heliodoro San Miguel

REFERENCES

Johnson, R. (1984) *Cinema novo x 5: Masters of Contemporary Brazilian Film*. Austin: University of Texas Press.

Johnson, R. & Stam, R. (eds) (1982) *Brazilian Cinema*. New Brunswick: Associated University Presses (Expanded edition, New York: Columbia University Press, 1995).

Paranaguá, P. A. (ed.) (1987) *Le cinéma brésilien*. Paris: Centre Georges Pompidou.

Salem, H. (1987) *Nelson Pereira dos Santos: o soho possível do cinema brasileiro*. Rio de Janeiro: Nova Fronteira. (Expanded edition, Rio de Janeiro: Record, 1996) (Spanish translation, *Nelson Pereira dos Santos: el sueño posible del cine brasileño*, Madrid: Cátedra/Filmoteca Española, 1997).

Stam, R. (1997) *Tropical Multiculturalism: A Comparative History of Race in Brazilian Cinema and Culture*. Durham, NC: Duke University Press.

Viany, A. (1959) *Introduçao ao cinema brasileiro*. Rio de Janeiro: Instituto Nacional do Livro.

LA CASA DEL ÁNGEL THE HOUSE OF THE ANGEL

08

LEOPOLDO TORRE NILSSON, ARGENTINA, 1956

Shot in June and July 1956, and premiered on 11 July 1957, *La casa del ángel* boosted the local and international reputation of Leopoldo Torre Nilsson and his style of film-making. The flamboyant and engaging discourse of the film did not sit easily alongside the 'traditional cinema' formula of Argentina Sono Film, the studio that produced it. Conceived as a 'quality film' in order to win the financial awards that the Instituto Nacional de Cinematografía (National Film Institute) were granting at that time, it won the Best Film award and the studio recceived 1,600,000 pesos. It also won the awards for its director, story (Beatriz Guido's novel *La casa del ángel*, which had previously been awarded the Emecé Publishing House literary award in 1954), cinematography (Aníbal González Paz), and music (Juan Carlos Paz). It was also presented at the 10th Cannes International Film Festival in May 1957. In a survey carried out by the magazine *Cahiers du Cinéma*, the historian Georges Sadoul and other representatives of *Les Lettres Françaises* ranked it among the best ten movies shown in France in 1957. It was premiered in France as *La maison de l'ange*, and in English as *End of Innocence*, although Roy Armes referred to it as *The House of the Angel* in the article he dedicated to Leopoldo Torre Nilsson in the *International Film Guide* in 1967. It also went some way to highlighting the presence of Argentinian film within the world cinema circuit.

Following its premiere in Argentina, many viewers and critics expressed reservations about the film, for the most part due to problems people had in understanding it. The Catholic Church frowned at Nilsson's daring view and audiences attending screenings out of curiosity made caustic remarks about the *mise-en-scène* and the film-maker's different approach to the 'naïve teenager' topic (also presented in *Graciela*, the film version of Carmen Laforet's novel *Nada*, which was premiered by Argentina Sono Film in May 1956). Audiences also objected to the unusual camera angles, the low positions of the camera, the use of light, the set designs, and the dissonant music. These arguments were welcomed at that time because they motivated some kind of unorganised reflection on cinema that spread to other areas of film culture, allowing the audience to participate in discussions on the concept of the film experience. Films by Torre Nilsson, as well as works by groundbreaking directors around the world, gradually began to receive screenings at cinema clubs, inspiring film discussions during coffee meetings, train journeys, bus rides and office hours.

During the opening credits, *La casa del ángel* begins with blurred images and the sound of footsteps. Juan Carlos Paz's sonorous rhythms are mixed with church or clock bells, palpitating with a deliberate lack of definition. From the start, Nilsson establishes the *film speech* in a space of 'unreality' or 'interior reality'. The unfolding action develops into a prologue. A female voice-over (Elsa Daniel) describes facts that correspond to the images; there is a certain visual deformation, however, produced by the low positioning of the camera and extreme close-ups of faces and objects. Shadows, accentuated by backlights have an ethereal quality. The woman's voice tells of an action that she claims is indefinitely repeated, from Friday to Friday. It is a prologue *en abîme*, without specific time or defined space. The action cannot be embraced; the retelling of quoted situations becomes undecipherable and the description goes beyond the fact of becoming an object itself.

If we consider Gilles Deleuze's notion of the *recollection-image* then Torre Nilsson's prologue never reformulates the *pure description* as narrative. The lack of definition cannot be decoded by the viewer's scrutinising attention; the voice-over of Ana (the main character of the film) uses verbs in an uncertain future tense that builds up a sense of immanent and continuous present. It is what Deleuze calls a *pure sound image*, an image that places itself only in its description. This description prevents us from seeing the object, since it is both a sensitive and intellectual displacement. What Deleuze says about Jean-Luc Godard's *Les Carabiniers* (1963) could be applied to the images of this prologue. 'He makes of each shot a description that replaces the object and that will lead to another description, to the extreme that, instead of organically describing an object, they are shown to us as pure descriptions that undo themselves at the same time that are being drawn.' In this sense, the result (an *inorganic image* in Deleuze's terminology) is an *audiovisual abstraction*.

In this initial sequence, it is surprising how Torre Nilsson is suggesting an elliptical language rather than establishing the ellipsis as a figure; only language (and the speech that derives from its comprehension) is specific and can be verified. If this filmic and abstract prologue is imposed upon us as a way of approaching reality, it would not be absurd to understand the sum of the *pure description* and the voice-over as Ana's mental confusion during her wakefulness, or during that second when she just awakes, when mind images and remembrances are chaotically, partially and poorly assembled because of her fear of every day's rebirth. In terms of narrative devices, the prologue acquires the form of an interior flashback (timeless – although it covers all times) whose only contact with reality is Ana's eyes, shot in extreme close-up. Following it is the second flashback, which is a return to the past, showing, with chronological coherence, the story of Ana's adolescence and the exposure of her body to its own development. 'Everything began that afternoon in Adrogué's manor', says the voice-over with the evident indication of a deictic phrase that points out a temporal beginning.

We soon learn that Ana is named Ana Castro and that she belongs to a family of certain lineage and murky political past, and that the action takes place at the end of the 1920s. Ana lives with her sisters, protected, if not suffocated, by the exaggerated Puritanism of her mother and by her father's old-fashioned life. He constantly tries to revitalise a political past of duels and barricade debates that has turned into verbal struggles of dirty content.

Ana is raised by Naná, a nanny with bulging eyes who may not look like a witch, but becomes unhealthily obsessed with the welfare of the children. Nilsson ridicules Naná because of her hypocritically sensual character. Ana meets street kids through hidden exit doors and among windows and terraces (the kids will be the main characters of Leopoldo Torre Nilsson's next two movies, *El secuestrador* (*The Kidnapper*, 1958) and *La caida* (*The Fall*, 1959)) and she receives information about life thanks to her self-confident cousin Vicenta, who unveils to her facts about sex that Ana's mother is determined to keep concealed. She is told of Buenos Aires' whorehouses, where politics are debated among well-shaped legs and double curtains, displaying the characteristic 'double content' of Nilsson's vision of life. Nilsson himself described this approach: 'I had a childhood of pretty aunts and blond cousins, among whom my dark hair and my easiness to learn naughty words and dubious habits with premature tobacco's taste played out of tune … I was too impatient to indulge in tennis' athletic idleness and preferred the exalted periphery of offshoot stems and leather … I got drunk with more or less subtle fine powders that made me allergic, sneezer and feverish in the sunsets … I was raised between Saxons and the suburbs.' (Taken from Torre Nilsson's 1967 novel, *Entre sajones y el arrabal*.)

In *La casa del ángel* two spaces are presented: the one that is open to Ana, and the one that is both hidden from her and frequented by Pablo Aguirre, her father's friend and political partner. There are also two eras. There is the one we see, where the action is settled, and a former one we imagine, probably of social and political splendour. In the current era we witness the decadence of a social class. Pablo Aguirre represents for Ana everything she wants to know in the moment of exposing herself, physically and willingly, to the tests of desire, exercising violence upon herself, turning her back on the church's teachings and proving the consciousness of sin. This description harmonises both a mannerist aesthetic developed by Torre Nilsson and the tendency to the demolishing of established norms, as presented in Beatriz Guido's literature. Ana gives herself to Pablo Aguirre not only because of her adolescent will, but also to demonstrate her challenge to the learned sin. When she objects to receiving Christ's body at mass, the film-maker manifests his aspiration to tell the story from the viewpoint of a real woman, in open opposition to the traditional 'male perspective' genre. Torre Nilsson's anxiety for making clear this new attitude was such that he emphasized the loss of Ana's virginity in Pablo's arms with the euphemistic fall of a picture frame from a shelf.

The following scene presents Ana in bed, suffering from insomnia but with a clear mind. She has just entered the adult world and hears in the upper floor the steps of Pablo, who is preparing for a duel. The sound of steps, a detailed and insistent description of fear in the pages of Beatriz Guido's *La casa del ángel*, creates in Torre Nilsson's film a new, mysterious and unknown space (the upper rooms) that is inhabited by two fears. There is the girl who has just given her body to someone else, and Pablo's feigned recklessness in agreeing to a duel. As the prologue created new spaces, so the insomnia imports new, ambiguous terrains. While Beatriz Guido contains the fear in Ana's mind, Torre Nilsson (tenacious with cinema's 'apparent realism') presents the upper rooms as a real, possible, or, at least, explicit space through the use of both exterior (the sound of steps) and interior sound (Ana's fear; her openly expressed wish; the death of Pablo, the executioner of her innocence – concerning the duel's resolution; and the measured recount of steps that will eventually decide who lives and who dies in the final fight).

Nilsson tries to construct an objective world through Ana's eyes. Visually, he destabilises the action now and then with angled shots that express the fear and insecurity of an unsteady gait. Thus, he is including Ana in the image – these shots seem to come from her own subjectivity. The use of the *indirect free style*, its expression and semantic description, is characteristic of this period in the director's filmography, and it coincides with his desire to impose the subjective character inside the objective image. In her initial novels, Beatriz Guido also used the first and third person singular to tell the story, making it difficult to establish whether this device is presented in her writings because of her fondness for cinema or because of her working with Torre Nilsson.

This conscious 'subjective/objective' alternation allows the viewer to remember that they are in the middle of a flashback, that the almost always hidden subjectivity will emerge every now and then. The flashback, as classical film theory understands it, expresses a recollection combining the subjective and the objective memory. In *La casa del ángel*, Ana represents the memory that produces the tale; but she is also the naïve observer of facts related to the 1920s history of Argentina and to the life at the National Parliament – constantly quoted in the girl's testimony and in the audiovisual narrative affected by her recollections. When dealing with the justification of the individual behaviors of a determined class (particularly, the high class) that participated in the political decisions of a period in Argentina's history not so distant to the 1950s, the Supreme Exterior Narrator – the film-maker and the book that comes from Beatriz Guido's pen – adds to these two voices a sharp social criticism.

Nilsson's film writing represents a vigorous struggle for the inclusion of an innovative aesthetic within an old narrative model. Though less obvious than *Graciela*, *La casa de ángel* still displays devices of insertion and displacement of the traditional narrative system in order to achieve a renewed and modern expressive modality. A provocative and daring *mise-en-scène* relocates the action between an apparent reality and a 'too realistic' fantasy. Expressionism is present in the distorted exposition of some elements rather than in the audiovisual *form*; in Torre Nilsson's oeuvre, contents and meanings will increasingly reveal a greater and more effective general unbalance, due to his emphasized mannerism and knowledge that the classical narrative model has displaced the transparent and neutral harmonisation of language. The mannerist writing functions from within the model itself, perverting it and evidencing it as an influential but destabilised and unproductive canon.

Following the prologue, the exhibition of Ana's extreme close-up (the pure present of the film between the prologue and the flashback), and after the long and organised recall of Ana's adolescence and rape, there is a fourth segment: an epilogue whose disseminated content relates to the prologue and is explained through the intermediate flashback. It is a return to the *continuous present*, always expressed in a new potential future, but in a more organised way than it took place in the dispersed prologue. At least, the knowledge of the totality allows now more orderliness than before; we are back to the information of those always-repeated Fridays of Ana, her father, and Pablo; back to her departure towards a never-ending and undefined walk in the street; back to the gaze of the stone angel that crowns the house and looks at her with a scrutinising, dominant, comprehensive and even *normative* gaze. Torre Nilsson emphasises the narrative subject in the final moment. The image is transformed in the streets, like it happened in *Días de odio* (*Days of Hatred*, 1953–54), and the walls suggest a horizon of perspectives.

Besides the narrative segments emphasised by interior or chronological remarks, *La casa del ángel* can also be divided, for semantic reasons, into four successive sections that are separated by three fade-outs. The rest of the transition effects are dissolves. The first two fade-outs relate to each other. Before the first one, we see how Ana (after being asked to dance by Pablo Aguirre, and once his requested has been fulfilled) enters her bedroom and dances with a doll repeating the dance steps; the second one, deep and silent, follows the sexual encounter between Pablo and Ana. These fade-outs present a 'black' screen that suggests the desire and the recently woken sexuality. Ana's voice-over had disappeared at the beginning of the intermediate flashback; after the second fade, however, it reappears unfolding an out-loud thought of fears and yearnings, but still remaining distant from that uncertain and demoralised consciousness she showed in the prologue and the epilogue. 'The only thing I want is (Pablo Aguirre's) death', her voice-over says.

The third fade comes after the duel in which Pablo murders his adversary and Ana's disease is revealed. The voice-over (Ana and the script) synthesises periods of time with a long ellipsis the sisters are married and Nana and Ana's mother is dead. Ana lost her innocence, became a woman, and decided to stay in the house, imprisoned by herself and by a certain eternity, like the one presented in *El crime de Oribe* (*The Crime of Oribe*, Leopoldo Torres Ríos and Leopoldo Torre Nilsson, 1950) through the fantasy of the perpetual but also broken Christmas. 'But', says Ana's voice-over in the epilogue, 'I had lost forever the shadow of the angel at my window, Barrancas' Square, the park, the wisteria's gazebo … I began to inhabit the moor that he [Pablo Aguirre] had opened for me the night of the duel … He was always waiting for me … I didn't know if we were two ghosts or what.' At the end of the film the camera looks at her as if it were the cold gaze of the stone angel. The fence through which Ana's departure is seen transforms the street into another prison.

One of the film's innovations is the interpretation of the action through the dissonant, unsentimental music. It reflects Nilsson's spirit of transgression. Deleuze is found again in the non-complaisant and apparently fragmented abstraction of Paz's score; the *pure description*, the missing object, with what Deleuze refers to as 'the acknowledgement of the optical image – perception [auditive, in this case] does not continue in the object [the visual image], because it does not depend on it– and is related with a *recollection-image* convoked by her'. In *La casa del ángel*'s soundtrack, the music demolishes what Michel Chion calls the *syncresis*, that is, a kind of *audiovisual diegesis*: to perceive 'as a single and unique phenomenon [both acoustic and visual] the concomitance of sound and visual punctual events at that moment in which both are simultaneously produced.' Chion insists in the need of dissymmetry, where sound and image are neither complementary nor balanced.

Leopoldo Torre Nilsson's merit is to have discovered this potentiality in cinema and its audiovisual match in a cinematographic era when tradition was being broken and spectral vestiges were being born from within the resulting fissures of that cracking. An era in which it was possible to try new devices as traces of a distant future in which researchers would develop the arguments of a theoretical challenge about the value of those film works.

Claudio España

REFERENCES

Cobos, J. (1961) 'La casa del ángel', in *Temas de Cine*, 12, April/May.

Di Nubila, D (1959) 'La casa del ángel', in D. Di Nubila (ed.) *Historia del cine argentino*. Buenos Aires: Cruz de Malta, vol. II, 217–21.

España, C. (2000) 'La casa del ángel', in C. España (ed.) *Cine argentino: industria y clasicismo, 1933–1956*. Buenos Aires: Fondo Nacional de las Artes, 2000, vol. II, 512–19.

Guido, B. (1954) *La casa del ángel*. Buenos Aires: Emecé.

Martin, J. A. (1980) *Los films de Leopoldo Torre Nilsson*. Buenos Aires: Corregidor.

Martin, M. (1993) *El gran Babsy. Biografía novelada de Leopoldo Torre Nilsson*. Buenos Aires: Sudamericana.

Martinez, T. E. (1961) *La obra de Ayala y Torre Nilsson en las estructuras del cine Argentino*. Buenos Aires: Ediciones Culturales Argentinas/Ministerio de Educación y Justicia.

Vieites, M. C. (ed.) (2002) *Leopoldo Torre Nilsson: una estética de la decadencia*. Buenos Aires: Altamira/Museo del Cine/INCAA.

DEUS E O DIABO NA TERRA DO SOL BLACK GOD, WHITE DEVIL

09

GLAUBER ROCHA, BRAZIL, 1964

A classic of modern Brazilian cinema, *Deus e o diabo na terra do sol* is a film-synthesis that presents the main issues in the work of director Glauber Rocha (1939–81). It is also a key film within the context of the first phase of Brazil's *cinema novo* (from 1962 to 1965), a cinema movement that rediscovered and gave visibility to the social and human landscape of the country's Northeastern region while creating a cinematic language in which aesthetics and politics could not be dissociated.

The country depicted in *Deus e o diabo na terra do sol* is a rural Brazil, the *sertão*, full of social conflicts and contrasts, a symbol of an unknown and archaic nation at the margin of history. This rural Brazil became the setting of many important works of the early *cinema novo,* appearing in other classics of that period such as *Vidas secas* (*Barren Lives,* 1963) by Nelson Pereira dos Santos, and *Os fuzis* (*The Guns*, 1963) by Ruy Guerra. These films thematicise the *sertão* as a territory of social borders and fractures (poverty, injustice, abandonment) but also, as is the case with Rocha's film, as a mythical territory, dotted with symbols and signs of a critically vital culture of resistance. The Northeastern *sertão* was always synonymous to an archaic Brazil; a place of misery, of mysticism, of disinherited people, a non-place while simultaneously a kind of perverse postcard, with its 'typical' landscape and its peculiar 'folklore', a source for histories born of adversity. It is an important symbol in the construction of the idea of 'nation' and 'Brazilianness', which emerges in the Brazilian literature of the 1930s, especially in the works of Euclides da Cunha, Graciliano Ramos and Guimarães Rosa. This mythic and imagined *sertão* remains a focal point of discussion in Brazilian culture. In *Deus e o diabo na terra do sol,* Rocha is able to synthesise and combine, in an exceptional and paradigmatic way, this entire literary tradition. More than that, he successfully reinvents the *sertão* through cinema, using realism and documentary language to arrive at the mythical and allegorical that achieves in this film a monumental and operatic form. The film also brings a genuine contribution to the studies on the relation between myth, politics, religion and popular culture, since it deals with contemporary topics such as land reform and social injustice at the same time that it recreates and politicises popular Northeastern myths.

The narrative of *Deus e o diabo na terra do sol* juxtaposes three important cycles of the Northeast: the *coronelismo* (a system in which large extensions of land are concentrated in the hand of a few powerful owners, the '*coronéis*'); the *beatismo* (the belief in saints, pious men – *beatos* – who led popular messianic movements); and the cycle of *cangaço* (social banditry that flourished in the *sertão* from 1870 to 1940). These are three distinct forms of power that combine crime and belief, religious, economic and political forces that bypassed governments and created their own laws.

By choosing as his main characters the cowboy Manuel, the pious man Sebastião, the bandit Corisco and the hit man Antônio das Mortes, Rocha creates synthetic types that carry in their actions and their pathos entire periods of Northeastern history. These characters were based on famous historical figures who are easily identifiable but, at the same time, achieve the stature of legendary and mythical figures, characters of popular backland fables often told in *cordéis* (popular paperback literature) or sung by *repentistas* (street fair singers). Rocha borrows from history and from realism but transcends them, transforming the *sertão* into a metaphysical territory. Like the literature of Guimarães Rosa, for Rocha 'the *sertão* is the world', a place of possible utopias and radical transformations, a place at once outside of time and permeated by the struggles of our days. It is this articulation between myth and reality, between an epic and didactic narrative (urged by Russian film-maker Sergei Eisenstein) that makes the film an exceptional work, capable of rivaling any sociological study without abandoning aesthetic and expressive issues.

The film is structured around the story of the cowboy Manuel and his wife Rosa, two common characters who endure three rites of passage, three very well delineated phases that synthesise the aforementioned historical cycles of the Northeast. The *first movement*, a kind of prologue, describes in an almost documentary fashion a Northeast that is still perfectly contemporary, marked by *coronelismo*. The unequal labour relations, the subsistence economy of the *sertanejo* (peasant), the small commerce of street fairs, are all presented to the viewer in a synthetic form. This is carried out in a raw narrative style of abrupt cuts, the story being told in song by a blind singer (a common character in the Brazilian Northeast) who 'witnesses' the events and circulates the legends and myths. Song makes the narrative move forward, anticipates and comments on the story, as in the ballads of the American westerns, a genre with which Rocha will dialogue in a most original form. Everything in these first sequences addresses the hardships and cruelty of life in the *sertão*, describing the land, a setting where ancient and recent fights take place, and the man who survives in that hell.

The images linger on in a movement of repetition and exasperation. The opening sequence shows the vastness of the land burnt by the sun, the natural theatre that will be transformed by Rocha into a Brechtian stage. In contrast to the vast landscape, the foreground shows the head of a dead steer and the solitary cowboy riding his horse.

Yet we can already see Rocha punctuating this realist aesthetic, marked by the use of monotonous sound, by the repetitious gestures involved in the making of flour and by the large, indifferent face of Rosa performing these chores, with a playful sight: that of a group of *beatos* who sing and pray whilst following the saint Sebastião, carrying flags in the desolate landscape like a magic apparition. The camera alternates between an indifferent description of the scene and the subjective view of fascinated Manuel watching the procession. 'I saw it!' he tells his wife arriving home. Manuel foresees a better future for the couple after the vision of the saint: 'A miracle may come!' The conversation is punctuated by the unbelieving, indifferent and exhausted face of Rosa.

In this setting of poverty and immobility, where actions and habits are repeated, the first rupture and turning point of the film will take place. In a gesture of revolt and individual unrest, Manuel kills his landowner boss after being cheated and humiliated by him. As a result, his house is invaded and his mother assassinated. This theme of someone exiled and outcast due to an act of individual rebellion, is another mark of the American western. The difference is that Rocha provides a political rationale for this revolt, whose horizon in the film is a radical transformation; that of a collective revolt in gestation. Contrary to the American westerns, the violence here is not 'natural' or 'a given', but a symptom of a larger change that Rocha would try to thematicise and explicate in his 1965 manifesto *Eztetyka da fome* (*Aesthetics of Hunger*).

The *second movement* of the film is put in motion with the transformation of the cowboy into *beato*, searching for an expiation for the crime he has committed, 'That was the hand of God leading me through the path of disgrace. Now the only way is seeking the help of *beato* Sebastião. Let's hurry, there's nothing for us to bring along except our destiny.' Rocha pulls away from the initial realism to create a grandiose vision of a mystical trance. Inspired by the descriptions of Euclides da Cunha in the book *Os sertões* (*Rebellion in the Backlands*), about the religious community of Canudos founded by Antônio Conselheiro and decimated by the Brazilian military, the director recreates the genesis of the popular religious leaders who form powerful religious communities, thus threatening the hegemony of the Church and the established powers. These 'imagined communities' rival the nation and the state that have abandoned them, beckoning a new 'reign' of justice and abundance.

From the personal revolt that leads to crime, Manuel arrives on the other side of misery. Through mysticism, the cowboy becomes a *beato*. The whole second movement of the film is an immersion in trance, messianism, religious utopia and in self-flagellation practices aimed at disciplining the body and the spirit. Humiliation, martyrdom, the exaltation of pain and suffering, penitence and redemptive expiations are the way to the Promised Land, described by the *beato* Sebastião as a kind of exuberant sertão: 'On the other side of Monte Santo there is a land where everything is green, where horses eat flowers and children drink milk from the river … There's water and food, there's abundance from heaven and every day at dawn Jesus Christ and the Virgin Mary appear, Saint George and my saint Sebastian, his chest all pierced by arrows.'

The ascension and initiation of Manuel takes place on Monte Santo (literally, Sacred Mountain) on a painful climb, a trail of penitents which becomes a type of natural and monumental Via Sacra (a path of pilgrimage that is still taken by the faithful of the North-eastern *sertão*). Using music, the monumental space of the hills and mountains, the sound of the wind and the voice of the *beato* Sebastião, the film builds an atmosphere of growing exaltation that arrives at hysteria, commotion and exasperation. 'I offer my strength to my saint in order to liberate my people!' cries Manuel. In some sequences the songs of prayer are mixed with the sound of bullets. Weapons and rosaries, crosses and rifles, transform the *beatos* into the armed guard of the Saint, 'Jesus has sent a warrior angel with his spear to cut off the head of his enemies.' Religion is depicted as a place of pacification, conformism and humiliation, but also as a theatre of violence, exaltation and ecstasy. In these sequences, the montage moves away from realism for a final effect of violence and pathos, a violence created by the movement of an unstable camera that watches, follows and circles around the characters.

Violence is treated in different forms, at once opposed and complementary, creating the rhythm of distention and exasperation perceived throughout the film. This violence ends up being experienced by the audience themselves. Rocha makes use of elongation of time, such as the sequence of Manuel's penance, as the character slowly carries an immense rock on his head while being flogged by the *beato*'s whip. But he also represents violence in a ritualistic and hieratic form, like in the sequence, recorded with live sound, in which the Saint sacrifices a child offered by Manuel. Here, the camera remains motionless, impotently contemplating the scene, in a narrative indifference that contrasts with the explosion of hatred and revolt in Rosa, who stabs and kills Saint Sebastião – a second, liberating crime that frees the couple from the Saint's influence. And there is yet another form of showing violence by the use of a hand-held camera that navigates through the characters. There are also sequences showing the delirium and pain of Rosa as she tries to save her husband from the influence of Saint Sebastião; sequences of mystic exaltation of the people of Monte Santo when they hear the prophecies of the *beato*; and, finally, scenes of massacre and horror when the people are decimated by the character Antônio das Mortes (played by Mauricio do Valle in a beautiful recreation of the 'lone rider' from western movies).

Trance is a privileged moment in Glauber Rocha's cinema. In fact, going into a trance or into a crisis is one of the key aspects of his work. Trance is transition, passage, becoming, possession. In order to go into a trance one needs to be pervaded, possessed by the 'other'. Going into a trance is getting 'in phase' with an object or situation, knowing it from within. Rocha makes trance a form of experimentation and understanding, presenting it with hand-held camera and rhythmic, syncopated editing. In *Deus e o diabo na terra do sol*, what we follow is the crisis and trance of landscape (the barren *sertão*), of men and of social formations. However, the images do not simply *represent* the trance, but rather *go into trance*, get 'in phase' with the characters, the setting, the props and the audience, which is shaken out of its immobility.

Trance and possession also characterise Corisco (Othon Bastos), the 'two-headed bandit' (one head to kill, one to think) that propels the *third movement* of the film: the transformation of the former cowboy, then pious man Manuel into a *cangaceiro* (bandit). Orphaned by the Black God Saint Sebastião, whose followers are massacred by Antônio das Mortes, Manuel sees in the White Devil Corisco, a new force of leadership and command, a new myth giving sense to the exploited life of the peasant.

The Saint, as well as Corisco, appear in Rocha's oeuvre as 'primitive rebels', in a state of revolt that also marks the character of the killer for hire, Antônio das Mortes. In *Deus e o diabo na terra do sol*, the saint, the *cangaceiro* and the killer carry a diffuse revolutionary hatred, emissaries of the ire of God and man. Rocha once again borrows from the imaginary of Euclides da Cunha in *Os sertões*, a literary piece where violence, ferocity, hunger and revolt are attributes or conditions of man and Earth. Yet he transforms these elements in such a way that all violence (from the environment, the religion, the banditry and the massacred people) and all rebellion (crime, mysticism and *cangaço*) will be the embryo of a revolutionary ire. Rocha tries to give political, ethical and aesthetic sense to this rebelliousness. Thus he transforms *beatos*, cowboys and hit men into agents of the Revolution. In *Eztetyka da fome*, Rocha writes, 'Only through violence and horror can the coloniser understand the power of the culture he exploits.' Violence is not just a symptom, but a desire of transformation, 'the most noble cultural manifestation of hunger'.

Rocha's Marxism has something sadistic and hysterical about it. In order to explode, a revolution must be preceded by a crime or massacre. The *beato* Sebastião inflicts penitencies and punishments upon the faithful; the bandit Corisco kills with his rifle 'so that the poor won't be left to die of hunger'. Antônio das Mortes kills *beatos* and bandits in the name of a Revolution to come, 'a war bigger than this sertão. An enormous war, without the blindness of neither God nor Devil', he claims, justifying why he kills with indifference religious mystics, bandits, saints and demons. These are figures of a past that must forever disappear, just as he must. The saint, bandit and killer are all primitive rebels. They are destabilising forces in their blindness, prophets and announcers of a 'bigger war' that shall come.

Rocha also subverts the Christian Gospel, combining Christianity, messianism and Marxism in an incredible political twist that appropriates immemorial symbols and myths in the construction of a pre-revolutionary mythology. The character of Corisco, handsome, violent, amoral and anarchic, a destabilising force that comes to 'mess up the orderly', functions as a character-synthesis of this revolutionary process. Upon seeing Corisco, Manuel falls to his knees, ecstatic before the figure of the *cangaceiro* claiming, 'This is my Saint Jorge' (the warrior saint of Christian mythology). Corisco accepts and baptises Manuel, giving him a new name, Satanás (Satan). Religion and banditry deal with the same forces of belonging and agglutination that give meaning to a group, reign, band or nation.

Corisco himself is a mystic character, but of a hybrid and syncretic kind of mysticism that mixes practices from different religions: baptism, exorcism, possession, 'closing of the body' (a ritual that invokes divine protection and shields one's body from all evil). Christianity, *beatismo* and *candomblé* (an Afro-Brazilian religion) take part in his religious experience, although Corisco exhorts the power of arms, rifles and force like instruments of transformation, replacing prayers and rosaries. Manuel and Rosa's acceptance into Corisco's band constitutes a new rite of passage, where the idea of rebellion and anarchy brings with it a sexuality devoid of taboos and prohibitions, involving and uniting Corisco, his wife Dadá, Manuel and Rosa. This free sexuality is expressed in three sequences: first, in the encounter of Rosa and Dadá, full of sensuality and admiration, where women desire and touch one another; second, in the scene when Rosa gives herself to Corisco, succumbing to the charms of the White Devil; and finally in the sequence when Corisco's band invades a farm and sets up a theater of orgy and cruelty, killing and raping.

In a parallel to the sufferings imposed by Saint Sebastião, Manuel is also humiliated and whipped by Corisco until he 'converts' to banditry, having at first questioned the bloody methods of the bandit. Manuel, taken by Corisco's hand, commits a new crime, affiliating himself to the band through the blood and the sacrifice of an innocent, just as he did in order to affiliate himself with Saint Sebastião's followers, through the sacrifice of a child. Mysticism and banditry are thus equated. They are worlds with their own ethics and rules, beyond good and evil, giving sense to the life of the disinherited and the outlaws.

The sequences that introduce us to Corisco's band make an extraordinary use of sequence shots and of the actors' movements across the natural setting. The white and endless *sertão* is a near-abstract scenery that emphasizes gestures and dislocations through space. The hand-held camera draws long-sequence shots that accompany the zigzagging of the characters in movements of hesitation, oscillation and restlessness that characterise the whole 'theatre' around Corisco. The anti-naturalist, Brechtian, almost operatic acting of Othon Bastos, who spins around, jumps and rotates in an admirable and dazed way, coupled with the Eisensteinian editing of Rocha, gives the character of Corisco an epic and monumental quality. In one sequence, Corisco receives the spirit of Lampião, another legendary *cangaceiro* of the Northeast. Possessed, he engages in a dialogue with himself, going from the voices and gestures of one to the other's, transformed into 'the bandit with two heads'. It is a possession that resurrects the dead: '[Lampião] died in the flesh but his spirit is alive here in me', says Corisco. The trance of possession is shown with anthological effects of editing and acting.

The second and third movements of the film, mysticism and *cangaço*, are brought to an end by the same agent, the killer for hire Antônio das Mortes, introduced in song as a man without God or law: 'Praised in ten churches, without a patron saint, Antônio das Mortes, killer of bandits'. He is constructed as a paradoxical figure, critical and conscious of his acts, serving the Church and the *coroneis* in the extermination of the religious fanatics and bandits who upset the business of priests and landlords. Antônio das Mortes kills out of the belief that mysticism and banditry are forces of a past that should disappear, like himself, in the name of a radical transformation. A blend of lone rider, mercenary, righteous person, bodyguard and Zorro, wearing a black cape and hat, rifle at hand, he belongs completely in the realm of legend. He is a character from western movies but also a kind of politicised killer who murders the fanatics gathered around the Saint and finally takes the life of Corisco. The shooting occurs in a stylised duel that ends with the bandit making a call to arms: 'Stronger are the powers of the people.'

Removing himself from the 'conciliatory' or paternalistic solution in the representation of the relationship between the Church, the landlords, the bandits, the mystics and the impoverished people, Glauber Rocha proposes a pedagogy of violence and revolt in pure state. In *Deus e o diabo na terra do sol*, not a single character is an intellectual, a legitimate representative or mediator of the people, nor is there a discourse of praise or victimisation of the people, a usual discourse in the 1960s. In the film, the people are whipped, humiliated, flogged and massacred on different levels. Instead of condemning the immorality of violence and exploitation of this people, Rocha depicts violence with such radicalism and force that it becomes intolerable to the viewer. He also points to new agents and mediators in this process of change (the bandit, the *beato*, the mercenary), who deprive the intellectual of their privileged position as an agent of change.

After so many trials and humiliations, Manuel and Rosa, free from both Deus and Diabo, from mysticism and banditry, become the embodiment of a people to come, a people in the process of inventing itself. A mythic couple, running desperately across the *sertão* in the long and magnificent tracking shot that ends the film, fulfilling cinematically the prophecy of Saint Sebastião, that 'The sertão will become the sea and the sea will become the sertão.' The film adopts a messianic or mythic vision, juxtaposing the image of the barren landscape with the image of an immense sea that covers everything, while the symphonic music of Heitor Villa-Lobos soars on the soundtrack. The blind singer praises the liberated peasant singing, 'So my story is told, both truth and imagination. I hope you can learn a lesson. Divided like this, our world goes wrong, for the land belongs to man, not to God or Devil.'

This is a cinematic utopia of transformation, a synthesis of the proposals of *cinema novo*, a movement that believed in film as a great vehicle of transformation not only for Brazil but for the whole of Latin America. 'A camera in your hand and an idea in your head', goes the celebrated statement of Glauber Rocha that defined this 'other cinema', based on the creation of a Brazilian movie industry, on aesthetic experimentation and on political engagement. With *Deus e o diabo na terra do sol*, Rocha constructs a narrative that expresses his infinite belief in transformation and becoming, in destabilising forces, even if they are impure, ambiguous or fragile. He also brings a new understanding to movements such as mysticism and banditry, viewed not as 'obscurantism' or 'alienation' but rather as expressions of discontentment and rebelliousness, capable of constituting powerful communities. By doing so, he tries to construct a new national mythology 'on the margins of a nation' and invent a 'people', calling attention to the different forms of identity and belonging created by mystic experience, by communities, gangs and groups formed by the disinherited and outcasts of a nation.

Within this proposal of constructing diverse, strong and autonomous 'imagined communities', a desire and an utopia that marks both Latin America and *cinemas novos* around the world, the cinema of Glauber Rocha is a vital and original moment. *Barravento* (*The Turning Wind*, 1961), *Deus e o diabo na terra do sol* (1964), *Terra em transe* (*Earth Entranced*, 1967), *O Dragão da Maldade contra o Santo Guerreiro* (*Antônio das Mortes*, 1969), *Der Leone Have Sept Cabeças* (*The Lion Has Seven Heads*, 1970), *Cabezas cortadas* (*Severed Heads*, 1970), *Di* (1977) and *A idade da terra* (*The Age of the Earth*, 1980) are, among others, film manifestos of an entire generation. Glauber Rocha was also a theoretician, having published *Revisão crítica do cinema brasileiro* (*A Critical Revision of Brazilian Cinema*) and *A revolução do cinema novo* (*The Revolution of Cinema Novo*), a writer, a polemicist and a major public figure in Brazil, with several interventions in the national press. Deserving comparisons to Pier Paolo Pasolini in Italy and Jean-Luc Godard in France, he spoke openly and provocatively until his untimely death in 1981 at the age of 42. Cinema was his battlefield and his experimentation medium, as well as a place of redemption. He believed that cinema itself, or 'a body of films in evolution could give, in the end, to the public, a conscience of its own existence'.

Ivana Bentes
(translated from the Portuguese by Vladimir Freire)

REFERENCES

Avellar, J. C. (1995) *Deus e o diabo na terra do sol*. Rio de Janeiro: Rocco.
Bentes, I. (ed.) (1997) *Cartas ao mundo: Glauber Rocha*. São Paulo: Companhia das Letras.
____ (1999) 'Transe, crença e povo: Glauber e a pedagogia da crise' and 'Romantismo, messianismo, marxismo', in A. M. Dias (ed.) *A Missão e o Grande Show: políticas culturais no Brasil dos anos 60 e depois*. Rio de Janeiro: Tempo Brasileiro.
Pierre, S. (1987) *Glauber Rocha*. Paris: Cahiers du Cinéma.
Rocha, G. *et al.* (1965) *Deus e o diabo na terra do sol*. Rio de Janeiro: Civilização Brasileira.
Rocha, G. (1981) *A revolução do Cinema Novo*. Rio de Janeiro: Alhambra/Embrafilme.
____ (1985) *Roteiros do Terceyro Mundo* (Orlando Senna, ed.). Rio de Janeiro: Alhambra/Embrafilme.
Xavier, I. (1983) *Sertão Mar: Glauber Rocha e a Estética da Fome*. São Paulo: Brasiliense.

MEMORIAS DEL SUBDESARROLLO MEMORIES OF UNDERDEVELOPMENT

10

TOMÁS GUTIÉRREZ ALEA, CUBA, 1968

Havana Airport, 1961. Sergio, a bourgeois intellectual, bids farewell to his family and ex-wife, who are leaving for the United States, fleeing from the changed living conditions imposed on them by the new régime, while he has decided to stay in the Cuban capital to 'see what happens'. From then on, the camera will follow his solitary wanderings over one year, through the city until October 1962, the date of the Cuban missile crisis. Sergio continues to live on the revenue from his property, which he still collects as former owner, while he stays in his cosy bourgeois flat, situated in the smart district of the capital. From there, using a telescope, he watches the city and its metamorphosis, following the rhythm of the brand-new Revolution. In an attempt to resume his short-lived vocation as a writer, he types down his reflections in diary form, analysing the situation, looking for clues, remembering the past and criticising the present. What is Revolution? What is an intellectual? How compatible are they? But in his identity quest, Sergio remains on the fringe of the revolutionary process and maintains a mode of living determined by class values, which are the values of bourgeois individualism. Seducing a working-class girl, he attempts to mould her as he did his ex-wife, according to the stereotypical patterns of fashion magazines.

Memorias del subdesarrollo, the fifth feature-film of Cuban director Tomás Gutiérrez Alea, was adapted from Edmundo Desnoes's novel, published in 1962, and became revelation when it was released in August 1968. The reviews published throughout the world following the film's release offer the same laudatory epithets whether they come from New York, Paris, London or Montevideo. The words 'remarkable', 'outstanding', 'extraordinary', 'perfect' were all applied to the film. 'One of the best films of all times', David Elliott wrote in 1978 in *The Chicago Sun-Times*, while Arthur Cooper stated in *Newsweek* that '*Memorias del subdesarrollo* is undoubtedly a masterpiece, a complex, ironical and extraordinarily clever film.' While Alea's former films had already focused international critical attention on the small Caribbean island which managed to produce films worthy of entering a universal history of motion pictures) such as *Historias de la Revolución* (*Histories of the Revolution*, 1960) or *La muerte de un burócrata* (*The Death of a Bureaucrat*, 1966)), with *Memorias del subdesarrollo*, interest turned into admiration. With hindsight, although conceived in the specific context of a post-revolutionary society, the film was clearly more than a work relevant only to what was taking place at that time. As the French critic Marcel Martin suggested a decade later in the journal *Cine cubano*, 'The film depicts a psychological and moral problem which is common to many intellectuals in a changing world. And it is a theme of universal value and import.' What is still fascinating today about this film, and what presumably fascinated audiences at the time, is the way Alea, by means of profoundly original aesthetics, put the issue of the relationship between the intellectual, or quite simply the individual, with the surrounding society in terms of a fundamental dilemma. To choose solitary or solidary, distance or fusion?

Such a universal dilemma was particularly topical in Cuba in the 1960s as it can be, in more general terms, in any country undergoing radical political and social change. The Revolution which triumphed in 1959 with the fall of the dictator Fulgencio Batista was an intellectuals' revolution, in the broadest sense of the word. Among the early revolutionaries, the *barbudos* who fought in the Sierra Maestra, two emblematic figures, Fidel Castro, a lawyer, and Che Guevara, a doctor, belonged, with many others, to the upper classes and they had given much thought to the destiny of their country. Besides, the Revolution would soon attract intellectual figures from all over the world who would bring their support to those who advocated Cuban-style socialism. Jean-Paul Sartre, Simone de Beauvoir and many others were to cross the Atlantic Ocean to look at the miracle with their own eyes. As for Cuban intellectuals, they contributed greatly to the Revolution. As early as 1961, in a series of historic meetings, writers and artists came together to discuss the place of art in the new revolutionary society. Fidel Castro then made a speech, later printed as *Palabras a los intelectuales* (*Words to the Intellectuals*), in which he guaranteed freedom of expression to artists providing they did not develop counter-revolutionary propaganda. As far as cinema was concerned, no sooner was the revolutionary process under way than the now famous ICAIC (Instituto Cubano del Arte e Industria Cinematográficos) was set up in order to foster the country's film industry. Its purpose, beside the material growth of the film industry, was to assist the Revolution. Tomás Gutiérrez Alea, originally trained as a lawyer, became one of its founding members; it was the ICAIC which provided him with the actual means to make films after he had started a career in rather difficult conditions under Batista with short or medium-length films (such as *El Mégano*, 1955). At the head of the ICAIC, Alfredo Guevara, one of Fidel Castro's companions, was at pains to lend Cuban cinema cultural credibility. It was in such a specific context, only a few years after the Revolution, and at a critical juncture in the history of the régime, that *Memorias del subdesarrollo* was conceived. It was a complex picture which assimilated in a radically original way the formal breaks which took place in film history after the Second World War. Far from being a propagandist and manichean representation of the Revolution, it offered a contrasted and dialectical picture of what the revolutionary break could mean. Through the figure of Sergio, an anti-hero on the margins of history, Alea put forward a number of issues that were inherent in the Revolution.

It was through the aesthetics inherited from Italian Neorealism that Alea built up his representation. Indeed *Memorias del subdesarrollo* is not strictly a Neorealist picture, since it was made long after the emergence of that historically determined movement, but it remains so in spirit. Well before the Revolution, in the years of his apprenticeship, the young Alea spent two years in Rome, between 1951 and 1953, at the famous Centro Sperimentale di Cinematografia, with a few companions of his generation, such as Julio García Espinosa and Gabriel García Márquez. There, the Cubans were in touch with the major film movement of the postwar period. Moreover, 'Neorealism was still the most vital movement and, like so many young people then interested in the cinema, I felt literally attracted to that tendency' (in Évora, p. 18). From Neorealism, Alea learned a fundamental lesson, that films must be in touch with history. The individual story is meaningful only if it connects with history. Against the Hollywood philosophy, centred on the individual, Neorealism broke with a stereotype of representation on which the Golden Age of American cinema was founded. This break remained one of the central characteristics of his films, from his first feature, *Historias de la Revolución*, in which the protagonists were used insofar as their personal story referred to a history which engulfed them, through to his last films, like *Fresa y chocolate* (*Strawberry and Chocolate*). Although the characters in his later work are extremely individualised, Alea was interested in them only because their personal destiny offered a basis for a critical reflection on history. This is at its most evident in *Memorias del subdesarrollo*. Even the title of the film combines the individual dimension (the 'memoirs') with a more general problem of underdevelopment. The latter, which was initially an economic phenomenon and was linked to a vision of economic growth as a factor of harmony among nations, is mainly treated, in *Memorias*, through its socio-cultural dimensions. Sergio, the main character, lives and thinks like a 'Westerner': his flat (its layout and its decoration), his cultural references, his dressing habits are imitated from a Western model which is made possible by his finances. But he is completely out of touch with Cuban reality, and following that, with Cuban identity. He is affected by an underdevelopment whose traces he detects in the course of his wanderings.

From that gap emerges Sergio's distanced vision, a vision both distanced and paradoxical since he is an insider and an outsider, a participant and a stranger.

Distance nevertheless allows a critical approach which gives the film its strength. 'Our ultimate purpose', Alea stated, 'is not to reflect a reality but to enrich it, to stimulate the sensibility and to increase it, to detect a problem. We do not want to soften the dialectical process according to ideal formulas and representations, but to give it an aggressive vitality, to build up a premise of development itself, with the amount of disturbance of reality it implies.' (*Cine cubano*, 45–6) This was to be one of Alea's constant preoccupations as a film-maker, creating protagonists who are out of step with history, in order to expose problems and to foster debate. In *La muerte de un burócrata*, for instance, the reflection on one of the evils born out of the Revolution – namely bureaucracy – does not stem out of the bureaucratic apparatus itself but out of a marginal character, the nephew, who is marginalised by the same bureaucratic apparatus, and whose outsider's vision of bureaucrats elicits a distanced and critical approach. In his last film, *Guantanamera* (1995), Alea approached the limitations of the system through the character of Georgina (Mirta Ibarra), who follows Adolfo, her husband, in his deadly cavalcade. Her progress is parallel to her husband's on a material plane, but her point of view grows increasingly distant until the final break, which concludes a road movie surveying the state of Cuba in the 1990s. The device of placing a character who is out of step with the world around them had been employed by the Italian Neorealists. Thus in Rossellini's *Europe 51* (1952), the external gaze of the female protagonist (Ingrid Bergman) leads the audience to question historical time and to challenge the values of a society in crisis.

Yet the big difference between Italian Neorealist films and Cuban cinema, especially Alea's films, is that the element of context determined by the Revolution makes the approach more complex. Cuban films produced by the ICAIC, which were explicitly designed to comfort the revolutionary impetus, were engaged in constructive dynamics. Now Alea's films, far from producing a consensual picture that would praise the régime's achievements, sustained through critical distance, such a fundamental irony which was meant to question assumptions and to probe the situation. The point is neither to praise nor to blame, but to suggest improvements through aesthetics which, true to Marxist terminology, Alea himself defined as 'dialectical'. This is precisely what makes post-revolutionary Cuban cinema so specific and what makes its approach complex, even ambiguous, yet never manichean, 'We must support the necessity of criticism as a necessity for the survival of the Revolution', Alea wrote in 1988, 'If we do not become aware of our problems, we cannot solve them. Criticism of the Revolution is fundamental to its development and this cannot be confused with the fact of equipping the enemy with weapons.' (*Juventud rebelde*, Havana, 10 September 1988)

On a formal level, Alea borrowed Neorealism's firm foothold in 'reality'. This was the great aesthetic revolution introduced by Neorealism on the wider scale of cinema history; to take the camera out of the studios, to shoot on location and to use non-professional actors. Its purpose was, on the one hand, to depart from Hollywood's aesthetics, which had turned into a gallery of endlessly recycled stereotypes and, on the other hand, to produce films at a lesser cost, in more flexible conditions. This approach would also favour a greater authenticity of representation. The relevance of such a formula to the Cuban situation is perceptible at once, as the virtually non-existent film industry did not offer the infrastructure required by studio production and the post-revolutionary economic conditions made the process of film production a precarious one. On the ideological ground as well, the preoccupation with authenticity was clearly relevant to the new revolutionary assumptions. As cinema was supposed to be subservient to the revolutionary impetus, reality in its immediate and contemporary aspects was to be the focus of any future investigation.

Having said that, *Memorias del subdesarrollo*, as a film of the late 1960s, is aware of the trends and attitudes that were filtering through world cinema at that time. Alea was conscious of what took place in Europe, particularly in France, where the Nouvelle Vague introduced a number of fundamental formal breaks. Jean-Luc Godard figured among the film-makers he admired, even though he considered the impact of his elitist pictures too narrow. Alea also developed his ideas on the cinema by analysing the Soviet production of the 1920s. With a Neorealist inspiration as a starting point, he would look at reality with a syncretic aesthetics which fitted his subject perfectly.

Memorias del subdesarrollo was shot entirely on location in Havana, where the action takes place. The streets of the Cuban capital are explored by a camera which details urban geography with precise, almost documentary approach. Its arterial street system now resembles typical North American planning. Yet within it are the vesitges of a bygone era (the old colonial palaces), standing side-by-side with more recent structures (the 1950s hotels). Contemporary history can be read on the walls, thanks to perfectly preserved revolutionary slogans. The interiors, such as Sergio's flat, with its vistas over the city, as well as the ICAIC offices and the meeting room where the round table on literature takes place, contribute to the feel of a documentary production. And the *mise-en-scène* is populated by the motifs and symbols of recent conflicts, whose incongruity in a revolutionary context would eventually belong to the Cuban townscape and the passers-by, who seem to have been captured in their daily lives by a particularly mobile camera.

But Alea pushes the referential game even further, with the insertion of actual 'slices of reality', which produce narrative breaks and contribute to some kind of post-modern bricolage. The most obvious breaks in the narrative continuity are caused by the insertion, at key moments, of images from other sources, newsreels of the crisis of October 1962, or photographs dating from the time of Batista. Those images, which refer to a reality outside the narration, work as a guarantee of authenticity through their historical dimension. We should remember that *Memorias del subdesarrollo* does not represent a reality which is strictly contemporaneous with the shooting of the film, but takes place over five years earlier (when Edmundo Desnoes' novel was written). Although it should not be considered a historical film, the gap of a few years between the shooting and the diegetic context made it necessary to highlight precise temporal marks. Alea therefore used the newsreels as historical markers which contributed to the general feeling of authenticity. 'Collage' was not in itself something new in the cinema in 1968, but Alea used it in a profoundly original way. Beyond its function as historical marker, the exported juxtaposed image introduced a different point of view, which ran parallel to Sergio's. As a consequence, this device throws into relief the subjective quality of Sergio's gaze but conversely, it also emphasised the discursive specificity of the newsreels. In the end the audience was left free to make their own judgment.

The feeling of collage is less striking, although the gesture is fundamentally the same, at two other key moments in the film. When Sergio attends a round table on literature, Alea filmed a real debate, which he inserted into his narrative by filming it from the point of view of his protagonist, whose commentaries are included through the use of voice-over. Furthermore, one of the members of the panel is the novel's author Edmundo Desnoes. This is no in-joke for knowledgeable audience members, or rather, the playfulness of the sequence does not exhaust its significance, for Alea uses that device again in another sequence, which takes place in the ICAIC buildings. Sergio's director friend is actually Alea himself, in the course of making a film which will eventually take the form of a collage and which therefore might well be *Memorias del subdesarrollo*. As it happens, the filmic fragments which the director friend wishes to insert into his film are themselves inserted into *Memorias del subdesarrollo*: they are sequences whose erotic content was censored by the previous régime and they are edited together. Sergio's comment is ironical, 'Do you really think that you will be allowed to edit them?' The reflexive game is therefore complex. The many mirrors offered to reflect reality contribute to the depth of the film, both in the representation and in the questionings related to it, which certainly accounts greatly for its impact on its release. The flirtation between reality and fiction produces breathtaking effects which refer the spectator to themselves, especially the contemporary spectator at the time of the film's release, whether it is the Cuban spectator of August 1968, when the film was shown in the Cuban capital, or the North American spectator of 1973, when the film could be seen in New York.

The context was indeed favourable. The years following 1968, when in various degrees a new moral, socio-cultural and political awareness was expressed, were years of crisis for intellectuals. What is the intellectual's role in society? What is their role with respect to politics? What is the function of an art that purports to be subversive? Such questions were to elicit diverse and contradictory answers but would henceforth make it impossible, for artists and intellectuals to act and to think without first taking a stand as to those dilemmas. *Memorias del subdesarrollo* echoed such preoccupations through the figure of the average intellectual, deprived of any outstanding qualities, who underwent an intellectual crisis in individual terms. Alea clearly took a stand and shunned any identification with the character, whom he constructed as an anti-hero: Sergio, as his mistress Elena tells him, 'is nothing'. He does not identify with the world that the Revolution wiped out, but neither does he miss Batista's régime. He does not go so far as to leave the country, unlike members of his family or his best friend. But he does not commit himself and in that respect the last images of the film are suggestive of an isolation that has grown throughout the narrative. At the time of the missile crisis, the people take up arms to resist, while he is watching them, carefully entrenched in his flat, which becomes for him both an observatory and a last refuge. As a character Sergio is condemned by history. What is going to become of him? Alea carefully avoids to conclude his film on anything which might look like a message. He leaves the spectator to himself and to his own judgment. In a first version of the screenplay, he was to commit suicide, an act seen as a materialisation of his failure. Eventually the writers judged such an ending too 'complaciente' (self-indulgent) and replaced it with an open one: 'It was more dramatic to let him live in those death pangs and to leave open the possibility of suicide, heart-attack or any other ending' (in Évora, p. 35).

Despite the open-ended quality of the film and Alea's sense of subtlety, or perhaps just because of it, *Memorias del subdesarrollo* suffered a form of censorship in the United States.

On 17 January 1974, the *New York Times* informed its readers that the Department of State had just rejected Alea's request for a visa, together with that of Saúl Yelín, who was to accompany him, to go to New York to receive the Rosenthal Award of the National Association of Film Critics ($2,000 and a trophy), on the official invitation of Andrew Sarris. Furthermore, any person who would come to receive the award on behalf of the Cuban director would face possible charges for breaking the law on trade with an enemy. The scandal that followed, the absurdity of the refusal at a time when, as the *New York Times* pointed out on 19 January, 'détente with the Soviet Union and the normalisation of relations with Communist China are rightly considered as diplomatic victories', only reinforced the international success of the film. On 22 January, in the Cuban daily paper *Granma*, the Cuban film-maker Pastor Vega concluded that 'With this new aggression, imperialism reveals its rage, dictated by blindness and impotence, faced with the cultural development of Cuba, which was made possible only thanks to the American socialist revolution.' The incident had just confirmed the notion that, subtle or not, manichean or not, films and, more broadly, cultural products were perceived as 'subversive acts' in the struggle which opposed the two ideological enemies, thus justifying the political use of artistic media.

Tomás Gutiérrez Alea thus pursued his career as revolutionary film-maker in Cuba until his death in 1996. He succeeded in sustaining throughout the double exigency which had made him an internationally acclaimed director, tirelessly exposing from within the limitations inherent in the system while adhering to criteria of aesthetic quality which naturally presented problems in a subtle and complex way. It was only on the release of *Guantanamera* that Fidel Castro (unaware that it had been directed by Alea and yet to have even seen it) judged that Alea was playing with fire, but this was to be his last film.

Nancy Berthier

(Translated from the French by Jean-François Baillon)

REFERENCES

Chanan, M. (ed.) (1990) *Memories of Underdevelopment (Tomás Gutiérrez Alea, Director) and Inconsolable Memories (Edmundo Desnoes, Author)*, New Brunswick: Rutgers University Press.

Évora, J. A. (1996) *Tomás Gutiérrez Alea*. Madrid: Cátedra/Filmoteca Española.

Fornet, A. (ed.) (1987) *Alea: una retrospectiva crítica*. Havana: Letras Cubanas.

Larraz, E. (ed.) (2002) *Voir et lire Tomás Gutiérrez Alea*. Dijon: Hispanistica XX/Université de Bourgogne.

Oroz, S. (1985) *Tomás Gutiérrez Alea: os filmes que nao filmei*. Rio de Janeiro: Anima. (Spanish translation, *Tomás Gutiérrez Alea: los filmes que no filmé*, Havana: Unión, 1989).

LUCÍA

11

HUMBERTO SOLÁS, CUBA, 1968

Lucía is a large-scale film, first by its length, with the three episodes lasting more than two and a half hours in total. The production also proved to be enormous, which included an epic re-enactment of the first encounter between the Spaniards and Cubans during the war of independence in 1895. The project was backed by the Cuban Institute of Cinematographic Art and Industry (ICAIC), which was created after the Revolution to develop cinematic activity on the island, of which Solás' film ranks among its most ambitious and expensive.

This venture illustrated the will that emanated from ICAIC, as it set about trying to promote a kind of cinema that would stand in opposition to pre-Revolution productions. Before its inception, Cuba had been used as little more than an exotic backdrop for melodramas. ICAIC saw the moment for greater artistic standards and a more genuine depiction of the country. For the revolutionary head of the institute, giving a faithful account of the country's history implied tackling the social issues that had been debated since the Revolution. Humberto Solás' film was part of this process, for national history was no longer seen as a pretext but as the heart of the matter. Every element in the film brings forward the sources and the idiosyncrasies of the Cuban Revolution. This is another element that was highly promoted by ICAIC – the representation on the screens of Cuban reality which was meant to bring popular success to the Institute's productions.

Didactic though it may now seem, the film never offers oversimplified answers, but conversely acknowledges that many social problems have found no solution, even following the Revolution. Indeed the third episode is permeated with elements of conflict; the general mirth that pervades most scenes stands in jarring contrast with scenes where the heroine is seen in tears, screaming and battling against her husband who is quite happy with the Revolution as long as it does enter his 'backyard'. Then again, Solás was representative of the ICAIC as it was immediately after the Revolution, that is, in favour of film-makers representing this period miles away from propagandist caricature, which certainly contributed to the diffusion of some of its production.

As far as narrative modes are concerned, the three episodes are similar. Indeed, each of them relates the experiences of a female character named Lucía in three different phases of Cuban history. The first episode takes place in 1895 during the Cuban war of independance against Spain; the second, in 1933 at the height of the rebellion against the dictator Gerardo Machado; and the final part which takes place circa 1960. The last part is not so historically specific, implying a general progression forwards, one that began with the Revolution.

Each episode gives an account of Lucía's relationship, both with her partner and the Cuban historical process, and as the chronology suggests, the film charts an evolution in Cuban history. In each case the association of Lucía with men and the historical context is different. In the first part, Lucía is a member of the aristocracy, living with her mother and friends in a frivolous atmosphere. She differs from them through her emotional and intellectual engagement with her brother's involvement in clandestine separatist activities. However, she falls in love with a Spaniard and naïvely discloses the location of the rebel's hideout to him, which he subsequently reveals. She thus becomes responsible for a massacre which she helplessly witnesses. Later, Lucía finally has her revenge when she locates her betrayer and shoots him on the street.

The Lucía in the 1930s is more directly commited to the revolutionary cause. She belongs to the bourgeoisie and meets Aldo, a rebel with whom she falls in love and shares an adventurous life, for better or worse. On the one hand they succeed in overthrowing the dictator through various actions by their group against the regime, with the men carrying out armed attacks while the women are involved in popularising their cause through the dissemination of propaganda and encouraging strike action in factories. On the other, Lucía must accomodate their injured comrades and above all cope with her lover's death. Indeed, in the second half of the film, both Lucía and Aldo realise that nothing has changed in Cuba and subsequently he perishes in a final and desperate attack. At the end of the film, she remains alone and pregnant, in a position of extreme loneliness but also carrying within her the seeds of hope.

In the last episode, Lucía is a countrywoman playing her part in a post-revolutionary country. The overall tone is jollier and the characters act more spontaneously, thus illustrating their freedom through the triumph of the revolution. And yet, Lucía is still defined according to her relation to men. Her husband Tomás is characterised by his brutal *machismo*, forbiding her to go out, albeit in order to visit her mother. Nonetheless, thanks to the Revolution, Lucía is on her way toward complete freedom, which she has demanded throughout the whole film. She is finally able to write a letter ending her relationship with Tomás – and thus rejecting obsolete traditions because she benefited from the literacy campaign, to her jealous husband's great dipleasure. The film oscillates between tenderness and violence in the couple as epitomised in the final scene where the two characters meet again, both hugging and fighting, under the mirthful gaze of a little girl who symbolises actual hope.

The ambitions of the new Cuban cinema have already been evoked both in aesthetic and thematic terms, in order to demonstrate how consistent with this intention *Lucía* was. For Solás as for others, a cinema that would be genuinely revolutionary means films made *with* the Revolution and not *about* the Revolution. These film-makers intend to show on screen what the Revolution is as a reality that the Cubans experience and not as a historical phase. That is why referring to other periods in Cuban history is essential; it presents the Revolution as the successful outcome of previous episodes. Therefore one considers the narrative progression in *Lucía* as a gradation which describes women being gradually emancipated from the chains of pre-Revolutionary social determinism.

According to Solás, cinema must be in congruence with the great concerns of the time. What matters is not revolutionary propaganda but a dialogue between the past and the present. In this respect the last episode is exemplary and it is evident that some deeply rooted prejudices have not been wholly eradicated. The film depicts a reality that remains problematic and as such contributes to social dialogue.

Even without attempting a depth-analysis of the films (many comments have already been penned, in particular by Michael Chanan in *The Cuban Image*) one may point out that each of them has been directed with a tone and a style of its own. And yet, some elements reverberate throughout the three episodes. For instance, the relation of the heroine with mirrors is significant. The first time Lucía feels the urge to gaze at herself is after her meeting with Rafael, thus discovering herself through a basic form of auto-eroticism. The second time, Lucía need not indulge in this narcissism, for her personality is more assertive. It is her mother, who embodies decadent bourgeois values (deserted by her husband, she smokes and drinks), who looks at herself in the mirror. Lucía even turns her back to a mirror during a conversation with Flora, who also loves a rebel but will eventually prove less intransigent than her friend. In this particular passage, by duplicating the image of the character of Flora, the mirror seems to fill the surrounding space that her interior emptiness has left void. In the last episode, it is Tomás, the narcissistic macho man, who combs his hair in front of the mirror, underlining his self-centred and dominant personality. Conversely Lucía resorts to her mirror merely to keep boredom at bay when she uselessly puts on makeup while her husband is away. This device shows that the Lucías are both the same and different; the evolution of the character both illustrates and alligns itself with the historical and social changes.

Lucía is one of the most typically representative films of the new Cuban cinema. Solás' work is part and parcel of a larger trend marking a break with the 'old', that is 'pre-Revolution', cinema. In order to illustrate how he participated in this creative renewal, let us broach his relationship with Raquel Revuelta, who plays the role of Lucía in 1895, for it seems that it exemplifies the radical change that the Cuban cinema undergoes.

On many occasions Solás commented on the way he worked with the actors of the film, and in particular, on his choice of an actress for the main part in each section. Once again, the evolution is characterised by a figure of gradation as can be seen in the structure of the trilogy itself. Indeed, as Solás himself suggested, the professionalism of the three main actresses is inversely proportional to the commitment of the heroines to their country's historical changes. Thus in the last episode, which represents the spontaneity of a Revolution in the making, he chose Adela Legrá, a countrywoman from the region of Oriente before she acted in *Manuela*, Solás' previous film. In the second episode, he hires Eslinda Núñez who was a professional but rather inexperienced actress. In the first part, Solás directs Raquel Revuelta, a renowed stage actress, who had also acted in a few films before the Revolution.

It is worth mentioning that indigenous film production before the Revolution consisted mostly of melodramas made in co-production with Mexico, especially in the 1950s. They are exemplified by the few films in which Raquel Revuelta acted; indeed she was part of the cast on two films by Miguel Morayta, a Mexican director who won renown through particularly frenzied melodramas (*Morir para vivir* (*To Die for Living*, 1954) and *La fuerza de los humildes* (*Power of the Humble*, 1954) were two titles that spare one the necessity of saying anything about the plots). Some historians of Cuban cinema categorise such films as 'melodramatic' or else 'tropical', again suggesting that the depiction of Cuba had hitherto been nothing but a string of clichés. Solás believed Raquel Revuelta was underused in such productions. Hence it appears that the renewal of the cinema also entailed the improvement of the roles it offered.

One explanation for the richness of style in *Lucía* could lie in the fact that Solás associated each of the three episodes with particular cinematic and cultural references that emphasise their singularity and originality. One may say that matter and manner are mutually enriching and in perfect congruence. Indeed the first episode describes the aristocracy in the late nineteenth century, and whose culture and lifestyle was characteristically influenced by European tastes. And Solás makes constant references to Visconti so that many critics point out possible comparisons between *Lucía* and *Senso* (1954) both in terms of filming and plot.

As for the second episode, it deals with the bourgeoisie in the 1930s for which the model is no longer the old continent but the United States. This is notably perceptible in the clothes of the female characters that are inspired by American fashions. It is particularly apparent in the middle of the film during the orgiastic party depicting a decadent society indulging in lust and intoxication. The viewer's disgust is made more acute by close shots on those scenes of pleasure Aldo witnesses from a distance. From a cinematic point of view, the episode can be linked to classical Hollywood productions from the 1930s. Nevertheless, Solás is no slave to such influences of which the above-mentioned scene is emblematic. Indeed, with this central scene, far from resembling the glamourous images of this classical American cinema, here Solás films very closely the characters' flesh, almost all of them hold a glass of some alcoholic beverage in their hands, men and women more or less drunk smile or laugh in a quite stupid way, and the sexual orientation of the party is not only suggested – as in the classical Hollywood movies – but clearly shown, as a man embraces a woman, putting his hand inside her dress. One could consider this particular sequence as a parody of the classical cinema, as it insists on what earlier movies never let show.

The last episode represents the Cuban people on the fast track to a new society and references are now indigenous. There is no need to imitate external models as the emergence of a national line of conduct freed the director from persistent and archaic burdens and representations. Solás resorted to shoulder-mounted camerawork in order to increase the effect of spontaneity. It perfectly renders a Revolution in the making.

Solás' ongoing goal of finding new cinematic forms to present a faithful account of the cultural and social actuality of Cuba is also illustrated in his use of music. In previous films the musical soundtrack has two main functions, either dramatic or ornamental. But in both cases it has hardly promoted Cuban culture. Film-makers were actually capitalising on successful themes; in films where cabarets and rumba dancers play such a significant role, commercial ends mainly justify the omnipresence of music.

In Solás' film, the musical themes are composed by the Cuban composer Leo Brouwer and the latter's comments on his work clearly demonstrate how different his attitude is. Each part of the trilogy is typified by a particular visual style, which the music effectively fosters. Brouwer took a great care to create a musical atmosphere specific to each period, and which functions as a reflection of the songs of the day and as a symbol of Lucía. According to the composer, music must be her 'second self'. Great emphasis is laid on the conceptualisation of music, which also must follow the transformation of the characters and of Cuban history. This is another instance of the intricate intertwining of thematic elements and the formal devices employed to represent them.

In Cuba, *Lucía* was a great popular success and was well reviewed, especially by the critics from *Cine cubano*, a Cuban film magazine that greatly contributed to the emergence of the new Cuban cinema. When the film came out, a special issue – with a reproduction of the film's poster on its cover – was dedicated to it. Its standing remains powerful. It is still among the best Cuban films, alongside Tomás Gutiérrez Alea's *Memorias del subdesarrollo* (*Memories of Underdevelopment*), according to surveys conducted in the local film industry in the late 1990s.

But this success was not limited to the domestic audience; it was also met with great critical acclaim abroad. In France and the United States, the distribution of Cuban films was problematic. In the US the film was not released until 1974, which critics attribute to the international context and in particular to the tensions between the two nations. Robert Reagan noted that a festival dedicated to Cuban films was banned in the US in 1972. However, when they had the opportunity to view it, American critics attached great importance to Solás' film.

Likewise in France, where it was released in 1970, it was widely reviewed and many critics complained about the limited distribution that the Cuban cinema had to endure. On this subject Jean-Loup Passek went as far to mention 'the ghetto of art cinema houses in the Latin Quarter in Paris'. Aside of a few occasional criticisms, the reviews were enthusiastic. The conclusion made by Michel Capdenac in *Les Lettres Françaises* illustrated how French critics tended to adopt a patronising tone which was not entirely free from clichés. For instance he welcomed a film that is 'perhaps heavy, but like a tropical tree loaded with tropical and sun-kissed fruit'. Though this statement sounds somewhat naïve (what ontological link between Cuba's flora and its cultural production?) it attests to a certain enthusiasm. Indeed critics open-mindedly treated themselves to a pleasant surprise with a film which unexpectedly (to them at least) 'ridicules social realism', as Guy Hennebelle emphasises. This shows all the originality of the Cuban cinematic project promoted by ICAIC. As mentioned above, the aim of this new cinema was not to celebrate the Revolution in a absolute and over-simplified way. On the contrary, the new film-makers, among which Solás is included, tried to represent the Revolution as a process and not as a given phenomenon that would solve the social and cultural problems in Cuba. This is why *Lucía* can be considered an open work, and it explains the surprise of some of the French critics. Where they expected a dense, ideologically loaded film, they found something else; an enthralling work that was attempting to question the revolution as a work in progress.

In such a wholehearted atmosphere, critics from Cuba and abroad saw in *Lucía* the seeds of a new Cuban cinema. In reality, the production in the 1970s did not meet the high expectations that sprouted from the excellent films of the late 1960s. In an interview he gave in 1988, twenty years after *Lucía* was first released, Solás was nostalgic about the period when he shot and released the film. He stressed that such films as *Memorias del subdesarrollo* or *Las aventuras de Juan Quinquín* (*The Adventures of Juan Quinquín*, Julio García Espinosa, 1967), and of course *Lucía* appeared at a time when Cuban film-makers were inventing a new form of cinematic expression. This kind of cinema gradually eroded through a lack of regeneration during the 1970s and the 1980s. He expressed a bitter judgment and opposed those years following the 1960s when the revolutionary experience matched the act of artistic creation, when film-makers were passionately and wholly dedicated to their work.

The *golden age* of the Cuban cinema, which reached its peak in the late 1960s, seems miles away from the 1970s when bureaucracy replaced spontaneity. Significantly, Ambrosio Fornet defined the first half of the 1970s as 'the grey years'. Whereas in the late 1960s opposing views regarding artistic culture were fruitfully exchanged, Solás believed that the Cuban cinema had lost its spark and that it dealt with its material in a passive and uncreative manner. Though ICAIC was traditionally independant, censorship was enforced due to the narrow-minded interpretation of instructions given by Fidel Castro in his address to intellectuals when he said 'Within the Revolution, everything; against the Revolution, nothing'. Paulo Antonio Paranaguá mentions 'a period of regression on cultural and political levels and hence a tendency to treat the public like children'. That state of affairs was poles apart from the creative dialectics that young film-makers and critics aimed to establish between their films and the audience. Solás suffered from this situation with *Un día de noviembre* (*One Day in November*, 1972) which he directed shortly after he completed *Lucía* and considers his most personal work. Though well received abroad, the film would not be viewed in Cuba until 1978. This painful experience led Solás to a crisis serious enough for him to consider giving up film-making.

But this discouragement was only temporary and Solás went back to work, producing films that confirmed his strained relations with the most intransigent Cuban critics. Indeed, he directed a film adapted from *Cecilia*, a novel written by Cirilo Villaverde that is considered as a mainstay in the process of building a national Cuban identity. He refused to obey orders from people he considered secretarian, thus provoking an angry response from some critics. Nevertheless such a disparaged film as *Cecilia* was selected for the Cannes Festival in 1982, the worthy descendant of *Lucía*, which had won many prizes in international competitions.

Lucía is in many ways emblematic of the early days of the new Cuban cinema. Indeed, as a production backed by ICAIC, it projects on large screens a grand vision of Cuban history culminating in the Revolution. As such it is consistent with the cinematic design of the young Cuban film-makers who rejected the old traditional Latin American cinema stuck in the mire of melodramatic folk representations.

Lucía offers a specific image of Cuban social reality in a historical perspective. Making a woman the central figure allows Solás to illustrate the evolution of an oppressive system through its more oppressed element. As he said in an interview quoted by Michael Chanan, 'The woman's role always lays bare the contradictions of a period and makes them explicit … *Lucía* is not a film about women; it's a film about society. But within that society, I chose the most vulnerable character, the one who is most transparently affected at any given moment by contradictions and changes.' Therefore, the final episode points out 'the problem of *machismo* … which undermines a woman's chances of self-fulfilment and at the same time feeds a whole subculture of underdevelopment'. This last word clearly expresses the link between his film and Alea's work, as they both perfectly represent the relationship between film-makers and the Cuban reality they intended to show. Yet the depiction of the Revolution they propose is neither Manichean nor simple. What they intend to do is give a dynamic image of a revolution which is still far from having solved all the cultural problems that exist in Cuba.

Although emblematic of the movement, *Lucía* is also representative of Solás' art. The latter may be defined by its nonconformism, reworking exterior models in order to reload them with new significance, and above all its anti-dogmatic vision of the Revolution. Even if it caused him many setbacks, one cannot deny that it is for his highly problematic and dynamic vision of the Revolution that he gained favour with the public and the critics. Re-viewing *Lucía* is therefore an excellent way to approach the most original, creative and revolutionary dimension of the new Cuban cinema.

Julie Amiot

(Translated from the French by Karim Chabani)

REFERENCES

Caballero, R. (ed.) (1999) *A solas con Solás*. Havana: Letras Cubanas.

Chanan, M. (1985) *The Cuban Image: Cinema and Cultural Politics in Cuba*. BFI/Indiana University Press, 1985.

Flores Gómez, L. E. (2000) *Tras la huella de Solás*. Havana: ICAIC.

González, R. (ed.) (2001) *Coordenadas del cine cubano I*. Santiago de Cuba: Oriente.

Various Authors (1968) articles about *Lucía* in *Cine cubano*, 2–24, 52–3.

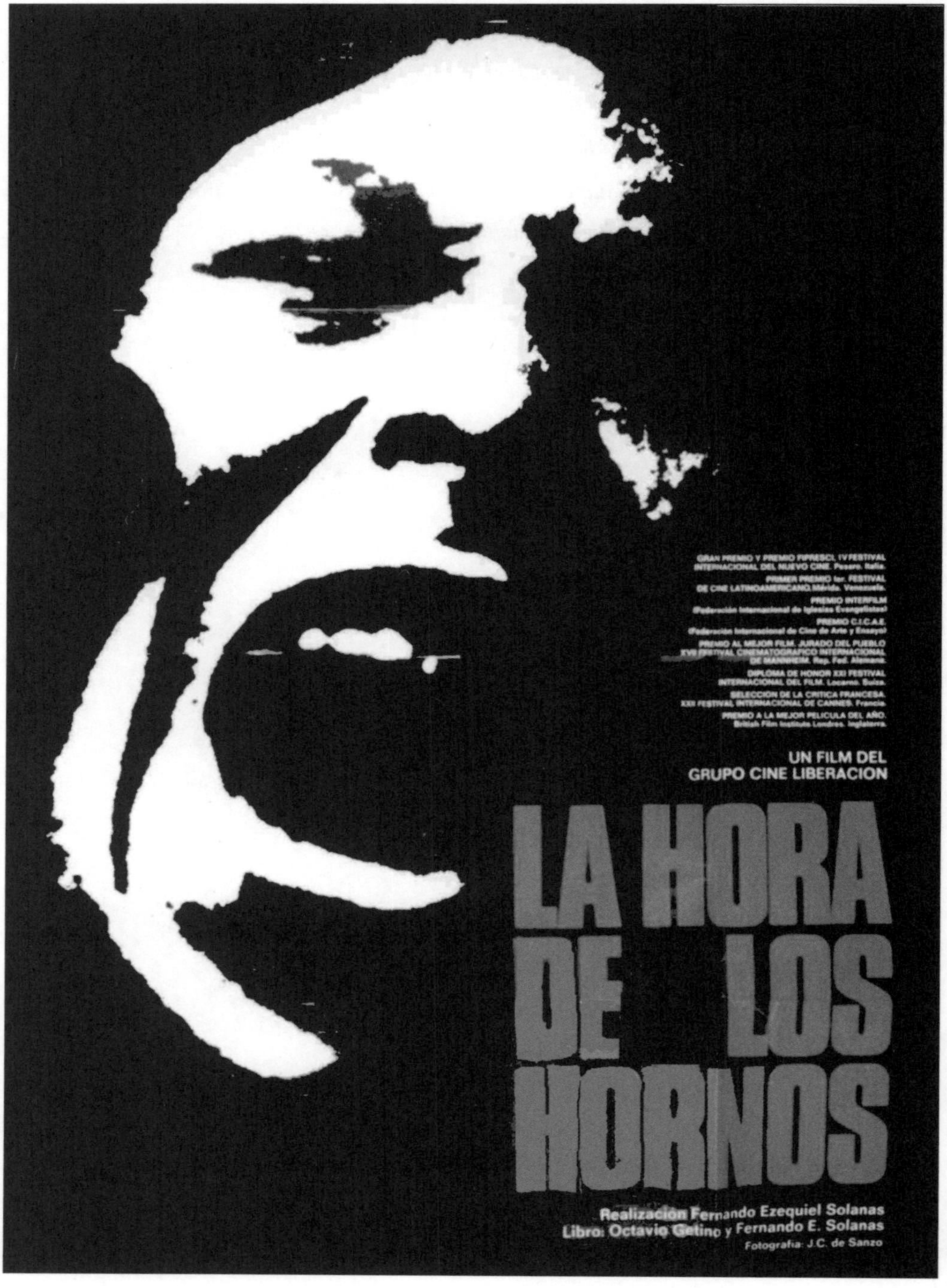
GRAN PREMIO Y PREMIO FIPRESCI. IV FESTIVAL INTERNACIONAL DEL NUEVO CINE. Pesaro. Italia.
PRIMER PREMIO 1er. FESTIVAL DE CINE LATINOAMERICANO. Mérida. Venezuela.
PREMIO INTERFILM (Federación Internacional de Iglesias Evangelistas)
PREMIO C.I.C.A.E. (Federación Internacional de Cine de Arte y Ensayo)
PREMIO AL MEJOR FILM. JURADO DEL PUEBLO XVII FESTIVAL CINEMATOGRAFICO INTERNACIONAL DE MANNHEIM. Rep. Fed. Alemana.
DIPLOMA DE HONOR XXI FESTIVAL INTERNACIONAL DEL FILM. Locarno. Suiza.
SELECCION DE LA CRITICA FRANCESA. XXII FESTIVAL INTERNACIONAL DE CANNES. Francia.
PREMIO A LA MEJOR PELICULA DEL AÑO. British Film Institute Londres. Inglaterra.
UN FILM DEL
GRUPO CINE LIBERACION
LA HORA DE LOS HORNOS
Realización Fernando Ezequiel Solanas
Libro: Octavio Getino y Fernando E. Solanas
Fotografía: J.C. de Sanzo

LA HORA DE LOS HORNOS THE HOUR OF THE FURNACES 12

FERNANDO E. SOLANAS, ARGENTINA, 1968

La hora de los hornos broke onto the international scene in a situation characterised by the consolidation of the New Latin American Cinema, the emergence of the new African cinemas, and the rise of a militant European cinema accompanying the climate of agitation in the main cinema forums all over the world following the events of May 1968. This was also a time of marked visibility for the cinematic 'thirdworldism' that nurtured the film and which in turn the film contributed to promote the Third Cinema Theory elaborated by its film-makers, a tendency of the 1960s which consisted of, as Fredric Jameson pointed out, a cinema of formal inventiveness and political ferment in which form was also an extra-aesthetic issue and whereby film-making and films were expected to have the effect of changing the world. Although *La hora de los hornos* was able to communicate with that world scene, the sense and orientation of the film was mainly associated with the Argentine situation, in which it sought to intervene.

In 1965 Fernando Solanas and Octavio Getino began working together on a documentary-based film that was to bear testimony to Argentina's reality. Thus they embarked on a process of collecting archive material, basically newsreels, and recording testimonies of militants of the so-called Peronist Resistance (a period of popular struggles beginning with Perón's fall in 1955), of intellectuals and university leaders. This search made the film-makers travel all over the country and was reflected in the film's subtitle: 'Notes and Testimonies on Neocolonialism, Violence and Liberation'. Throughout this process (spanning from late 1965 to mid-1968, and including the participation of Gerardo Vallejo towards the end), the directors gradually modified their original proposal and part of their ideas. They incorporated the revisionist view of history and a look on the Peronist working class as the main subject of Argentina's revolutionary transformation. They experienced, as well as many other intellectuals in those years, a passage from traditional left into national left. With a new military regime coming to power in 1966, because of the film's adhesion to proscribed Peronism and in particular to its most radicalised wing, its revolutionary proposal and the will to inscribe it in the struggles for social change, they had to resort to an alternative exhibition circuit.

The formal organisation of *La hora de los hornos* is inextricably linked to these objectives. Its total runnning time of 4 hours 15 minutes is structured into three parts, each with a different formal treatment, theme and even objective. The first section, 'Neocolonialism and Violence', was conceived as an essay-film, which discusses the neocolonial nature of Argentine and Latin American dependency throughout 13 chapters. The second part, 'Act for Liberation', is divided in two, reflecting specific time periods: 'Chronicle of Peronism' and 'Chronicle of Resistance'. Conceived as a *film act* and dedicated to the 'Peronist proletarians', these two chronicles respectively deal with an analysis of the ten years of Peronism in power (1946–55) and a critical reconstruction of the ensuing struggles (1956–66). The third part, 'Violence and Liberation', dedicated to the 'new man who is being born out of this liberation war', presents itself as a study on the meaning of violence.

Some critics have highlighted the way in which the film articulates an original experimental language with its revolutionary project, making possible – as Robert Stam put it – the confluence of political and formal avant-gardes. For the construction of this language, *La hora de los hornos* incorporates and works with a wide range of cinematic resources and techniques (newsreel sequences, interviews, documentary material and reconstruction of scenes, extracts from other films, still photographs, intertitles, graphisms, freeze frames, advertising images, editing effects, collage, the contributions of direct cinema), while it absorbs and re-works various influences, including the film-makers Eisenstein, Vertov, Rocha, Alvarez, Ivens, Godard, as well as perspectives on art and politics as exemplified by artists such as Brecht. As opposed to cinematic entertainment, particularly in its Hollywood form, the first part integrates various strategies to attack the spectator's passivity, where counter-information and agitation (agit-prop) are combined without any conflict, while the following parts advance in a more classic, reflective documentary line, critically incorporating and reviewing a series of experiences about which the viewers are invited to draw conclusions, and then act.

From the beginning, an omniscient voice-over expounds an argument about Argentine and Latin American history, which functions as the textual dominant. It is not by chance then that the first part of *La hora de los hornos* is considered an 'essay-film', for it incorporates, following Bill Nichols' modes of documentary representation, the mode that is closest to the essay or the classic expository report. But this mode becomes more complex as the materiality of forms is constantly used to address spectators' emotions and reason, disquieting and provoking them. This dialectics of appropriation of images, texts and sounds dynamises the film through an impressive process in which we can highlight the meticulously organised composition of every section, the intensity and the sound rhythm, the bold and precise montage which makes the sound and the image tracks work in counterpoint or in unison, incorporating intertitles in the style of Vertov, camera movements, and fragmentation and manipulation of images. This last procedure shows a very elaborate technique that was the result of Solanas' previous experience with the language of advertising.

The film establishes a close relationship between form and content, seeking to sensitise its ideas and varying each section according to the topic dealt with. The political-ideological perspective, in a strongly Manichean register typical of the period, mainly combined a historiographic revisionism which contested the liberal version of Argentine history – the main issues discussed in the Havana Tricontinental Conference and an uncompromising Fanonian-rooted 'thirdworldism'. Frantz Fanon's influence was certainly remarkable; in every exhibition, a sign with his motto 'Every spectator is either a coward or a traitor' hung below the screen.

In the prologue, a torch appears on the black screen and is followed by intermittent footage of acts of repression and protest that match the increasingly loud percussive rhythm of the soundtrack. Accompanying this are legends and intertitles with quotes from Aimé Césaire, Frantz Fanon and Che Guevara, the Argentinean national thinkers Scalabrini Ortiz, John William Cooke and Juan José Hernández Arregui, and political leaders from Perón to Castro. The claim that 'the history we were taught is false' preceeds the first, essay, section.

This first section presents the *other* history, with its claim of neocolonialist penetration in Latin America and Argentina, a country where everyday violence, represented by alienated work in the factory, reigns. The camera travels across its premises while we hear the broken echoes of the workers' testimonies, superimposed on the machine sound so that they become a uniform and disturbing noise in which randomly heard words do not allow us to catch their meaning, yet materialise this concept of alienation.

Latin American statistical data on working conditions, latifundium and rural life, urban shanty towns or diseases of poverty are illustrated by images of impoverished rural and urban sectors, and *ollas populares* (outdoor soup kitchens) in the sugar mills. Then, the film processes a certain social hypocrisy through the counterpoint of the soundtrack reproducing *Aurora*, a traditional song, with its references or connotations of purity and patriotism, and two successive sequences of social violence: a hand-held camera reconstruction of a knife fight between two young men in a slum (reminding us of scenes by Pier Paolo Pasolini or

Jean Rouch), followed by the *mise-en-scène* of a precarious brothel shown with a slow camera movement over the prostitute and the faces of her marginal clients waiting for her services.

The images that follow are extracts from Fernando Birri's medium-length film *Tire dié* (*Throw us a Dime*, 1958). The use of this is known 'filmic citation', an original resource in part consisting of the inclusion of sequences of what is regarded as a 'culturally valid testimony-cinema'. Thus, there is footage of Joris Ivens' *Le ciel, la terre* (*The Threatening Sky*, 1965), of Leon Hirszman's *Maioria Absoluta* (*Absolute Majority*, 1964) and sequences from Humberto Ríos' *Faena* (*Work*, 1962). 'Filmic citations' constitute one of the ways in which this film maintains a dialogue with the documentary tradition it comes from. However, it also strives to differentiate itself from it, a move very much in keeping with a time when Latin American cinema was discussing the passage from documentary characterised by recordings and testimonies to a new, offensive and more aggressive stage. In the case of *Tire dié*, the extract used is the sequence where bare-footed children ran along the train, catching the coins tossed by passengers. Solanas' editing recovers the look of the last boy at the train and, as Emilio Bernini noted, projects it onto the big city buildings recorded by a low-angle camera at the beginning of the next section, as if the camera eye were the child's. A pan shot from a car over the buildings introduces an omnipresent and omnipotent Buenos Aires as a 'Europeanised' city.

The composition of the following section, 'Oligarchy', highlights the work with images and sounds so as to parody or even satirise this social class in the traditional livestock exhibition held in Buenos Aires. Images of the imposing bulk of the heavily ornamented award-winning bulls are juxtaposed with shots of their owners watching the parade and the cattle auctions from the crowded grandstand of the Argentinean Rural Society. These images are accompanied by a voice-over providing data on the wealth of this agrarian oligarchy. Image track references to the symbols of its power, consumption and leisure activities are edited together with reflections of their members on their ancestors, Argentina's founding fathers. In this and other parts of the film, dominant classes are confronted or ridiculed through their own anti-popular testimonies, in which certain voice modulations, tone patterns and mannerisms connote class. But the film's treatment of oligarchy transcends denunciation to characterise this class through their visible signs of decadence. Their dream of 'making the future into the past' is addressed in a remarkable sequence in Recoleta cemetery, the Neoclassic Holy Sepulchre of Argentina's dominant class. Statues and monuments appear to become animated as if talking to each other, with a montage rhythm matching an opera, one of the favourites of this social class, creating the aristocratic 'aura' that the film manages to de-legitimise at the same time.

The film also provides a systematic and didactic analysis. Some sections denounce issues such as political violence. In 'Neo-racism', images related to popular culture accompany a genealogy of the proscription of popular classes, establishing a link between the historical persecution of *gauchos*, *montoneros* (popular rural movements) and Indians, and the contemporary persecution of *cabecita*, *grasa* or *mersa*, pejorative names for those new workers who had migrated from inland provinces and were mostly Peronists. In other cases, they seek to unveil less evident oppression mechanisms of the System. Similarly, after characterising economic dependency through the off-screen comment, concepts like underdevelopment are discussed. The introduction of work in a slaughterhouse illustrates a central feature of this dependency – meat exports. These images have antecedents in the history of political cinema like the metaphor created by Eisenstein in *Stachka* (*Strike*, 1925) but in this case the footage is taken from the Argentinean film *Faena*, by Humberto Ríos. The sequence is more complex because the shots of labourers in the slaughterhouse, of their violent work, of bleeding cows and sheep and of butchering, are mixed with advertising icons and matched with an atmospheric soundtrack, an Americanised Bach 'comparable to the abridged versions of Don Quixote by the Reader's Digest', as Solanas has said.

Culture, and particularly the position of the intellectual, is addressed in significant sections. Within the framework of a certain anti-intellectualist Manicheism typical of the period, but mainly under the influence of Argentinean popular-nationalist thinkers, Solanas and Getino propose the intervention of the 'national' or 'revolutionary' intellectual in political and ideological struggles: the dispute between the national version of history and culture and the colonised intellectuals (a group associated to liberal trends and including the traditional left) or intelligentsia dominated by the establishment.

Thus, another section, 'The Models', outlines the mechanisms of pedagogic colonisation, whose 'major instrument' is the University of Buenos Aires. A long-distance shot of a solemn ceremony is followed by a camera panning over the people in attendance, while a voice-over outlines the University's role in creating an anti-national consciousness. The comment is suddenly interrupted and a speech by the professor presiding over the ceremony is foregrounded', ending with a sentence spoken in Latin. That is, a type of composition in which the solemnity of the event, its protagonists (stereotyped like the scholar) and the final sentence are constructed as if they were the evidence of the film's argument, 'the myth of the University's autonomy contributes to making intellectuals cut off from the people-nation'.

In 'Ideological War', the voice-over heard above background music stresses how 'ideological war in Latin America is mostly waged in men's minds', while a hand-held camera shows crowded downtown pedestrian streets by night. This camera pans over different culture industry symbols until it finally stops at a record-store where modern young people are listening to foreign music. An intertitle, 'artists and intellectuals are integrated into the system', introduces a sequence on the Di Tella Institute, the modern art centre. As expected, the most ludic and frivolous side is selected among the institution's wide range of cultural activities. The camera enters an eccentric cultural party held there, stopping to show the young participants dancing and fooling around.

Following it, a long and remarkable montage of images and sounds opens up a wide range of issues to be denounced, unveiling mechanisms of 'cultural penetration'. Shots of the wealthy elite are intertwined with those of poverty-stricken people, cultural frivolity, consumerism and advertising, repression on Argentinian and other Third World streets. The soundtrack includes fragments of television and mainstream cinema discourse, adverts, music and the voices of those 'modern and universalistic' young people and aristocrats. The interpretation of the varied sensations generated by this complex and uninterrupted editing is oriented by the intertitle, 'Monstrosity is disguised as Beauty'. This segment is closed by a staccato montage of still photographs of the same type, matching the rhythm of machine gun fire in the soundtrack, with an editing style reminding us of the end of the short-length film *Now!* (1965) by Santiago Álvarez.

The last section presents 'The Option'. A sequence about the burial of a man from the marginal classes in the north of Argentina, an 'ordinary man', is followed by images of Che Guevara's corpse: his lifeless body laid out on a concrete table, followed by a static shot of his face, which lingers on screen for the last five minutes of this section, accompanied only by percussion sounds. The image presents a Christ-like Che, whose example could function as an icon of liberation.

The second part of *La hora de los hornos* is also organised into sections following a chronological development. 'Chronicle of Peronism' (1945–55), following the historical documentary pattern, includes newsreel sequences which generally function as an illustration or proof of the text delivered by a voice-over whose argumentative rhetoric about the Peronist Movement in power and its subsequent fall plays the role of being a textual dominant. Hence, the images of Peronist mass demonstrations in Plaza de Mayo are presented as if they were pieces of evidence of the government's popular support. In contrast to the demonstrations after the 1955 civilian-military coup, they purportedly prove the class difference between one crowd and the other. Images of planes dropping bombs over the civilian population in Plaza de Mayo present evidence of the violence of the new regime.

This section caused the greatest degree of controversy internationally. The recovery of Peronism as a revolutionary popular movement, and particularly of Perón as a charismatic leader, was called into question. However, other critics rescued the new treatment of Peronism which the film came to offer, as well as the more complex reading of a phenomenon which most of the European traditional left had wrongly and hastily associated with fascism. In turn, Solanas and Getino insisted that the film sought a critical discussion of this experience. In an interview conducted by Louis Marcorelles in *Cahiers du Cinéma*, Solanas rescued the historical meaning of Peronism, the place of nationalism in liberation processes, and maintained that many had failed to understand the film's theses: the limits of bourgeois nationalism; the impossibility of a democratic bourgeois revolution if it was not continued as a socialist revolution; the Latin American horizon of national struggles.

In any case, this revision was there to be discussed by the audiences. In this sense, the most interesting aspect was the fact that the film's very structure incorporated an explicit call for the spectator to continue it through a collective discussion and a transforming praxis. Thus, after 'Chronicle of Peronism' was over, a legend announced: 'Space open for dialogue'. That was the point when a member of the militant group hosting the exhibition had to coordinate the *act*, as a unique communication moment among the viewers. A tool to make the spectator (in traditional filmic terms) into a protagonist of the exhibition and actor (militant) in the political process. Prior to this, the film-makers' voice addressed *compañeros* (comrades – a privileged kind of spectator), those 'protagonists of the process which the film somehow attempts to bear witness to and deepen', reaffirming the idea of openness (and even collective authorship) contained in the concept of *film act:* 'The film is a pretext for dialogue, for the search and the meeting of wills. This is a report we place before you for your consideration to be debated after the screening. What counts is the conclusions you can draw as the real authors and protagonists of this story … Above all, what counts is the action that might spring from these conclusions … That's why the film stops here and opens up for you to continue it.'

This open nature is reiterated from the beginning of the 'Chronicle of Resistance', drawing parallels with a more reflective documentary approach, also drawing on the *mise-*

en-scène of the film's construction, revealing the process of interviewing and reflecting on it. This has a special significance. While 'Chronicle of Peronism' drew on a reservoir of familiar images forming part of the audiovisual memory of Argentinian popular classes, 'Chronicle of Resistance' incorporated a fresco of reports and testimonies about Argentine popular struggles during a long period of proscription. Of course, the two sections incorporated these materials through a narration reaffirming their meaning or resignifying it in the line of the discourse of a growing Peronist left, which the film-makers embraced.

The sections included in 'Chronicle of Resistance' also borrow from familiar footage and through the *mise-en-scène* of interviews with leaders and militants, mainly from trade unions. Its central thesis refers to the limits of spontaneity and the need to organise revolutionary violence. Most footage with or without original sound, functions as an illustration of the interviewees' words, and to this extent can be seen as supporting evidence of what is said. This effect is also achieved by the reconstruction of certain events such as factory occupations, when the account of a factory occupation through the testimony of the trade union leader who participated in it (in a epic register pervaded with a fine irony) and of the ensuing argument with a police chief who was trying to evict them, is edited with alternate images of both, in order to illustrate the dialogue.

The testimonies themselves largely appear as the evidence of the persuasive argument which reappears in the voice-over at the end of each section. Towards the end of this second part, for instance, protagonists of Resistance tell of their experiences and make explicit their limits in being able to change the system. This is exemplified by the testimony of a young man preparing *miguelito* nails to sabotage public transportation vehicles during general strikes, or the woman remembering how she used to throw pepper at police horses during confrontations, only to see the powder blown away by the wind. Somehow, the prominent position occupied by interviews with militants makes the textual authority of the film shift to the social actors, whose comments and responses provide an essential part of the film's argument, as Bill Nichols notes with reference to the role of interviews in the interactive documentary. However, these and other previous testimonies are also incorporated and articulated by the dominant voice-over. Whether through the omniscient narrator or the voice of film-makers, the voices of others, either friends or enemies, are usually intertwined and largely subordinated, in a persuasive textual logic which orchestrates them to follow the orientation of the film's theses. Thus, the voice-over is always supported by the images or testimonies. In the example mentioned above, the off-screen comment develops the idea that, in spite of its participants' courage, resistance had found a limit in repression and thus it was time for it to shift from isolated sabotage actions to a higher form of organisation. This solution is developed in the third part.

The last part of the film is presented as a study supported by testimonies (letters from fighters, interviews, reports) relating to the meaning of violence in the process of national liberation. From the beginning of this part, there is an insistence on the open nature of the film, related to its disposition to encouraging open dialogue. There is also a specific explanation of its 'unfinishedness', as it intends to incorporate new materials which might arise from the process of liberation itself in which the film seeks to be inserted. In this part we can highlight two extensive interviews with an old anarchist fighter reconstructing his experience after the events of the 1919 Tragic Week, and with Julio Troxler, a key figure of Peronist Resistance and a survivor of the 1956 shooting of Peronist civilians after Perón's fall. The film ends with footage images of Latin American and Third World struggles, accompanying a discourse questioning the possibility of pacific coexistence, as well as a song on violence and liberation, written by Solanas himself.

The appearance of *La hora de los hornos* encouraged militant cinema in Argentina. As soon as the film was finished, Grupo Cine Liberación started to screen it on a clandestine exhibition circuit, supported by 'mobile units' in the most important cities. At the same time, the group published documents on political cinema, with a dialectics whereby, after the initial guidelines, the militant dissemination of films contributed to nurturing new technical elaborations and these in turn promoted further exhibition practices. Their best-known manifesto, 'Towards a Third Cinema', establishes the basic principles of what would later be their actual practice, but due to its early appearance (October 1969) it failed to take account of most of the exhibition experience triggered by *La hora de los hornos*. In this sense, the systematisation of their conception of a militant cinema was reached by 1971 with 'Militant Cinema: An Internal Category of Third Cinema'.

The proposal of Third Cinema is associated with the above-mentioned 'thirdworldist' perspective, but at the same time it refers to a 'cultural decolonisation cinema' for the Third World that is defined in opposition to Hollywood Cinema (First Cinema) and seeks to surpass the limitations attributed to the so-called 'Auteur Cinema' (Second Cinema). Militant cinema was conceived as the most advanced category of Third Cinema and associated to a more immediate type of intervention. Thus, the notion of *film act* occupied a crucial position. In several documents, Cine Liberación dealt with the way of organising debates, the moment of the *act*, which, regardless of the guidelines thus provided, usually tended to fit the kind of work the mobile units articulated with local groups (particularly belonging to the *Juventud Peronista* (Peronist Youth)) who accrued political gain after the exhibition. This articulation determined the main political objectives as well as the type of material exhibited. In this sense, one of the most singular aspects was the tendency to use different parts of the film depending on the kind of audience. On many occasions, the first part was exhibited for discussion with intellectuals or middle-class professionals, and the second one for working class and popular sectors. The third was exhibited much less often.

On the other hand, on an international level, after its successful premiere at the Pesaro Film Festival (Italy), in June 1968, *La hora de los hornos* appeared at numerous alternative cinema forums all over the world and was incorporated into the catalogues of the major alternative distribution companies. The public's reception differed from that of the critics. Its cinematic form was generally acclaimed, but its political dimension gave rise to heated controversy.

It is interesting to note that even though in the European reception of Third World political cinema, as Paul Willemen pointed out, a 'Second Cinema' reading very often prevailed, prioritising the artistic-authorial dimension of works at the expense of their political aspects, the case of *La hora de los hornos* shows that this kind of reception coexisted with a different use of those films and their insertion in militant circuits also in the First World. An early Italian example is that of the exhibition of *La hora de los hornos* in early 1969 as part of the political events staged by the Students' Movement, *Ombre Rosse* magazine and the powerful Collettivo Cinema Militante in the university circles of Perugia, Turin, Trento and Milan. This was a militant use of *La hora de los hornos* abroad which also reached working class and popular circles, similar to the Spanish collective of Catalonian film-makers associated to the Comisiones Obreras trade union in the last years of Franco's regime, or in Italy around 1971–72 with the Centro de Documentazione Cinema e Lotta di Classe. In all cases, this Argentinian film was one of the titles most often requested for exhibition.

The international impact of *La hora de los hornos* and the Third Cinema Theory throughout the 1970s thus reached the most important forums, as it was reflected in the discussions published in specialised magazines and encounters about new cinemas and political cinema in several Third World countries, Europe and North America.

Mariano Mestman

(Translated from the Spanish by Libertad Borda)

REFERENCES

Bernini, E. (2001) 'La vía política del cine argentino: los documentales', in *Kilómetro 111. Ensayos de Cine*, 2, September, 41–60.

Ortega, M. L. (1999) '*La hora de los hornos*', in A. Elena and M. Díaz López (eds), *Tierra en trance: el cine latinoamericano en cien películas*. Madrid: Alianza, 210–15.

Pines, J. & Willemen, P. (eds) (1989) *Questions of Third Cinema*. London: British Film Institute.

Solanas, F. E. (1989) *La mirada: reflexiones sobre cine y cultura. Entrevista de Horacio González*. Buenos Aires: Puntosur.

Solanas, F. E. & Getino, O. (1973) *Cine, cultura y descolonización*. Buenos Aires/Mexico: Siglo XXI.

Stam, R. (1980/81) '*The Hour of the Furnaces* and the Two Avant-Gardes', in *Millennium Film Journal*, 7–9, Fall-Winter (Reprinted in J. Burton (ed.) *The Social Documentary in Latin America*. Pittsburgh: University of Pittsburgh Press, 1990, 251–66).

Tal, T. (1997) 'History, Politics and Aesthetics in the Films of Fernando Solanas: Cinematic Representation of Changes in Argentina's National Left Discourse, 1968–1972', Tel Aviv University: Master of Humanities Dissertation.

REED: MÉXICO INSURGENTE REED: INSURGENT MEXICO

13

PAUL LEDUC, MEXICO, 1971

Fiction films about history should not be taken seriously as a reliable source of information on the topic they are talking about, because these films are conceived merely as spectacles, a set of actions slotted into a tight structure that audiences would easily understand and, above all, enjoy. History films and especially those about revolutionary movements fail to become precise reconstructions of historic facts. In short, it is rare that a serious scientific analysis may become a fiction film. History films are not a genre apart from drama or melodrama, but a subdivision or subgenre of any of these, where dramatic progression is the rule that controls these films, rather than transcriptions of historic facts.

In general, films about revolutions emphasize the figure of a particular historic character, usually a revolutionary leader, instead of focusing on the importance of the movement or its achievements. As film historian Marc Ferro says, fiction films about history are melodramatic renderings of actual history; therefore, they should not be taken as accurate to the facts. With respect to the depiction of the Mexican Revolution in cinema, the characteristics of fiction films have not been drastically different from the depiction of other revolutionary movements. The pattern of melodramatic, hero-oriented staging remains the same. However, the link beetween cinema and the Mexican Revolution is unique, for it was the first one that took place in the twentieth century and, coincidentally, it was the first one that cinema was able to photograph in the actual battlefields.

The Mexican Revolution as a theme was present in Mexican cinema in its earliest stages. The cinematograph of the Lumière brothers arrived in Mexico in 1896, and in that very same year some nationals interested in it became the pioneers of Mexican film (Salvador Toscano, Guillermo Becerril, Enrique Rosas, Carlos Mongrand to name but a few). For a number of years, Mexican cinematographers struggled to make cinema acceptable to Mexican society and they traveled around the nation carrying their own screens and a set of films to project in public squares everywhere, even in small villages and remote areas. When the Revolution exploded in 1910, Mexican cinematographers had already mastered documentary techniques well enough to make cinema the main source of information available to the people. The need of people to know about the latest events was such that these documentaries easily found a captive audience. Active film-makers of the period such as Jesús H. Abitia and the three Alva brothers and their uncle, who often risked their lives visiting the battlefields, produced remarkable documentaries, many of which were feature-length. The pioneer Enrique Rosas was also producing montage documentaries. It is true that newspaper had the news available earlier than these precursors to cinematic newsreels, but the power of the image overshadowed the immediacy of written media at a time when the majority of the population in Mexico was illiterate.

As the revolutionary strikes reached an end, so did the documentaries. Later, when fiction film became the standard in Mexican cinema, some films that dealt with the Revolution still stood out, because of their quality, with some still considered masterpieces today. One such film was *El automóvil gris* (*The Grey Automobile*, Enrique Rosas, Joaquín Coss and Juan Canals de Homes, 1919), which was one of the first to allude, albeit indirectly, to the events following the Revolution. Film historians agree that some of the best Mexican fiction films about the Revolution were made in the early 1930s, when director Fernando de Fuentes produced his trilogy: *El prisionero trece* (*Prisoner Number Thirteen*, 1933), *El compadre Mendoza* (*Godfather Mendoza*, 1933) and *¡Vámonos con Pancho Villa!* (*Let's Go with Pancho Villa*, 1935). The third is a remarkable analysis of the then recent civil war that had changed the strata of Mexican society. In *¡Vámonos con Pancho Villa!*, the director depicts the life of humble people; the anti-heroes, peasants and workers that left all behind to fight for elemental rights in Mexico. De Fuentes offered an honest yet pessimistic portrayal of the Revolution. Despite de Fuentes' achievements, his narrative's excellence and sober vision would not be found again in Mexican cinema until four decades later in 1971, when Paul Leduc directed *Reed: México insurgente*. In between, approximately fifty films dealing with the Revolution had been produced in Mexico. Most of them verged on caricature; blurred sketches of that historic period, using events to foreground stories of love, betrayal or passion against the perilous backdrop of the Revolution.

In terms of international cinema, America has been the most interested in creating narrations about the Mexican Revolution. It was, in many ways, Hollywood's distorted view on the topic that shaped the image of this historic period in the minds of audiences around the world. With respect to early American newsreels made during the Revolution (1910–20), sociologist Margarita de Orellana argues that these films can hardly be called documentaries. They were performances, focused on seducing American viewers for marketing purposes.

Hollywood producers realised that the American public was interested in the Mexican Revolution and they decided to take advantage of this situation by sending cameramen to photograph battles. However, since getting into the battlefields was not an easy task to accomplish for the camera operators, the studios opted to stage some of the battles in their backlots. One of the studios even signed a contract with the revolutionary general Francisco Villa to perform some battles for them to shoot. Villa had a good relationship with both the Mexican and international press and had no problem in accepting the offer. The outcome of all these productions was a series of unconvincing films of little value as documentaries, bearing minimal actual information or links to reality. It would not be imprecise to say that these films were closer to what is known today as fiction films (westerns, more precisely) than to our concept of documentary.

As far as Hollywood was concerned, its accounts on the Mexican Revolution were biased by the ambivalent position of the American government, which at times supported leaders such as Pancho Villa. But when Villa entered American territory, he became a hateful character and then, as a result, admiration of him dissipated (and yet, somehow, a fascination for him as a mythological character has remained in US media). The American reaction to Pancho Villa's activities on US soil helped inspire a trend for racist films that remained unchallenged for decades, in which negative stereotypes of Mexicans (betrayers, bandits, lazy, simple minded, comic people) were created and perpetuated across different genres. Later, Hollywood attempted to deal with the facts of the Mexican Revolution in a more consistent way, in *Viva Villa!* (Howard Hawks, 1934) or *Viva Zapata!* (Elia Kazan, 1952), for instance.

In contrast to the hybrid newsreels of the time (1911–14) that were unable to convey actual information, the reports of John Reed for the left-wing oriented *Metropolitan Magazine*, offered a more reliable account of events. His goal was to send objective and accurate reports to his magazine. At that time, mainstream American newspapers frequently highlighted the brutality of Mexican battles and exaggerated the actual cruelty with which some revolutionary leaders treated their enemy prisoners. Consequently, the cameramen sent by film studios repeated this trend. Reed aimed to redress the balance through objective reportage.

John Reed was born in 22 October 1887 in Portland, Oregon, to a wealthy family. He attended Harvard University where he openly displayed an interest in socialism. Long before, he had been influenced by his father, C. J. Reed, who was actively involved in state politics. After graduating, Reed began his career as a journalist in Manhattan. He was sent to report on the Mexican Revolution by *Metropolitan Magazine* in 1911. At the same time, his human-interest stories were also published in Joseph Pulitzer's *New York World* and, later, in the independent magazine *The Masses.* Even before leaving for Mexico, John Reed was recognised as a distinguished member of the American left. Following his return to the United States, he continued as an activist who participated in strikes, demonstrations against militarism and became one of the founders of the American Communist Party. He traveled to Europe in the midst of World War One as a war correspondent, following which he left for Russia to witness the Revolution there and where he befriended Lenin. His reports were collected in the book *Ten Days that Shook the World*, which enhanced his reputation as a writer. He died in Moscow in 1920 and was buried in the Kremlin.

The collection of articles that Reed wrote on the Mexican Revolution was published in 1914 in the United States, with the title *Insurgent Mexico* (ironically, it was not published in Spanish until 1954). Reviewers of Paul Leduc's adaptation generally agreed that the film was very much in keeping with the tone of Reed's original writings. His two main ideas were present in the film: the unpassionate narration of the historic battles that he witnessed while accompanying Pancho Villa's Northern Division and the vivid description of the routine of the anonymous revolutionary soldiers who were little more than peasants who travelled by foot to fight the Revolution. The film starts with Reed's arrival in Mexico with the remit of fulfilling his mission as a reporter. He interviews prominent leaders of the Revolution such as Francisco Villa and Venustiano Carranza and meets many simple Mexicans who fight for this cause. As his journey unfolds, he develops solidarity with the revolutionary ideals and as the film concludes, we see that John Reed has had a leap of consciousness.

Paul Leduc's take on *Insurgent Mexico* foregrounded Reed's experience as a reporter accompanying Pancho Villa's Northern Division. Leduc may also have been influenced by the recollections of his uncle Renato who, during the Revolution, was a teenage telegraphist working in the same division. He had met Reed, who was known to the revolutionaries as Juanito or Johnny – at that time, however, Renato Leduc had no idea who the nice American reporter would later become. As a result, the film observes the routine of soldiers and officers before and after the battles. To emphasise the private side of life, Leduc rejected any sense of the epic, avoiding discussions of the great battles that constituted the major achievements of Villa's division. In direct contrast to Reed's referencing specific battles in detail, Leduc stops short of showing any of the conflict, preferring to stay with the film's central theme; the account of Reed's leap of consciousness as a man committed with ideals. Throughout, the spectator is invited to reflect on this theme.

It is clear that Leduc chose not to make an epic film with large crowds and special effects. Instead, he decided to present a minimalistic approach to Reed's stay in Mexico during the Revolution. As film critic Dilys Powell once wrote: '*Reed: México insurgente* describes the Mexican Revolution as Reed saw it, and I must say it is a startlingly persuasive view. Or perhaps, startling is the wrong word, for the film is deliberately low-key, the violence merely suggested, the setting arid, undramatic.' In such a way, the director leads us to empathise with John Reed's discovery of his inner self. For instance, at the beginning of the film, when Reed arrives in Mexico, his attitude suggests that he feels like an observer of the action. Later, as he meets more struggling Mexicans, he is confronted with his personal fears, or what he calls 'his cowardice', as he afterwards acknowledges in a conversation with one of Villa's subordinates, Longino. Reed tells him that he is not courageous enough to participate in the battles, despite the fact that he would like to. However, the soldier replies that his duty is to be a witness and to inform the readers in his country about the harsh existence of the revolutionaries.

It seems that Leduc's objective of telling the story of a foreign observer of the Revolution who finds himself is a way to break from the tradition representation of the Revolution within Mexican cinema. His second objective is to touch us by depicting the private life of the humble revolutionary soldiers, showing their sad, hazardous way of life and how they managed to live in such poverty, breaking up with this filmic tradition. Again, this aspect is present in Reed's book. In the context of Mexican cinema about the Revolution, only two directors before Leduc have shared the same interest: Fernando de Fuentes in *¡Vámonos con Pancho Villa!* and José Bolaños in *La soldadera* (1966). The other films about the Revolution were grandiloquent melodramas in which historical truth was diluted, the highlights being the exploits of revolutionary heroes, often depicted in a Manichean way.

Leduc's film is also different in the way it offers a very humane account of these simple people, placing aside negative stereotypes. It even goes further, making some sort of homage to the forgotten team within the battalions, the *soldaderas*, that is, the women who left their home and children to take care of their soldier husbands. These women would gather food where possible, cook, and in general look after the soldiers' well-being within the disastrous setting of the Revolution. Occasionally, a few women fought in the battlefields as men, and in the film there is a scene in which one of these revolutionary women, wearing trousers, passes by. In the iconography of mainstream Mexican films, this image would have been the object of negative remarks implying that she is a tomboy or at least, a very extravagant person. In traditional films, the *soldaderas* are often regarded as tragic, caricatured figures, while Leduc's view remains impartial.

These details reveal the subtlety at the heart of Leduc's approach. Subtlety in the cinematography (long, descriptive tracking shots and images that evoke the texture of rotogravure photographs), staging (there is not a clear dramatic climax and the acting is low-key and naturalistic), editing (elegant sequence shots) and in the use of sound (the absence of incidental sound and music adds distinction to the narration, in direct opposition to the practice of an ever-present soundtrack in commercial films). With time, all these features would become trademarks of Leduc's style. In particular, he would refine his style to the point where parallels could be drawn with silent cinema.

Nevertheless, *Reed: México insurgente* is not a perfect film. Leduc's debut feature contains flaws ranging from sound mismatches to unconvincing acting. However, there is more to admire in this independently produced feature, than to dislike. For example, there is the scene in which Reed is running among wounded people and the horses of the revolutionaries, all of whom are fleeing the battlefield, where the platoon he is traveling with, is losing. In classic Leduc style, the scene is almost silent, save for the sound of few isolated gunshots and the horses hooves on the ground, as the revolutionaries retreat past Reed. As it starts, it is difficult to understand the scene, but as it progresses, we can tell what is going on and finally, share Reed's angst and bewilderment. What happens in this particular scene is akin to the reflection of two mirrors facing each other. As Reed the character, we are no longer observers, for we become his accomplices in one of the few moments of the film in which the spectator is invited to share the feelings of the character.

Reviewers have often labelled this film as semi-documentary, because it appears to bear more authenticity than some documentary films, if it is possible to make such a statement. In other words, it may seem a documentary because there is not conventional dramatic progression, resulting in a fragmented narration, despite the film making no claim to being anything but a fictional account of real events. Aside of a few scenes, mentioned previously, where the audience is invited to empathise with Reed's anger and confusion, the film attempts to keep a critical distance from them, so that they can analyse the action. This is in some way aided by the contrast between such devices and the evocative sepia photography, which creates a transcendent, yet contradictory, tone.

The verisimilitude in *Reed: México insurgente* probably comes from the position of the director's gaze, which avoids being judgmental and interventional on the characters' behaviour. The camera acts as a fly-on-the-wall, which offers another reason for some spectators confusing the film with a documentary. Additionally, there is no conventional use of music, that is, music emphasising and controlling emotions as it can in commercial feature-films. Therefore, the spectator is on their own to confront the action with their own personal ideas and feelings. Furthermore, the film does not comment on or offer an easy explanation for most of the action, as this was not Leduc's intention. Moreover, the film does not follow a tightly-organised plot in the Hollywood fashion, which can account for the difficulty of enjoying the film in any conventional manner. This is another way in which this film moved away from conventional Mexican cinema's representation of the Revolution. In those films, the viewer's opinion was something to be manipulated, because they portrayed characters as black and white, poorly drawn stereotypes of good and evil.

After directing a number of documentaries, Leduc grasped the nakedness of the genre to use it in a fiction-film, where he had no intention to attempt to tell the whole truth about the Revolution, only aiming to show an aspect of it which was the American reporter's experience. As mentioned above, the film is a fiction-film unwilling to take a position about the Revolution and its heroes, and conversely does not want to build up the image of new heroes. Another film maker probably would have decided to emphasise the qualities and good deeds of John Reed in Mexico, knowing that he later became a champion of international socialism. On the contrary, Leduc portrays a very human character who is troubled by his indecision to take a rifle and fight in the battlefield. Other aspects of his personal life, such as his refusal to fight with a macho revolutionary and even that Reed had a possible affair with a *soldadera*, in Leduc's hands, remain ambiguous.

As an adaptation, a document that speaks about the actions the journalist witnessed, the film is a perfect match by being non-judgemental. It merely describes daily life within the Mexican Revolution as Reed saw it, like a diary. However, it remains questionable as to what extent a narration – whether it is a film or a written text – can be objective or unbiased. A comparison with some other films inspired by John Reed's powerful and romantic personality, such as Warren Beatty's *Reds* (1981) or Sergei Bondarchuk's two-part *Campanas rojas/Krasnye kolokola* (*Red Bells*, 1982), co-produced by Mexico and the USSR, could be an instructive way of constructing some kind of 'truth'.

A significant fact to note is that Paul Leduc was 28 years old when this film was made and he was working with an equally youthful crew. Most of the actors had just finished their drama studies at university. Through their enthusiasm they displayed a determination to overcome the limitations of making an independent film. Some of the problems encountered related to working with direct sound recording on location, as well as coordinating all the outside studios locations, which totalled 10 separate sites in 12 weeks. Conversely, Leduc made very wise decisions in the selection of film techniques, such as the format he would use. The film was shot in 16mm film in order to lower production costs. Leduc thought that this format would allow him to shoot more footage than if he had chosen the 35mm format, the standard for feature-length productions. In post-production stage, the film was blown up to 35mm to meet the standards of distribution but also as an artistic choice. When blown up, the grain of the emulsion in each frame breaks apart, giving the film an aged quality.

Leduc's decision to follow the path towards independently made films, disregarding the commercial structures and mode of the time, derives in part from his education. He was one of the first generation of Mexican film-makers that studied film in schools, and consequently, their view on cinema was substantially different to that of previous generations who would make things difficult for new directors interested in entering commercial film production. Along his career as a film director, Paul Leduc stood firm to his principles. None of his films were produced by the film council of the Mexican government.

Reed: México insurgente, was well received by the Mexican press and audiences, going on to achieve international acclaim. It was scheduled in the international film festivals at Berlin and Cannes (Quinzaine des realizateurs) a few months after its national exhibition (it premiered in January 1972 in Mexico). It was awarded the Georges Sadoul Prize as the best foreign film screened in France in 1972. Before Paul Leduc, only two other Mexican directors had attracted such international attention: Emilio Fernández and Luis Buñuel (who obtained Mexican citizenship in 1949). After such a warm reception, Leduc's film raised hopes amongst a number of critics for Mexican cinema. The film was regarded as opening the gateway for a new trend of more politicised films where critical revisions on the subject of Mexican history would take place. Conversely, bureaucratic structures did not favour the production of similar artistic films, and more importantly, young film directors in Leduc's generation were interested in dealing with other subjects, supposedly more universal. After a fruitful cinematic career, in the mid-1990s Leduc ceased shooting on film and concentrated on video, making a number of videos on music in 1998 under the title *Bartolo y la música*.

Carmen Elisa Gómez

REFERENCES

Ciuk, P. (2000) *Diccionario de directores del cine mexicano*. México: Consejo Nacional para la Cultura y las Artes / Cineteca Nacional.

Delgadillo, W., and Limongi, M. (2000) *La mirada desenterrada: Juárez y El Paso vistos por el cine (1896-1916)*. México: Berumen Campos / Cuadro por Cuadro.

Ferro, M., and Passek, J.-L. (eds.) (1989) *Révoltes, révolutions, cinéma*. Paris: Centre Georges Pompidou.

Orellana, M. de (1991) *La mirada circular. El cine norteamericano de la Revolución mexicana (1911–1917)*. México: Joaquín Mortiz.

Powell, D. (1974) 'Films', in *The Sunday Times*, 13 January.

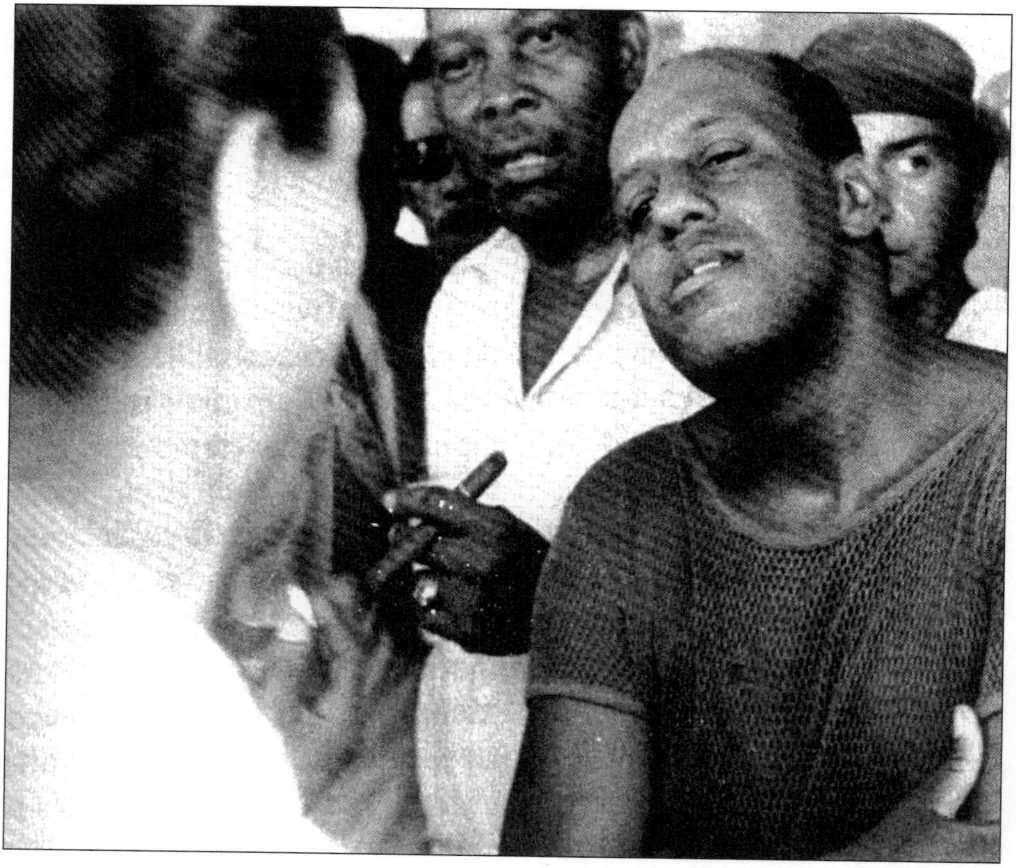

DE CIERTA MANERA ONE WAY OR ANOTHER

14

SARA GÓMEZ, CUBA, 1974

The young film-maker Sara Gómez died at the age of 31, victim of an acute asthma attack, without seeing a completed version of her first full-length feature, *De cierta manera*. Her mentors in ICAIC (the Cuban Institute of Cinematographic Art and Industry), Julio García Espinosa and Tomás Gutiérrez Alea, together with Rigoberto López, completed the post-production process. The film had been shot on 16mm, but a first restoration forced by problems with the negative delayed its screening until 1975 and then only at the Pesaro Film Festival. It finally premiered in Cuba only on 6 October 1977.

It is regretable that this strange and beautiful film should be seen as the extraordinary culmination of Gómez's brilliant career. She entered ICAIC in 1961 after studying journalism and piano. With the arrival of outstanding foreign film-makers in Cuba, backed by the renewal and open-door policy of production adopted by Julio García Espinosa (one of ICAIC's directors under the presidency of Alfredo Guevero), Gómez accompanied Agnès Varda on her trip throughout the island, from which Varda's short film *Salut, les cubains* (1963) was produced. Gómez's cinematographic training resulted in her co-working with the first-generation directors and founders of Cuban post-revolutionary cinema – she was the assistant director on *Cumbite* (Tomás Gutiérrez Alea, 1964) and *El robo* (*The Robbery*, Jorge Fraga, 1965) – and her work in documentary cinema, which was ICAIC's unavoidable and determining trademark in its first years and a necessary step in her training. From 1962 to 1973, she directed 18 films that were categorised as anthropological documentaries, very different from the classical documentary established by Santiago Álvarez and symbolised by his *noticieros* (newsreels). In these short and medium-length films her visual boldness and good use of music as counterpoint to the action was already in evidence. Along with Gómez's work, Octavio Cortázar also made documentaries in which he tried to thread the procedures of social sciences – such as interviews and social and historical investigation – through cinema, always engaging with revolutionary reality, popular with documentary production of the time.

Throughout her short career, Sara Gómez searched for the issues that best shaped the creation of a reflexive background about Cuban revolutionary culture. Her style never lacked complexity or engagement with her own female and Afro-Cuban identity. The existential crossroads of constant renewal, of a developing thought process and of personal analysis, highlighted that the topics we see foregrounded in her films – popular culture, musical production, popular democracy, volunteerism, the raising of children, tobacco production, civic education, the personality of neighbourhoods, etc. – do not prevent themselves from facing the creeks of the revolutionary process, where documentaries do their best to highlight its most undetectable faults and to denounce basic issues such as delinquency, racism and, of course, machismo.

Her most acclaimed documentaries drew from her personal standpoint, on the edge of a new Cuban world, at that time under construction. She opted for a personal and familiar vision in *Iré a Santiago* (*I'll Go to Santiago*, 1968) and *Guanabacoa: crónica de mi familia* (*Guanabacoa: A Chronicle of My Family*, 1966). Following these personal films, she shot a beautiful triptych – (*En la otra isla* (*On the Other Island*, 1967), *Una isla para Miguel* (*An Island for Miguel*, 1968) and *Isla de tesoro* (*Treasure Island*, 1969)), focusing on the island of Pinos and its youngsters who assume their part as narrators, thus avoiding the use of the voice-over. The mid-length film *Mi aporte* (*My Contribution*, 1969–72) is interesting in that it is a precusor to the issues raised within the discourse of *De cierta manera*. The title itself is meaningful, displaying the personal feminist imprint Gómez left in a film that attempted to analyse the integration of women in post-revolutionary society and the hindrances they faced with that integration. Paulo Antonio Paranaguá highlighted the film's controversial subject matter stating, 'It is unreleased, among some other films of hers, due to its trespassing of the limits of feminism tolerated by "machismo-leninism".'

The epigonical *De cierta manera* follows this line, offering a pattern for reflection and explanation to each of her previous questions. This film cannot help its inclination towards presenting some preliminary conclusions to the historical meaning of the revolutionary process after its first decade of existence. That is why it is impossible not to link its contents and aims with her teacher's film *Memorias del subdesarrollo* (*Memories of Underdevelopment*, Tomás Gutiérrez Alea, 1968). Such a formally complex film that contained a deeply critical scope and filmed with a specific style set the standard from which film-makers could question the course and achievements of Cuban society at that time. Alea's film aimed to search, from the ideological premises of development, for a structural and almost emotional process to assume as a transnational Latin American historical and cultural continuum. To do so, the director did not waste the formal and visual resources that open the narrative discourse, and that evoke and strengthen, not only self-parody, but also the sense of melancholy for a future that was originally a great deal more vague than what the renewing direction of political spaces – not only Cuban – of renewal and reappraisal of modernisation and its social theories, could indicate. *Memorias del subdesarrollo* embodied the principles of Garcia Espinosa's notion of 'imperfect cinema', an idea defended by Cuban cinema and the New Latin American Cinema movement.

In this sense, *De cierta manera* takes from *Memorias del subdesarrollo* an intention of opening up to the political ideas and the production of a cinema that confesses, as Latin American, and engaged precisely with the reality that it does not want to evoke, but to specify and rebuild through the new systems for its interpretation, unavoidably, from privacy to collectivity. Both films include documentary images without losing their texture and their documentary character, so that, as a counterpoint to fiction stories, they shape narrations whose analytical value breaks through the 'clouds' and whose political meaning stays open for reflection, due to the exposition of contradictions, much thicker and more complicated than the famous political dialectics previously showed. The result of that cinematic pattern allows the use of procedures materialised and proposed by *new* cinemas – especially *cinéma vérité* – with all the Latin American imagery of documentary vocation, whose references can be carried back to *Los olvidados* (*The Young and the Damned*, Luis Buñuel, 1950), and including emblematic pieces such as *Rio, 40 graus* (*Rio, 40 Degrees*, Nelson Pereira dos Santos, 1955), *Tire dié* (*Give Me a Dime*, Fernando Birri, 1956–60) and *Los inundados* (*The Flooded*, Fernando Birri, 1961). *Memorias del subdesarrollo* uses all the visual wealth materialised by those films and their genre partners to establish a background which evokes Latin American history.

Six years later, Sara Gómez's first feature shows an absolute harmony with the generic proposal, the theoretical category for cinema, proposed by *Memorias del subdesarrollo*. *De cierta manera* delves even deeper into an exploration of generic syncretism, and along with it Gómez assumes a more radical standpoint, perhaps a more explicit – if not more idealistic – engagement, with her ideological legacy. Her aim is to make her work more complex, elaborating a discourse which never leaves a didactic and intellectual level. Througout the film, there is an intentional attempt at some form of bewilderment in the presentation of images, where the specific rhetorics of fiction and documentary are offered explicitly, yet deliberately never lacking calm and clearness in the framing. The flow of sequences is structured in visual and thematic to-and-fros, which form constant counterpoints. From the initial titles we are informed that what we are going to see is a 'feature film about characters, some real and some fictional', so the way is clear to experiment with the formulas to both worlds, legitimatising the homogeneous texture in which both meet.

The formal structure is attractive. Before the titles appear, without any introduction, there is a long, live-sound, sequence shot of a disciplinary board at a Cuban factory. A man explains that he has stayed away from work because he had to travel urgently to Santiago to visit his mother, who was ill. In a submissive tone he states that if the disciplinary board accuses him of a misdemeanour, he will accept hard work on a farm, despite the fact that he believes the trial was prompted by some people who dislike both him and his normally happy disposition. When he finishes, another man among the attendants stands up and reproaches him for his lack of respect to everyone because he has lied. Outraged, he adds that he knows the whole story of his journey to the East, and that he is determined to reveal it all, 'like men do'. Humberto had actually stayed away from work and travelled to Santiago in order to spend a couple of days with a woman. His mother had in fact died many years before. This man is Mario, one of the main protagonists of the film. The scene ends, cutting in Eisenteinian style, to footage of a demolition ball hitting the wall of a building being demolished. This contrast, with its purely metaphorical intention, repeats throughout the film. This specific image is used on two more occasions to symbolise the destruction of those things that hinder the evolution of revolutionary society.

The explanation of this first sequence, which will be repeated towards the end of the film – because the film is in fact one long flashback – has a double relevance in understanding the multifaceted structure of the film. Though we will become more familiar with these two men, the introduction of such a verbally violent sequence presents itself to the audience as the epicentre of the film's ideological structure, its climax. By taking it out of the narrative, it is set up as the point of contention, but also as a catharsis from the issues proposed, which will be clearly exposed throughout the fictional plot and its documentary counterpoints. In a similar way, the introduction of the montage, which implies the solution of the conflict with such a direct intellectual association, predisposes to a logic narratively assumed in various content and reflection levels, which will be present throughout the film.

From this opening moment, we learn from the two voice-overs that narrate the documentary sequences, that the real demolition was carried out in order for the creation of a 'reparto', a renewed neighbourhood in the old quarter of Miraflores. This depressed area in Havana was being restored following a urban plan to demolish all areas where poverty and social exclusion ran counter to the renovating rhythm of the country. Together with this complete renewal of buildings, an education programme was being carried out, echoing the great literacy campaign initiated between 1960 and 1961. These measures aimed at the thorough renovation of those sectors, improving their living conditions. As highlighted by the various voices who present the discourse, in those places the surviving social layer, a victim of chronic unemployment and of a fragmented matriarchal family, permitted the study of how conservative and anti-social values of the most traditional and reactionary nature survive. The film gathers two key elements in the social and political renewal undertaken by the Revolution: urban sanitisation and the creation of an educational structure, both aimed to erradicate social exclusion and the backwardness of the most underprivileged layers of Cuban society.

Both protagonists of the fictional story work in Miraflores, embodying the problems that are expressed and specified. Yolanda, a school teacher, and Mario, son of the president of the disciplinary board and a worker in a factory, are having an affair. Both work within the set of ideas of the Revolution, but their social origins are completely different. Their romance polarises questions that allows both of them to engage with the film's central issue which is the social and cultural renewal of the neighbourhood. The dramatic structure allows us to observe how both live their lives in the process that leads them to a greater understanding of the new world they are living in, but also the pain inherent in developing and in adjusting their reality to the requirements of idealism.

Mario and Yolanda's mode of co-existence and personal adventures are skilfully introduced. In the first part of the film, the narrative weight lies on Yolanda and her difficult experience at the school where she teaches, exemplified in her pupil Lázaro, son of one of the single mothers that live in the neighbourhood, and whose lack of discipline will lead him to youth court. Lázaro is one of the real characters. Yolanda's toughness collides with a world whose reality she refuses to accept. She tells him off for throwing down all his school books and for his uncontrollable and noisy behaviour. Her dealings with him leads to her visiting his mother in order to beg her not to beat him. In a similar way, she goes to the youth court to learn of Lázaro's fate, allowing the spectator to attend all the physical and psychological examinations the boy undergoes. When Lázaro leaves hospital, Yolanda takes his hand, buys him an ice cream and takes him for a walk in Havana, whose atmosphere is presented as bouyant. One way or another, Yolanda bravely assumes that she has to include Lazaro in a world he had never been part of, but which belongs to him.

Throughout the film, the reasons for the opening sequence begin to take shape. Humberto and Mario are friends, who 'became men' in the streets. The male behaviour of playing games and flirting with women is apparent in the neighbourhood's common spaces. Nearly every scene in the neighbourhood shows such behaviour, to the margins of both the camera's and film's attention, creating a counterpoint to the moral 'cleanliness' with which the revolutionary emphasis appears to transform everything. As a contextualisation for the cultural weight of machismo, Mario confesses to Yolanda that as a boy he wanted to become an *abacuá*, but he was freed from it thanks to the Revolution. At that moment, as an expositive and explanatory parenthesis, we see a documentary, preceded by its title 'Sociedad abacuá: Análisis documental' ('Abacuá Society: A Documentary Analysis'). Through historical images and an ethnographical documentary, we are presented the rite of passage of that exclusively male Cuban society. The *abacuás* follow a Calibar rite from southeastern Nigeria based on a vitalist and magic mythology of oral tradition, which fitted in perfectly with the patriarchal and machista creole society of colonial Cuba.

The relationship between Humberto and Mario wears down, despite Humberto's attempts to remind Mario from the very beginning of the film that men should share their time and secrets, that they should protect each other. Mario experiences an additional pressure due to his father Cándido's firm political standpoint, but also due to his relationship with Yolanda which is by nature an achievement of a new world where social and class differences are blurred. All this forces him to think that his world is not his friend's any longer, even though their neighbourhood is governed by unchanging rules. The tension reaches breaking point during Humberto's trial. Paradoxically, Mario feels lonely, misunderstood and fearful. Nobody, not even Yolanda, her ex-husband – his new friend – nor his own father, are able to calm him or console him in his despair of not being aware of what kind of 'man' he has become with that supposed betrayal to male social order.

As previously noted, the disorientation of both characters before their own problems and questions of their ability to change, given the new situation, is evoked and materialised in the relationship they share. The differences between them are constant, and break-ups and reconciliations repeat throughout the film; even in its very open ending when we see them going away, once more, arguing. From their two worlds – his world of social exclusion, her middle-class world – the undetermined future of an uneven couple like theirs is enunciated both in a direct and indirect way. The toughness of Yolanda taking charge of her career when she unpatronisingly confronts the other teachers at school contrasts with Mario's fear towards assuming that he is not the man he used to be. Once again a documentary digression through a real character – Guillermo Díaz – is used to explain the link between them, the feeling that keeps them together in spite of everything. The ex-boxer, musician and singer appears in one of the breaking-up moments that weave the cyclothymic relationship between both lovers. Even though he re-interprets for Mario what masculinity should be in the new social space and encourages him to leave Humberto, Guillermo embodies the singer-songwriter who is creating a world of new meanings through his melodic music. In a concert he plays one of his songs, a song that is also a film theme used as intellectual counterpoint, which is the main narrative resort of the film. The song 'Ríndele' explains how reality should not tarnish love relationships because it is there where fidelity and the search for personal and social improvement lie. The re-formulation of love, the romantic ideal, acquires a political meaning, in which involvement takes the part of the logic of daily work, but also of the logic of daily love. At the end of Guillermo's song, to which they are listening together, moved, but each in their own way, a new montage begins, showing the same demolition hammer. The third and last appearance of this sequence takes place in the middle of a collective conversation among Humberto and Mario's workmates, condemning Humberto and emphasising the need of a respect for work. This last demolished wall seems to evoke the destruction of a machismo logic, parasitical of a society that has no place for it.

Sara Gómez claimed for her movie two clear lines, which compose her view of the revolutionary process with its achievements and its defects: the feminism through which all the revolutionary common space is reinterpreted, and the culturalism with which the critical balance of the Revolution is drawn up; a positive revision with a passionate tendency to Cuban culture with which a new surfacing identity must be negotiated and built.

With regards to feminism, Yolanda's leading role, with her tough and unpatronising character, her direct look to the camera when she speaks about her worries for the destiny of the women in the neighbourhood, and especially her demanding but loving relationship with her partner, does not just make her a charismatic character. She also reveals the director's strict and combative outlook. Yolanda succeeds in creating constant elements for self-affirmation, despite everything and everyone. It is precisely this that affects Mario, who symbolises the hidden spectrum of sexist relationships revealed from an ethic based on social equality. Two of the most important works on feminist cinema – Annette Kuhn's *Women's Pictures: Feminism and Cinema* (1982) and E. Ann Kaplan's *Women and Film: Both Sides of the Camera* (1983) – refer to the film to emphasise the otherness of its discourse as a way of undermining the patriarchal values of American traditional or classic cinema. In this sense, the story of the protagonist couple undermines melodrama, a classical expression of women's cinema. It is showing their relationship through conversations, in which they try to learn who they are, together or as individuals. In particular, they show us their love for each other, avoiding passion and searching for it in the involvement of a similar interpretation of the world, pointing out a radical and breakaway redefinition of cinema and generic exposition of love.

On the other hand, the treatment of Cuban contemporary culture endows the images with beauty and pride. Cuban specificity as a space for self-reflection is not neglected; from traditions dissected with iconographic material to those spaces in Havana that are lovingly presented, as a collection of habits that shape national identity and unite all the characters. These range from Mario's mother's altar full of saints, the ice-cream and the pier, to the avenues full of light and warmth, the dancing bodies and the animals, which share their space with a specific nature. And the counterpoint is best represented by a soundtrack. As well as Guillermo Díaz's songs, which are repeated throughout the film, Mario hums 'La canción de la nueva escuela', a popular anthem composed by Silvio Rodríguez, the inhabitants sing traditional songs, and the composer of the soundtrack Sergio Vitier continues – as was usual in the ICAIC Experimental Sound Group, founded in 1972 and responsible for the renewal of Cuban *trova* – with the blending and re-elaboration of Afrocuban rhythms, which perfectly accompany the illustration of a neighbourhood with the same cultural identity.

The legacy of *De cierta manera* can be seen in the cinematic cycle for which it is a symbol. According to Marvin D'Lugo, a female character in Cuban cinema can be explained as an emblem of a new mythology, through which the revolutionary development and set of ideas could be specified. So Gómez's film and its protagonist would be bound to all those heroines of the Cuban Revolution who had appeared before, as the women in Humberto Solás' movies such as *Manuela* (1966) and *Lucía* (1968), or the protagonist in *En días como éstos* (*In Days Like These*, Jorge Fraga, 1964), which analyses the problem of a bourgeois school teacher confronted with the literacy campaign. But that presence is outlined in Yolanda's heirs, in films that could be considered its more direct legacy: *Una mujer, un hombre, una ciudad* (*A Woman, a Man and a City*, Manuel Octavio Gómez, 1978) which tells the militant life of a woman in the construction of a pilot town through the narration of those that met her before she died, *Retrato de Teresa* (*Portrait of Teresa*, Pastor Vega, 1978) about a female textile worker who does not manage to open her home to a real modernisation of herself, and especially *Hasta cierto punto* (*Up To a Certain Point*, Tomás Gutiérrez Alea, 1983) which follows the interesting silent dialogue between the work of both film-makers, and even though at first Alea wanted to show the differences between the intellectual and working world, *Hasta cierto punto* became a reflection on the survival of machismo in Cuban society. Alea himself confessed that the title's ambiguity and revelation of the limits that hinder the equality between men and women was 'a tribute to Sara Gómez's *De cierta manera,* which is an important precedent of this movie'.

The memory of her work and the images of her films are a living document of Cuban society and its constant interpellation. Among them, *De cierta manera* emerges as a marvellous, lively and complex movie which made space for the forces of regeneration.

Marina Díaz López

REFERENCES

D'Lugo, M. (1997) 'Transparent Women: Gender and Nation in Cuban Cinema', in M. T. Martin (ed.) *New Latin American Cinema.* Detroit: Wayne State University Press, 155–66.

López, A. M. (1990) 'Parody, Underdevelopment, and the New Latin American Cinema', *Quarterly Review of Film and Television*, 12, 1–2, 63–71.

____ (1990) 'At the Limits of Documentary: Hypertextual Transformation and the New Latin American Cinema', in J. Burton (ed.) *The Social Documentary in Latin America.* Pittsburgh: University of Pittsburgh Press, 403–32.

Paranaguá, P. A. (1997) 'Cuban Cinema's Political Changes', in M. T. Martin (ed.) *New Latin American Cinema.* Detroit: Wayne State University Press, 167–90.

CREAR PODER
PARA BARRER EL

LA BATALLA DE CHILE THE BATTLE OF CHILE

15

PATRICIO GUZMÁN, CHILE, 1975–79

> Without this film, perhaps those years would not exist.
>
> – Jorge Ruffinelli

11 September 1973. The Casa de la Moneda, official Residence of President Salvador Allende, is attacked by armed forces led by General Augusto Pinochet, putting an end to the government of the Unidad Popular and its peaceful road to socialism. The familiar images of this event open *La batalla de Chile: La lucha de un pueblo sin armas* (*The Battle of Chile: The Struggle of a People Without Arms*), a three-part film told in flashback, from exile, providing a unique example of how the technique, aesthetics and expressive achievements, the signification and the excellence of a documentary film could result in a complex framework in which the contexts of filming, editing and audience are equally relevant. Considered one of the best political films of its time, and the most outstanding example of the militant documentary cinema made within the parameters of the New Latin American Cinema movement, along with *La hora de los hornos* (*The Hour of the Furnaces*, Fernando Solanas, 1968), *La batalla de Chile* is, first of all, a global film in which factual history, narrative and memory become irremissibly intertwined.

Patricio Guzmán's film was born from the urgent task to document what, even at that time, was seen as a historic moment, the same certainty and sentiment that were in the origins of his preceding works – *El primer año* (*The First Year*, 1972) and *La respuesta de octubre* (*The October Answer*, 1972) – but in a subtly different way, since *La batalla de Chile* represented the shift from a rejoicing mood to having a more analytical and explanatory purpose, due to the foreboding threat of armed confrontation.

As with many leftist Chilean intellectuals and film-makers, at least in a broad sense, Guzmán felt engaged with the project of the Unidad Popular for the sake of the social and political transformation of Chile, and was attracted by the energy and excitement in the streets, where people were protagonists, the main characters, to be represented in his films. Therefore he postponed his fiction-film projects from his return to Chile in 1971 – the year in which Salvador Allende won the presidential election – after his four years of studying film at the Escuela Oficial de Cine (State Film School) in Madrid. The hopes and illusions of being a witness to history in the making manifested itself in the Unidad Popular documentary production and in Chile Films' newsreels, as well as in that first collective film project led by Guzmán, which aimed to register, document and 'celebrate' in a political sense, 'el primer año' (the first year) of Allende's government. As in *La batalla de Chile*, that film avoided a conventional journalistic treatment, instead – in the case of the first film – being conceived as a film work that wished to transform the newsreel form into a dramatic storyline.

Nevertheless, there is a great difference between *El primer año* and *La batalla de Chile* in their shooting and editing processes. Even though *El primer año* was far from a piece of government propaganda, it was made from the standpoint of the party in power. As other films produced during the government of the Unidad Popular and in the framework of Chile Films, the official film agency, it represents, along with Soviet Cinema, Bolivian film produced under the government of the Movimiento Nacionalista Revolucionario and Cuban revolutionary cinema, one of the few moments in history in which cinema has taken an active and creative part in a revolutionary process from the top. For this reason, and especially taking into account documentary cinema, there are some common features between these national cinemas and the structure and narrative resources of *El primer año*, such as the before/after rhetorical exposition and the disturbing representation of social groups (indigenous people, for example) in the process of being integrated in a national project. But historic events made it impossible for *La batalla de Chile* to be a part of this celebratory tradition. History created a different and exceptional signification framework for it, though the ideological position and film strategies were similar. When it was filmed, the political and social confrontation in the streets and the unknown but palpable threat substituted and avoided the celebratory tone and its discourse-from-the-power narrative. Pinochet's coup d'état gave the dramatic and structural narrative to the film during the editing process, mainly in its first two sections, and has also rewritten and connoted the power of the images in the spectator's mind.

In the last months of 1972, when the third year of Allende's government was about to begin, the struggle to achieve a socialist state by pacific means seemed seriously challenged and threatened, and the social and political confrontation began to manifest itself in the streets. A civil war was perceived as one of the eventual outcomes of that situation. Patricio Guzmán decided to regroup the team that had collaborated on *El primer año* and *La respuesta de Octubre*, now given the name, 'El Tercer Año' (The Third Year), which was also the provisional title for a new film that was going to describe and analyse the political and social clues of this critical period of the government of the Unidad Popular, in order to mobilise people against the forces of reaction supported by foreign organisations, such as the CIA. From this point of view, *La batalla de Chile* is closer to a militant film made from the political fence of the opposition, hence the use of powerful images associated with the combatant discourse of resistance. The 'Second Year' team of Müller, Elton, Menz and Pino were joined by young people like Angelina Vázquez. The Spanish writer José Juan Bartolomé co-wrote the successive screenplays with Guzmán, developing ideas, schemes and working papers that would orientate and guide the shooting schedule. A central role was played at this time by the political magazine *Chile Hoy* and its director Marta Harnecker, harnessing political and ideological support for the film, which continued in exile by Harnecker's consultation during the editing process in Cuba. Chris Marker supplied the required film material, which was difficult to obtain in Chile due to the US blockade. Guzmán described the principal features of the project to him. It would be 'a free-form film, that will use journalistic reportage, still photography essay, the drama structure of a film, vertiginous editing and the sequence-shot, all this edited according to circumstances, according to the requirements of reality'. However, the situation forced them to overlook all but a few of these structural characteristics.

The shooting began around the time of the local election campaigns in March 1973 and was only interrupted by the army coup. During this period, Guzmán's team worked in a semi-clandestine way, as they acquired shooting licences by forging different identities in order to avoid revealing the real project they were working on. The situation was especially hazardous when they infiltrated the right wing or risked their lives in violent confrontations. They were even kidnapped for a short period in August 1973. Hiding the footage in different places was a part of these security measures that ensured the safety of the team and the material they were shooting. Not that they remained completely safe; members of Tercer Año were arrested and underwent interrogations and searches. Guzmán himself was detained for two weeks in the Estadio Nacional in the period following the coup and the cameraman Jorge Müller became one of the multitudes who were to disappear permanently. Fortunately for the crew, the footage was smuggled out of the country in a diplomatic bag.

The analytical and testimonial aims were constantly in question during the shooting process, which were as important as the resulting film, since *La batalla de Chile* was to be a true document of the complex historic moment. But analysis and testimony did not conflict because of working methodology and ideological viewpoints. Far from being spontaneous or unpredicted, the filming was highly selective and orientated. The cases, events and situations to be shot had been identified, given their political and social relevance in the explanation of the conflict. Before and during the shooting, Guzmán and his team discussed the theoretical and methodological framework with which they could find, visualise and film 'invisible' events underneath the obvious political and social manifestations, so the film would not become a mere agitprop and militant documentary. In April, the group produced a nine-page document identifying problems and anticipating alternatives or complementary patterns for the editing process (whether it is divided chronologically, or in chapters, depending on problems or specific cases, in addition to using the dialogue between opponents or the testimony as main structural leitmotif) that would be followed in the final decisions concerning the editing.

The identification of crucial problems and the decisions about which aspects of the conflict would be followed, in order to construct an explanatory, dialectic structure, endowed the film with two of its most outstanding characteristics: the structure in parallel between the actions of both opponents that was born during the shooting and reinforced in the editing, and that gave the main dramatic power to the first part of the film; and the use of some shooting techniques and aesthetic treatments not common to documentaries of testimony, such as establishing and sequence-shots, that are in tension with the pure direct style also present in the film. These last elements replace aspects of the same strategy. On the shooting site Guzmán guided Jorge Müller's camera with the far-sighted instinct of a skilled documentary director, even though he had never studied documentary techniques nor had he seen the work of his contemporaries of the *cinéma vérité* and direct cinema movements. But by doing so and never losing freshness and spontaneity, Guzmán also put in practice fiction *mise-en-scène* strategies, only made possible thanks to the clearness of the project in their minds.

Ninety-five per cent of the finished film was shot by Tercer Año. The remaining footage was taken from Chile Films' newsreels (the cameraman Leonardo Henricksen's shooting of his own death), the German crew, Heynowski and Scheumann (the images of the bombing of La Moneda) and Pedro Chaskel.

Despite the relevance, quality and power of the original footage, the film was born as a post-11 September product, because the armed coup and the ensuing exile cast a new light on the material. The structure was determined by the tragic and well-known end, which determined the story and the comprehensive exposition of Chilean reality of the times that the film wanted to offer from the beginning; the same 'external' agent also conditioned and it still does – the significance and meaning of almost every action and face, music and sound, registered by Guzmán's team, which consequently became evidence, track and sign of the betrayal. The editing was however a very hard and difficult task in which a restrictive selection of the material was necessary, and clear, explanatory and coherent narrative and exposition had to be found without killing the fluency of the events.

As soon as he could, Patricio Guzmán travelled to Paris to thank Chris Marker for his collaboration in the film production and to look for post-production support, which he did not find in France. But the trip was not fruitless. He met Alfredo Guevara, then director of ICAIC (Instituto Cubano del Arte e Industria Cinematográficos), who offered him the equipment and personnel to finish the film. At ICAIC, Guzmán´s footage gathered a new working team. The Chilean film-maker Pedro Chaskel, one of the most interesting and active documentary directors in the New Latin American Cinema movement, who went into exile following Pinochet's coup, edited the film with Guzmán. Both Marta Harnecker and Julio García Espinosa not only played an advisory role, but orientated the film towards an ideologically and politically coherent discourse that would meet the satisfaction of the major Chilean opponents of Pinochet's regime.

Without economic or time restrictions, Guzmán and Chaskel edited together a series of rough cuts of the film, with a two-part film appearing to be the best way of presenting the film. After this, hard work continued on the film until the internal structure of both parts was properly defined. They were finished in 1975 and 1977 respectively, and given the subtitles *La insurrección de la burguesía* (*The Insurrection of the Bourgeoisie*) and *El golpe de estado* (*The Coup d'État*). They work well as independent films, whilst simultaneously complementing each other because of the chronological linkage between them. The third part of *La batalla de Chile*, entitled *El poder popular* (*The Popular Power*), has a different story and structural relationship with the rest of the film. It was finished in 1979 and was edited with footage previously rejected due to its lack of dramatic power, as well as with material from *La respuesta de Octubre*. The aim with the final part was to create a parallel story to that witnessed in the first two parts, in which Chilean people play the main character. It was presented as a tribute, from the film-makers, to the resilient spirit of an oppressed nation.

La insurrección de la burguesía was released in Cuba in August 1975. Structured in the form of a flashback, it deals with those subversive stratagems and moves against government undertaken by the Right and the Bourgeoisie, their manipulation of mass-media and their campaigns, financed by imperialistic – that is, US – interests, in order to attract and galvanise the support from the middle class, the Army and certain working-class groups, such as El Teniente copper miners. The film explains how the atmosphere of social and political confrontation, fostered by the opposition forces, led to the future events which resulted in Allende's government being overthrown. The structure, though determined by the film-maker's thematic concerns, remains dramatic, with an underlying chronological flux determined by its beginning, which announces a retrospective narrative, and its final sequence that describes the 'Tancazo' in June 1973 when the 'Blindado Número Dos' regiment entered the government.

After a prologue that features footage of the coup, the film begins with a thirty-minute sequence in which the tense political atmosphere is presented as a natural consequence of the development of the events within Chile. The electoral race gave the framework for a picture of political, social, cultural and ideological differences that ran throughout the country, both at a local and national level. As in the best moments of the *cinéma vérité* foundational film *Chronique d'un été* (*Chronicle of a Summer*, Jean Rouch and Edgar Morin, 1960), seemingly neutral questions presented in a traditional journalistic style trigger meaningful and sometimes unexpected reactions. The investigative techniques employed present the spectator with an idea of the wide spectrum of political difference present. In some cases clues lie in the answers provided in interviews with the camera probing for a physical reaction to the subjects raised. But occasionally, the camera provides a more telling account of feelings and resentments than words alone could provide. In one scene, when the film-makers enter a bourgeois home pretending they are representatives of a television station, it is the camera that is really carrying out the investigation and not the interview, which was merely an excuse to gain access.

The remainder of part one consists of five chapters: 'Acaparamiento y mercado negro' (Monopolizing and Black Market), 'El boicot parlamentario' (The Parliamentary Boycott), 'Asonada estudiantil' (Students Riot), 'Ofensiva a los gremios' (Offensive against the Guilds) and 'La huelga del cobre' (The Copper Strike). These chapters become more expository and explanatory, investigating the opposition strategies and social agents involved in Allende's fall. The omniscient present-tense narration creates a strange tension throughout the film, because the story's outcome is always foretold. Images, interviews and present-tense narration seem to offer a direct access to the real, to the history in the making, while the contents and style of the voice-over, which knows and explains everything from a teleological point of view, create a distant form of address.

The tragic end of part one preludes the final outcome with powerful images, taken by Leonardo Henricksen's camera. The footage was edited by Chile Films for its newsreel, in which Henricksen's film is presented twice. First, in its raw and original form, then later on in slow motion, the seemingly frozen images providing a damning document against his killers. The footage was shown in Chilean theatres as well as on television screens around the world. Guzmán acquired a copy that had been hidden together with other footage shortly after the coup took place. In this last sequence of *La insurrección de la burguesía*, Guzmán retains the Chile Films presentation, changing only the soundtrack, constructing a realistic representation of the sounds that might have been heard in the moments leading up to Henrickson's death.

El golpe de estado opens with a very different version of Henricksen's footage. This time it was edited with the images recorded by the Tercer Año team, presenting a different point of view, with a soundtrack that only contains the narrator's voice. These images and their relevance to the ensuing film unfold within a chronological and detailed account of the events that would result in the bombing of the presidential palace. The voice-over continues in the present, but the narration is now more compact, due in part to the course of events it follows, which are arranged as a cause-and-effect chain. At the same time, it becomes denser, slower and more complex. The principal focus is the different strategies adopted by the Left to resist and restrain the insurrection, in addition to the differences they were experiencing internally. Whereas part one paints a sociological portrait of the political upheavals, part two is closer to a political film, as much in its analytical devices as in its political accusations, even then mere hypotheses that would only be proved later, such as the involvement of the CIA in the destabilisation of the government. If part one presented an expository pattern through which dialectic analyses could be carried out in order to create a construct similar to fiction in which to present the opposing sides of the looming conflict, part two carries the dramatic tension of a country on the brink of a military coup and a party collapsing under the weight of its own internal difficulties. Within this maelstrom, Guzmán's team continued to search for a way of presenting the film, recovering for documentary cinema those almost magical and revealing features that Dziga Vertov and Jean Vigo attributed to non-staged filming, which is able to catch life by surprise. The power of documentary images transforms the faces of army officers, filmed as members of loyal forces during Arturo Araya's funeral, powerful symbols of betrayal, a fact only discovered after the events had passed into history. Likewise, the footage of the first addresses to Chilean people by the military Junta and the different speeches of its members present another chilling portrait of deceit; the audience's knowledge of Pinochet, with hindsight, lead to an alternative reading of his speech.

The story – also a great chapter in the history of Chile – would seem to end in those speeches made by the members of the military Junta and transmitted by television. But Guzmán's film does not end here, as there was an untold story in which Chilean people, who could be presented as the social and historically victorious agent instead of as defeated subjects. Guzmán and Chaskel were able to make an unnoticed history visible and constructed a third film that goes back to the October 1972 crisis. In *El poder popular*, the history of the government of the Unidad Popular is told again, but from a different point of view. According to Jorge Ruffinelli, the whole of Guzmán's film incorporates all the elements of an expertly constructed narrative: struggle in part one, brutal outcome in part two, and alternative end in part three. In this last part, the coup is not even mentioned. The film is seen from the point of view of the people and the story is of their desire to transform their country, in order to achieve peace and justice. The focus is directed at this invisible popular movement that was represented at its broadest extent by the *cordones industriales* (industrial belts), which even unnerved the government and trade unions because of its potential as counter-power.

El poder popular includes new stylistic elements, including music by J. A. Quintano, which creates an emotional address not present in the previous part. The film is also more self-conscious, with cameras and microphones regularly visible on the screen. The voice-over continues to be the main information source, proving essential in providing the backdrop to the rise of the people's movement. Nevertheless the interview remains a privileged instrument in making this invisible and powerful reality visible, in recording the existence of a powerful collective agent written on the faces and in the voices of workers and housewives, who describe their efforts for the sake of political and social transformation.

The film finishes with a coherent discourse that explains, from the point of view of Marxist orthodoxy, what has been seen and heard in the film. Rather than a direct address performed by the narrator, it is an indirect one in the voice of Ernesto Malbrán, identified in the film as a trade unionist, who projects an insight into the future with his last words 'I will see you, comrade'. He appears again in Guzmán's *Chile: La memoria obstinada (Chile: The Stubborn Memory*, 1997).

La batalla de Chile is very much a film of its time. It can be included in Zuzana M. Pick's description of the documentary production of the Unidad Popular, to such an extent that it also surpasses the idea of documentary as memory or witness of reality, aspiring to transform into an instrument for historical analysis. But Guzmán's film is much more than that: memory and historical analysis are married in a way perhaps difficult to achieve had the film-maker not been able to inscribe the unique historical circumstances in a complex cinematic form that allows various levels of signification. According to Ana M. López, the complex and contradictory textual operations of the film – in which direct and dramatised, immediate and mediated, modes of representation are constantly in tension – are shaped by the confrontation between the context in which the filming took place and the experience of the exile. The grasp of historical events by this use of distancing and empathetic cinematic devices is the result of placing the events of the coup in a meaningful framework. It creates a balance between the urgency of the situation and the calm and steady view of the exile, who has access to both the past and the events which followed it.

Despite its political militancy, mood and content, the film transcends the mould of political cinema to become an exceptional example of historical and memory cinema. The film garnered praise amongst critics and audiences at film festivals; more importantly, it would leave an indelible mark on the spectator. Hardly will our memory be able to dissociate the facts that changed Chilean history in 1973 from the images, sounds and voices that *La batalla de Chile* presented. The film embodies individual and collective memory at once, opening the path to Guzmán's future works, *Chile: La memoria obstinada* and *El caso Pinochet* (*The Pinochet Case*, 2001).

María Luisa Ortega

Burton, J. (1986) 'Patricio Guzmán: Politics and the Documentary in People's Chile', in J. Burton (ed.), *Cinema and Social Change in Latin America. Conversations with Filmmakers*. Austin: University of Texas Press, 49–68.

Guzmán, P. and P. Sempere (1977) *Chile: el cine contra el fascismo.* Valencia: Fernando Torres Editor.

López, A. M. (1990) '*The Battle of Chile*: Documentary, Political Process, and Representation', in J. Burton (ed.) *The Social Documentary in Latin America*. Pittsburgh: University of Pittsburgh Press, 267–87.

Pick, Z.M. (1993) *The New Latin American Cinema. A Continental Project*. Austin: University of Texas Press.

Ruffinelli, J. (2001) *Patricio Guzmán*. Madrid: Cátedra / Filmoteca Española.

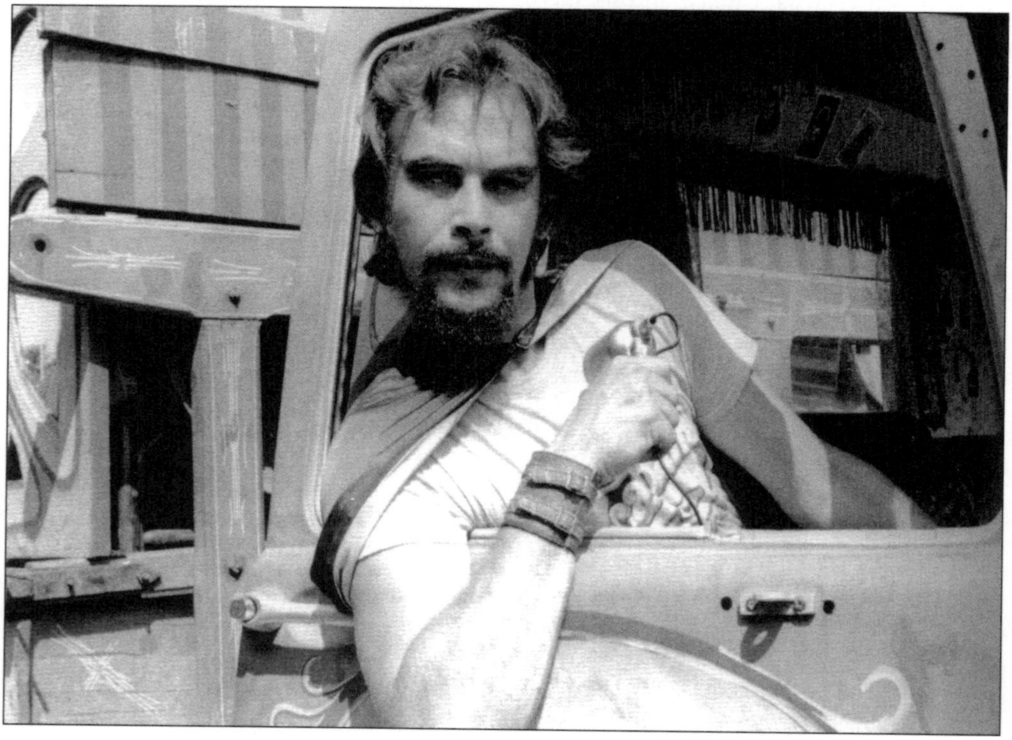

BYE BYE BRASIL BYE BYE BRAZIL

16

CARLOS DIEGUES, BRAZIL, 1979

> The idea was to make, precisely, a film about a country shortly to be born in the place of another on the brink of disappearence: the change of one country by another and at the very moment when such a change had not yet been made. A moment in which the archaic co-existed with the modern, when that old Brazil was still there, together with the new Brazil ... in a certain way, I am announcing a new Brazil, different from the one we knew, a Brazil, above all, based and inspired in the mixture of all those different cultures, being them of our origin as a nation or the ones that daily affect us today. Therefore, I think this film was made with lots of love, a love all too great for the country as well as for the characters that cross this country ... In this sense, I think *Bye Bye Brasil* is, above all, a film about change.
>
> – Carlos Diegues

Carlos Diegues' *Bye Bye Brasil* was dedicated to the Brazilians in the twenty-first century. That millennium has now arrived and with it some of the bleak horizons anticipated in the film have, unfortunately, materialised. To quote Néstor Garcia Canclini, *Bye Bye Brasil*, in many ways, anticipated some of the concrete ideas of Brazil and the rest of Latin America as *postnational suburbia*, identities as a multinational spectacle, and the 'Americanisation' of spectators.

One of the keys to experiencing *Bye Bye Brasil* lies in its title. There is also one image that seems emblematic of the general pessimistic overtones of the film towards what it poses as the 'end' of an idea of 'Brazil'. After the main characters encounter a group of wandering Native Brazilians in the forest, one shot depicts an older Indian woman seated by a river, ears glued to her transistor portable radio. The song she is listening to is *Bye Bye Love*. To her left, behind, one boat bears the name of Brasil and she herself mumbles the words 'bye bye', as if bidding farewell to a jet airplane, which had just taken off in the previous shot. Such an image projected a frozen representation of the Native Brazilian population at that time. However, by the time the twenty-first century arrived, we have witnessed the emergence of indigenous media with the appropriation of audiovisual technology (mostly camcorders and VCRs) for cultural and political purposes unsuspected at the time *Bye Bye Brasil* was made. Modern technology, at its best, became an empowering weapon for some communities struggling against geographical displacement, ecological and economic deterioration, and perhaps, most importantly, cultural annihilation. As Faye Ginsburg and Terence Turner have already noted, such work is not locked into a bound traditional world but rather is concerned with mediating across borders, mediating ruptures of time and history and advancing the process of identity construction by negotiating powerful relationships to land, myth and ritual. Nevertheless, the emblematic image of the old Indian woman with her portable transistor speaks eloquently of a time when the country was experiencing a rapid process of transformation, moving at great speed from an agricultural economy to industrialisation. Some Indian tribes, notably in the state of Pará, were caught in the middle of this process and were on the verge of extinction as national and multinational companies were being introduced to the riches of the Amazon region, bringing with them pollution and decimating the region's natural resources. As Randal Johnson has aptly pointed out, *Bye Bye Brasil* develops metaphors of prostitution and penetration at the same time it denounces the 'decharacterisation' wrought by internal and external cultural dependence.

Other emblematic images in the film also guide us throughout the allegorical interweaving of its episodic structure. A brief close-up of a crushed armadillo, probably hit by a truck along the Trans-Amazonian Highway, is 'living' proof of the many changes faced by that region. Images like this bring to mind the pervasive pedagogical role played by allegory in Brazilian cinema, since the heroic times of the early *cinema novo* films. Partly due to its continental size, allegorical strategies have always favoured the cinematic treatment of microscopic situations, which evoke Brazil as a whole, developing a fragmentary discourse to insinuate coded political messages. Two good examples from the 1970s are Joaquim Pedro de Andrade's *Os inconfidentes* (*The Conspirators*, 1972) which centres around the abortive eighteenth-century revolt against Portuguese colonialism led by Tiradentes, and Walter Lima Jr's *Joana Angélica* (1978), which mixes present-day documentary sequences of the popular celebrations of 2 July, in Bahia, with, once more, re-enacted references to independence from Portugal. These festivities go back to the days after the official Independence Day in Brazil when the Portuguese still had control over some provinces, especially in Bahia, Maranhão and the territory of Cisplatina (Uruguay) then occupied by the Portuguese. The bloodiest of the conflicts between both troops took place in Bahia and two heroines came out of these battles: Joana, Abess of the Lapa Convent and Maria Quiteria de Jesus who, crossdressed, enlisted in the Brazilian front under the name of José Cordeiro. Joana hid some Brazilian soldiers in Lapa who were fleeing from the Portuguese troops. For this feat she paid with her life on 19 February 1823. On 2 July of that same year the Brazilians finally succeed in expelling the Portuguese from Bahia. The date is celebrated in Bahia in the same way as the whole country celebrates 7 September. Bahians are proud to have concluded the liberation process from Portugal and even now parade on the streets of Salvador rendering hommages to the syncretic character of the *caboclo* population (actually Native Brazilians) and their strength. Until recently, the figures of Joana and Maria Quiteria were also part of the parade, a tradition which faded with time. Walter Lima Jr, in 1978, brought Joana back to the public's attention by placing her once more in the parade. This was a pretext to have some of his assistants in the film 'improvising' the chorus '*abaixo a repressão*' (down with repression) which is heard in the film's soundtrack, a direct reference to repression by the military dictatorship then in power.

Bye Bye Brasil weaves a picaresque allegory in which the Caravana Rolidei, a colourful troupe of wandering artists, travel around Brazil to witness the advance of modernisation. Here the social contradictions compressed into a single apartment in *Tudo bem* are anamorphically expanded over the wide screen of Brazil, moving from the arid Northeast (Piranhas, Maceió), through the Amazon Forest (Altamira, the Trans-Amazonian Highway) to the Central Plateau (Brasília, Rondonia). More recently, Sergio Bianchi's *Cronicamente inviavel* (*Chronically Unfeasible*, 2000) through a careful and sharp editing style, also assumes a concept of a socio-geographical totality for Brazil when he moves his narrative from one region to another. Hence he cuts from the more developed South to Bahia, Santa Catarina, Mato Grosso (Midwest), Rio de Janeiro, São Paulo and all the way up the Amazon borders. In the film's narrative, such a strategy has the effect of transposing the mechanics of capitalist social relations. He mixes the social with the geographical to represent the internal diaspora of contemporary migratory movements. Both *Bye Bye Brasil* and *Cronicamente inviavel*, as well as other films such as *Iracema, uma transa amazônica* (*Iracema*, Jorge Bodansky and Orlando Senna, 1974), *A opção* (*The Option*, Ozualdo Candeias, 1982), *Jorge, um brasileiro* (*Jorge, a Brazilian*, Paulo Thiago, 1989) or even, to a certain extent, *Central do Brasil* (*Central Station*, Walter Salles, 1998) can be considered Brazilian *allegorical* road movies in this respect.

In *Bye Bye Brasil* the wandering Caravana is made up of Lorde Cigano (Lord Gypsy) who promotes himself as the 'King of Magicians and Clairvoyants', the dancer Salomé, 'Queen of the

Rumba' and Andorinha, the strongman. Together they arrive at the Northeast town of Piranhas, where they pick up a local accordionist, Ciço, and his pregnant wife Dasdô. The group's final destination is the town of Altamira, deep in the Amazon jungle, where they envision a utopian land of plenty. On their way, the troupe confronts internal obstacles (including amorous complications) and external ones, most notably the television that leads the troupe's audience to passively consume the vapid audiovisual production of Rio and São Paulo television stations.

Contrasting with the film's theatrical elements, *Bye Bye Brazil* develops a style that flirts with the documentary, registering the aftershocks of the 'multinationalisation' of the Brazilian subcontinent. The exploitation inherent in the Brazilian model of development takes on a particularly predatory form in the interior. The Amazon region, the government's trump card ('After all, there's always the Amazon') is being transformed into a vast bordello administered by a legion of hustlers and entrepreneurs. In this sense, the transformation of the Rolidei truck into an ambulatory neon-lit whorehouse metaphorizes a much broader process. American millionaires such as Daniel Ludwig tried to extract profits from cheap Brazilian labour through 'floating factories' shipped from Japan in the infamous Projeto Jari. The futuristic city of Brasília, designed by the Communist architect Oscar Niemeyer during the developmentalist euphoria of the 1950s, is now ringed by the mini-slums into which two of the characters are graciously ushered by a social welfare assistant who, at first, welcomes them with a parodic sightseeing tour of the more salubrious neighborhoods of the capital, the *super quadras*. The countryside, usually the site of perennial hope, has merely magnified Brazil's historical contradictions.

The film's title also encapsulates the 'disappearance' of Brazil. It bids farewell to what it sees as outmoded visions of the country, not only to rightist dreams of capitalist development, but also to leftist dreams of popular resistance. The film's Indians do not play the symbolic role conventionally assigned them in Brazilian art and in the national collective unconscious. They are not the heroic representatives of quintessential Brazilianness, as they were for the Romantics. Nor are they the symbols of anti-colonial resistance, all 'cannibalised' and consuming Europeans in allegorical meals, as one would expect, for example, from Nelson Pereira dos Santos' *Como era gostoso o meu francês* (*How Tasty Was My Frenchman*, 1972). *Bye Bye Brasil* breaks with this metaphorical discourse by showing Indians in the process of physical extermination and cultural annihilation. The Cruari Indians in the film, the last remnants of a once proud tribe, are now thoroughly impacted by modernity, as encapsulated in the previously mentioned image of the chief's mother with her ears glued to a transistor radio. Neither mythical heroes nor stereotypical victims, the Indians are presented simply as members of the urban poor, trying to survive with dignity.

The film also provides visual confirmation of the Americanisation pointed out in the lyrics of the title song. Pinball machines in the jungle, Indian chiefs sporting designer jeans, backlands bands that sound like the Bee Gees, all contribute to the image of an encroaching culture and a culture encroached upon. One sequence in particular lampoons this kind of cultural colonialism. Lorde Cigano anoints his audience with a bogus snowstorm (actually shredded coconut) to the accompaniment of Bing Crosby's 'White Christmas' thereby realising the 'dreams of all Brazilians' to have snow like 'civilised countries'. At the same time, the film highlights a process of reciprocal cultural anthropology, which is not without its positive side-effects. Even the name of the travelling caravan, Caravana Rolidei, a phonetic transcription of the Brazilian pronunciation of 'holiday', illustrates the Brazilian 'creative incapacity for copying'. Another of these famous appropriations is the term *udigrudi* (from the English underground) to refer to a group of young Brazilian film-makers in the late 1960s who questioned and offered alternatives to *cinema novo*, proposing an 'aesthetics of garbage' as a radicalisation of Glauber Rocha's influential 1965 manifesto *Uma estética da fome* ('The Aesthetics of Hunger').

The loudspeaker of the refurbished caravan plays Frank Sinatra's version of a Brazilian song (*Aquarela do Brasil*), rendered in the style of American swing, much as Bossa Nova musicians melted the sounds of cool jazz with those of samba. The Americanisation of Brazilian music, that is to say, goes hand in hand with the Brazilianisation of American music, detectable in artists as diverse as Dionne Warwick, Paul Simon, Stevie Wonder, David Byrne, Pat Metheny, Al Jarreau and others. However, the problem, for Carlos Diegues, is not the interterming-ling of different cultural traditions, but rather the unbalanced and exploitative terms under which these exchanges often take place.

The same observation about unequal exchange applies to the other media treated in the film. One sequence has a provincial mayor place a television set on what appears to be an altar in a public square, to be worshipped as an icon of modernity. The sequence eloquently speaks of the rapid expansion of television as the new agent of entertainment and conditioner of the social imaginary; an emblem of the 'national unification' so desired by the military dictatorship still in power at the time the film was made. Television, the image suggests (in an analysis reminiscent of Frankfurt School depictions of the narcoleptic audience), has inherited the ideological role of religion as a mass opiate. Northeasterners watch

Dancin' Days, a popular TV-Globo prime-time soap opera set among the disco crowd in Rio de Janeiro (again, the original title was also in English). The programme encodes a double mode of cultural colonialism; that of Brazil by the United States, since the show's function is to disseminate American top forty hits and that of the poorer Brazilian North by the more developed South. But the film uses television soap opera stars (most notably Jose Wilker and Betty Faria) to make contact with the television audience. And although television fosters cultural homogenisation, it also brings the events of the world into the lives of rural people. Only very recently the hegemonic role and aesthetic unilateralism of TV-Globo has been challenged by another network, SBT. The more recent battles for audiences took place, between the *Human Zoo* reality shows pioneered by Bandeirantes (*Casa dos artistas*, 2001) and followed by Globo's *Big Brother Brasil* (2002). As television rapidly expanded as the hegemonic agent of entertainment it also flattened regional diversity and rendered obsolescent the Caravana Rolidei's old-fashioned entertainment. At the same time, Diegues presents an ambiguous position towards television, incorporating it into its diegesis. By the end of the narrative, television is both part of Lorde Cigano's new high-tech truck and Ciço's new life in Brasília, where he re-structures television practices to his own use, playing on a stage behind six television sets that transmit his new lavish image to the immediate public. The sequence is visionary in the sense that it indicated, back in 1980, a market for the large scale and expanding consumption of *forró* music, a phenomenon that took place throughout the 1990s and continues to do so today. It is interesting to note that such an ambiguity would be later acknowledged by Diegues who premiered two of his films on television, before they even made it to the big screen (*Dias melhores virão*, 1989 and *Veja esta canção*, 1992), reaching audiences never before imagined by film exhibition alone. So, far from being an 'enemy', as presented in *Bye Bye Brasil*, television, at its best, can contribute to the revitalisation of Brazilian film production as it has in some European countries, notably Spain.

Bye Bye Brasil also speaks of cinema itself. The crisis situation of the ambulatory troupe evokes that of cinema, also challenged by the ubiquitous fishbones (antennas) of television. As Randal Johnson has pointed out, the film constitutes a kind of good humored yet critical retrospective of the development of Brazilian cinema from the 1960s to the late 1970s. *Bye Bye Brasil*, he suggests, reworks the different phases of that national cinema through its *road* narrative. There is the documentary style of its beginning, showing a street market, the quintessential locale of dozens of short film documentaries. There are also the similarities between the locations of an instant classic of *cinema novo*, *Vidas secas* (*Barren Lives*, Nelson Pereira dos Santos, 1963) and the *sertão* where Ciço tells his father that he is leaving home to join the Caravana. Finally, there is the search for the wide audience that patronised the *chanchadas* of the 1940s and 1950s and who, by the 1960s, migrated *en masse* to television. Lorde Cigano functions as a fictive surrogate for the cineaste. He represents a latter-day incarnation of a typical *cinema novo* character, the mediator, the *magister ludi*, at once inside and outside the fiction. His self-description as a magician capable of realising the dreams of all Brazilians echoes Diegues' own view of himself as the interpreter of the 'utopias of the people'. The film's central concerns (What is the current state of Brazil? What is popular culture? What is cultural colonialism? What is the relation between artist and public?) are largely inherited from earlier stages of *cinema novo*, but Diegues clearly rejects the 'aesthetic of hunger' in favour of relatively high production values. Beginning with its pop-pastel credits, *Bye Bye Brasil* is lush, colourful and sensual. Its soundtrack is elaborate and polished. A film about poor people, for Diegues, need not look poor. And unlike earlier *cinema novo* films, it offers no omniscient political analysis and no models to be followed. Instead, *Bye Bye Brasil* displays a Renoir-like tenderness for all its characters, without completely forgetting the social contradictions in which they are enmeshed.

João Luiz Vieira

[*Author's Note*: This text reworks some of the issues presented in the collective and extensive essay 'The Shape of Brazilian Cinema in the Postmodern Age', written in six hands by Ismail Xavier, Robert Stam and myself for R. Johnson & R. Stam (eds) *Brazilian Cinema*. New York: Columbia University Press, 1995, third edition, 387–472].

REFERENCES

Johnson, R. (1984) *Cinema Novo X 5. Masters of Contemporary Brazilian Film*. Austin: University of Texas Press.

Johnson, R. & R. Stam (eds) (1995) *Brazilian Cinema*. New York: Columbia University Press.

Mauad, A. M. (2001) '*Bye Bye Brasil* e as fronteiras do nacional-popular', in M. de C. Soares & J. Ferreira (eds) *A História vai ao Cinema*. Rio de Janeiro: Record, 75–86.

Stam, R. (1980–81) '*Bye Bye Brasil*', *Cineaste*, 11, 1, 34–6.

TIEMPO DE REVANCHA TIME OF REVENGE 17

ADOLFO ARISTARAIN, ARGENTINA, 1981

Tiempo de revancha, Adolfo Aristarain's fourth film, is a political thriller about the clash between a mining dynamite expert and a corrupt multinational company specialising in mineral extraction. Of all the Hollywood genres exported to Latin America, the thriller was the most successful during the *golden age* of Argentine cinema. However, differing from its American model, local films often told stories from the perspective of the Law, imprinting them with a bias that was strongly moralistic and edifying. As a rule, the tragic detour from the institutional legality was used in order to confirm the convenience of remaining within the frame of the system. This is precisely what happens in most of the landmark films of the genre: *Fuera de la Ley* (*The Outlaw*, Manuel Romero, 1937); *Camino al crimen* (*The Path to Crime*, Don Napy, 1951); *Mercado negro* (*The Black Market*, Kurt Land, 1953); *El rufián* (*The Scoundrel*, Daniel Tinayre, 1961), among others. If Aristarain really did revitalise the tradition of the thriller, he expropriates these codes in order to rewrite them in the opposing paradigm. The film-maker executed his so called 'thriller trilogy' (*La parte del león*, *Tiempo de revancha*, *Últimos días de la víctima*) during the final days of the military dictatorship in Argentina. In those films, the characters that deviate from the law represent a questioning of the totalitarianism of the regime and a denunciation against the atrocities of the State's terrorism.

Aristarain began as an assistant director in Argentina, but after some minor collaborations he traveled to Europe, where he worked under the direction of Mario Camus, Sergio Leone, Lewis Gilbert, Gordon Flemyng, Melvin Frank and Robert Parrish. Upon returning to his country, he was the assistant director to Daniel Tinayre, Juan José Jusid and Sergio Renán until he directed his first film, *La parte del león* (*The Lion's Share*) in 1978. Already in this first work Aristarain showed a strong interest in *film noir* despite the fact that the protagonist of the film lacked the tragic romanticism that characterises the genre. Bruno Di Toro (Julio de Grazia) is a failure without any hope of improving his situation; but, suddenly, he finds a large sum of stolen money and realises that this is his salvation. Succumbing to his greed, Di Toro reveals his most unscrupulous side and falls into a series of crimes and betrayals that leave him alone. The film was a cruel portrait of a man who had lost all of his ethical principles in a merciless society. Aristarain successfully adapted and reformulated the rules of the genre in order to present local situations and characters. But in spite of his solid narrative and his talent for creating suffocating atmospheres, the film went unnoticed.

Nevertheless, the film-maker's technical solvency was evident, and he was contracted by Aries Cinematográfica to direct *La playa del amor* (*Love Beach*, 1979) and *La discoteca del amor* (*Love Disco*, 1980). Both were clearly commercial productions, aimed at younger audiences. The weak narrative thread allowed a dozen musical scenes to be placed throughout the piece in order to promote some of the pop singers sponsored by the record label that co-produced the film. They were light and escapist comedies, starring popular television actors, that avoided any allusion to reality. And they were not an exception in the cinema of the period. The financial troubles of the film industry, the economic crisis, the obstacles to free expression and the prevailing climate of terror created the conditions that favoured these types of superficial undertakings, trivial and created with the sole purpose of making a profit.

With the producers enthused by the box-office success of these musical comedies, Aries proposed a third film that would be a sequel to the same series and would be called *Las vacaciones del amor* (*Love Vacation*). But the success of his two previous films allowed Aristarain to impose certain conditions on the producers. He presented a brief summary of *Tiempo de revancha* to Fernando Ayala and Héctor Olivera, both of them established film-makers and the owners of Aries. They agreed to back the film. At the end of that year, Aristarain had finished the script and began working on pre-production. Soon after, he encountered several problems that delayed the shoot. At first they feared that the project would be rejected by the censors due to its political content and denunciation of official corruption, be they camouflaged within its narrative. Likewise, the political situation of the main actor, Federico Luppi, was a problem. Since his name was included in one of the many blacklists of the time, there were doubts over his being allowed to star in the film. Finally, the script was approved, Luppi was granted permission and the Instituto Nacional de Cinematografía (National Institute of Cinematography) agreed to the budget. The filming took less than two months, but the date of the premiere (30 July 1981) had been arranged beforehand and Aristarain was lucky to complete the post-production in time.

Tiempo de revancha recovers the *film noir* style of *La parte del león*, but incorporates powerful allegorical elements about the political situation at that time. After five years of being unemployed, the union activist Pedro Bengoa is contracted by the mining company Tulsaco (the same name of other powerful companies that will represent the symbol of exploitation in *Un lugar en el mundo* and *La ley de la frontera*). Sent south to work in a copper mine, Bengoa meets up with an old political comrade, Bruno Di Toro, a name the filmmaker had used in *La parte del león*. Di Toro informs him of the company's dubious business and of the dangers in working under these inhuman conditions. He also tells him of his plan to blackmail Tulsaco and get the compensation he needs to retire. He will cause an accident and feign dumbness as a result of it. At first, Bengoa resists participating in the scam, but finally agrees to take part. However, the plan does not go as planned and Di Toro dies in the explosion. As a result, Bengoa decides to take his friend's place and, upon being rescued, refuses to speak, as if he suffered a nervous breakdown. The unscrupulous company tries to reach a monetary agreement in order to avoid a trial that could bring to light its irregular business; but just when it seems as though they have reached a suitable agreement for both parts, Bengoa rejects the bribe and files a lawsuit against Tulsaco. Persecuted, hounded and tormented, he knows that they are watching him at all times, waiting to take him by surprise as soon as he lets his guard down. His life becomes an unending ordeal. Finally the worker defeats the company, yet this does not end the intimidation. The dead body of one of the witnesses who testified in his favor is thrown at Bengoa's feet from an unregistered Ford Falcon automobile (reproducing the modus operandi of the state police during the time of the military dictatorship). Realising that he is cornered, Bengoa cuts out his tongue. It is the hopeless image of a man who knows he is being watched and persecuted, but it also expresses a vehement determination to resist to the last. A small victory and an individual revenge but, in the context of that dark period, it was understood as a hidden political message. All of the action in the film takes place between one Christmas and the next. For the Argentine spectator, who had suffered the military dictatorship, this end of a cycle seemed to announce a new beginning.

Aristarain shows great skill in the staging, a sensitive ear for dialogue and a solid visual intuition for organising his narrative material. With only a few contrasting scenes, he manages to deliver in an expressive manner the information needed to set up the conflict. In the first scene, when Bengoa is interviewed by the head of personnel at Tulsaco, he is seen to have an impeccable record including an absence of any political activity. In the scene that follows, Bengoa visits his father to tell him the good news. It is at this point that we realise he falsified the references that allowed him to get the job and that he had been a combative union leader, at times persecuted and, with his new career move, had lost the respect of his father. The truth is thus seen to be an illusion. The story is set in a country under repression and has as its central character a man who seems to have lost his ideals. Aristarain proposes an impeccable mechanism of action and reaction; he constructs a system of credibility in which the characters' motivations and the dramatic strategies imprint the story with an autonomous, convincing logic. At first, Bengoa turns down Di Toro's proposition because he does not want to make trouble. As his friend says (and as his father has said before), it looks like the company brain-washed him. Regardless, the accidents that occur during the mining and the sudden death of his father pull him out of his political inertia. The quarry transforms, now resembling some sort of hell and the only salvation is to defeat the corrupt mining company. Things are organised in such a way that the plot naturally pushes the character to what becomes an inevitable ending.

Just like Aristarain's first film, *Tiempo de revancha* demonstrates not only a solid understanding of the mechanisms of classic narration but also its malleability in using it in local and contemporary stories. When the end of the trial is near, Tulsaco's lawyer warns Bengoa, 'Don Guido never loses; sooner or later he always wins. A hard-headed Basque cannot change history.' In a country dominated by an appalling dictatorship, the theme of an individual facing the system adopts the concrete form of a call for rebellion. The film revolves around the different uses of silence: when Bengoa complains of the dangers of using large amounts of dynamite to mine for copper, one of the company's engineers assures him that none of the workers will protest three days before their paychecks; and when the first accident occurs, his boss insinuates that he would be better off not assisting the police investigation. 'You want me to keep my mouth shut', Bengoa clarifies. 'It's just that there are certain things they do not need to know', replies Rossi, and categorically rejects the possibility that other workers will dare to speak. 'Everyone has a price.' This is a crucial moment, because later, when Bengoa fakes his own accident and the owner of the company offers him a large amount of money to stop the lawsuit, he rejects the bribe and explains that he is not for sale. His silence has become a powerful instrument that will topple Tulsaco. Opposed to a cowardly omission, a different connotation of silence as resistance is implied here.

Since silence is his only defense, Bengoa understands that he will have to carry out this performance to the end if he wants to crush the powerful. Larsen, his lawyer, warns him, 'they will drive you crazy, they will make you talk'. In effect, silence becomes a kind of torture. During the trial, Tulsaco constantly harasses him in order to make him speak and betray himself; but Bengoa tolerates it all without saying a word. Aristarain knows that in cinema, the smallest details can convey a great deal of information when they are developed through a precise visual strategy. While preparing the fake accident, Di Toro had burned his arm with a cigarette butt in order to test his unshakable determination. 'No one can make me talk if I don't want to', he had said. Now it is Bengoa who trains himself with self-inflicted pain until he proves that he can remain silent. He moves into his father's small room, and noticeably Bengoa starts to imitate his father. He takes his job as a bookbinder and even wears his clothes. Symbolically, after the trial, when it is obvious that Tulsaco will not leave him in peace, it is with his father's blade that he cuts out his tongue. With this extreme gesture, Bengoa demonstrates that no one will make him speak against his will.

Tiempo de revancha was a great critical success. It received several national and international prizes (in the film festivals of Montreal, Biarritz, Havana, Chicago and Cartagena among others) and was extremely popular with audiences. The film opened at a time when the military dictatorship still had a considerable power to prevent all dissidence, but Aristarain's work was presented as a simple thriller, which enabled him to cloak numerous allusions to the socio-political context in Argentina. In fact, *Tiempo de revancha* does not belong to the genre of political cinema in the way that the films of Costa-Gavras or Pontecorvo did. It is not a political plot under a fictional format but a piece of fiction impregnated by political denunciation. The film is not a vehicle with a particular message. Rather, the horror of the years of military repression surface in it like an optical unconscious that breaks through the images in an unmistakable manner. On all levels, even those apparently irrelevant, the film holds the memory of an impossible daily life hounded by the omnipresent sense of torture and death.

At that time, the suffocating and persecutory tone that runs through the film was an indicator of the paranoia that had been generated by the State control implemented by the military government. Even without direct allusions to the regime, *Tiempo de revancha* denounces the corruption of multinational corporations allied with the economic plan of the dictatorship, and insinuates their hidden connection with political power. The film is traversed by usual problems in a country dominated by terror; the political restraints, the blacklists and prohibitions, the repression and the torture, and the disappearances and assassinations. This does not necessarily transform it into testimonial cinema, but the denunciation is incorporated into its narrative. There was a message between the lines that escaped the censor yet was clearly understood by the audience. It was logical that in a context of furious repression, the silence that the protagonist submitted himself to would be accepted as a metaphor for a possible political action. Silence could also be a weapon of resistance.

If in *La parte del león* an honest man could become a delinquent, in *Tiempo de revancha* the feigned accident turns into validation of the struggle against unjust power. In this case it is not someone on the margins of the law but someone who consciously challenges it within its own rules. This mix of thriller and political denunciation would be developed in more depth in the subsequent film, *Últimos días de la víctima* (*Last Days of the Victim*, 1982), where Aristarain departed from the theme of the hunter being hunted, instead representating the military regime as a monstrous mechanism of control and repression. Even though this film was also received well by the public and critics, it did not repeat the success of *Tiempo de revancha*.

Tiempo de revancha thus contributed to the rebirth of the *film noir* genre in Argentina. With the return to democracy, the abolition of censorship and the absence of political coercion over acceptable themes, it was possible to review the episodes of the dirty war, the shady deals and the corruption, together with the exploitation of a sordid eroticism. After 1983, Argentine cinema frequently performed a superficial connection between urban violence and paramilitary action, justifying the liberalisation as a supposed political denunciation. But as opposed to these opportunistic films, Aristarain's work is notable for its authenticity. His disrespect for the law is not based on a nihilism derived from a vindictive or cynical conception of justice but rather from an idealistic rebellion against a repressive system. Skeptical, tragic, moved by unshakable ethics, Pedro Bengoa is a romantic outsider whose inability to negotiate is conveyed as a repudiation of a regime of terror.

In the years that followed, there came an interval in which Aristarain would experiment with the thriller in Spain (*Las aventuras de Pepe Carvalho* (*The Adventures of Pepe Carvalho*), 1985: an eight-part made-for-television miniseries) and in the United States (*The Stranger*, 1986). But when he returned to Argentina, he showed a great interest in recapturing the same notion of resistance proposed in *Tiempo de revancha* and applied it to other genres; *Un lugar en el mundo* (*A Place in the World*, 1991) a modern re-working of classic western themes, and in *La ley de la frontera* (*The Law of the Border*, 1995), a comedy of adventures. 'He is a *frontera*', someone says about the protagonist of *Un lugar en el mundo* to indicate his uncorruptible and uncompromising temperament: 'drunk or defeated, a *frontera* never loses its dignity'. In the story of an exiled sociologist who returns to his country in order to organise a rural cooperative and face the powerful landowners of the region, the film manages to capture the vital sense of utopias. However, as Aristarain expands his body of work, he will suffer more and more from a tone increasingly sermonised with every film. In *Martín (Hache)* (*Martin H.*, 1997), a father's preoccupation for his adolescent son makes the plot a mere accumulation of advice about life and moral lessons. The dialogue becomes exasperatingly explanatory, the characters are stereotyped and the story is absorbed by common places. Instead of expressing the characters' conflicts, the film ends up suffering from them.

If we go back to consider *Tiempo de revancha* from the perspective of the later films, it is possible to notice some negative elements that were not so evident at the time. Twenty years after it premiered, the film shows certain signs of deterioration. Some dialogue insinuate the use of local customs as a genre that is so characteristic of Aries productions and more than one dramatic situation is defined by means of a tendency for explanation that would be accentuated in later films. Nevertheless, its narrative mechanism remains unspoiled, and so does the power of its rebelliousness and its capacity to reflect the social discontent in the country during the early 1980s. In this sense, the film constitutes a landmark not only because it definitively consolidated the professional prestige of the director, but also because it evidenced the beginning of a reaction to the military regime that would emerge more fully the following year with the defeat in the Malvinas War.

David Oubiña

REFERENCES

Anon. (1982) 'El arte de narrar (entrevista con Adolfo Aristarain)', in *Cine Libre*, 1, 3–7, 46–7.

Barnard, T. (1996) '*Tiempo de revancha*', in T. Barnard & P. Rist (eds) *South American Cinema. A Critical Filmography, 1915–1994*. New York: Garland, 59–60.

Brenner, F. (1993) *Adolfo Aristarain*. Buenos Aires: Centro Editor de América Latina/Instituto Nacional de Cinematografía.

Oubiña, D. & Aguilar, G. (1997) 'La intuición del relato (entrevista con Adolfo Aristarain)', in D. Oubiña & G. Aguilar (eds) *El guión cinematográfico*. Buenos Aires: Paidós, 153–72.

LA HISTORIA OFICIAL THE OFFICIAL STORY

18

LUIS PUENZO, ARGENTINA, 1984

When democracy returned to Argentina in late 1983, the cinema began to flood with the issues and images that had been forbidden during the so-called 'Proceso de Reorganización Nacional' (Process of National Reorganisation). *La historia oficial* is the emblematic film of this 'opening', because, besides proposing a revision of some aspects of recent history, it received some of the most important national and international film awards.

To understand the meanings involved in the film, it is necessary to highlight certain dates which will let us shape the historical context that determines the narration. On 24 March 1976 the Military Junta, headed by General Jorge Rafael Videla carried out a coup d'état that toppled the debilitated democratic government led by María Estela Martínez de Perón. From then on, the armed forces imposed State terrorism on Argentine civil society, which took the form of kidnappings, torture, disappearances and assassinations. When democracy was recovered in 1983, the government of President Raúl Alfonsín created the CONADEP or Comisión Nacional sobre la Desaparición de Personas (National Committee on Missing People), and was joined by respected personalities from different cultural and political fields, and entrusted with the mission of producing a report on the workings of the recently-ended State terrorism, the repressors and their victims. The resulting report was entitled *Nunca más* (Never Again) and proclaimed: 'We have the certainty that the military dictatorship produced the greatest and wildest tragedy of our history ... Thus in the name of national security, thousands and thousands of human beings, most of them young, even teenagers, were included in a terrifying and phantasmagoric category, the *desaparecidos* (the 'disappeared'); a word that is nowadays written in Spanish in the world's press.' The report detailed how the persecutions, house searches and seizures, as well as all types of violations of human rights, were perpetrated leaving as a result innumerable victims, among whom were found the children of the disappeared born in captivity.

The cultural world went on with this process of opening and reflecting on the tragedy that happened in the 1970s, trying to insert all of the absences that called for a response in their artistic representations. The cinema too became stocked with images referring to this long night in Argentine history. Artists and audience projected the deep wounds of society in the cinema as a manner of preserving the memory of the events.

The plot of *La historia oficial* focuses on the family of Roberto and Alicia, and their young adopted daughter, Gabi. The action takes place in Buenos Aires in March 1983, a moment marked by the withdrawal of the military regime and the strengthening of civil society. This family also goes through unsettling circumstances. The order imposed during the dictatorship begins to crumble when Alicia gradually becomes aware of the true nature of the past years. Roberto is an executive in a company that flourished thanks to the implementation of neo-liberal policies and that keeps some kind of bonds with American finance companies and high-ranking officers of the regime. He displays distress at the 'withdrawal' of the military and, although his relationship with the regime is never explicit, constant references are made to the existence of business and ideological links. Things, however, change for Alicia, a teacher of Argentine history in a school, and for Gabi, who Roberto had brought home illegally five years before. Alicia begins to cross a path that takes her from a reactionary social milieu, characterised by repressive attitudes and stultifying sentences, to a world where a diversity of voices denounce the injustices and conflicts of power. Her safe and harmonious life begins to fall apart with the arrival of Ana, a dear friend who has just returned from exile. During dinner, Alicia innocently asks about the reasons of the sudden trip that took Ana abroad, seven years before, and gets an answer that evokes the search and seizure of Ana, her 36-days kidnapping and the application of the 'full treatment'. Alicia shudders and asks, 'Why did they do that to you? Did you file a report?'

These questions reflect her lack of awareness about the reality of Argentina. She had preferred not to hear or learn about what was happening, but now the armed forces are leaving power and the stories of the victims come to the surface, together with the increasing presence of their families in the streets. But the most important aspect of the encounter is that Ana acts as the emissary of a reality that affects Alicia personally. She tells Alicia that she was imprisoned in a crowded place, where there were pregnant women that gave birth and that those new-born children were given over to 'those families who bought them without asking where they came from'. This sentence functions as a detonator that destabilises the constructed order. As in a Greek tragedy, Alicia begins the search for a truth that she intuitively knows will destroy her harmonious life. The question about the identity of her daughter leads her to investigate in old records and finally takes her to the office of the Abuelas de Plaza de Mayo (Grandmothers of Plaza de Mayo). Meanwhile, these changes are not easy for

Roberto, who sees his security gone. With the end of the dictatorship arrives the end of his businesses and his impunity. He cannot elude Alicia's questions, but neither can he answer them. He turns violently on his wife when he discovers that she is investigating the true identity of Gabi. Finally Alicia meets a grandmother with a white scarf who thinks she sees some resemblance between Gabi and her disappeared daughter.

Undoubtedly, in *La historia oficial*, female characters have a greater relevance because they became a focal point of the conflicts and stood out because of their courage. One can easily relate this outlook to the relevance of social women's movements that actively resisted Argentine military dictatorship. The role of women in society was redefined through the birth of organisations such as Madres de la Plaza de Mayo (Mothers of Plaza de Mayo) and Abuelas de Plaza de Mayo (Grandmothers of Plaza de Mayo), identified by the white scarfs they wore over their heads while carrying out their silent protest in which they asked for information about their lost relatives, a relentless search that faced all kind of adversities. In this way the quartet composed of Alicia, Ana, Gabi and the grandmother allows us to catch a glimpse of a wounded society. Each of them has been affected by the social tragedy in different ways, but all of them understand that the search for the truth is the only tool they can count on to move on, even though they ignore the consequences that each discovery may entail. This particular dimension was aptly highlighted by Norma Aleandro's reflection about her performance, 'Those shy, almost absent characters, always careful not to falter or disturb, who never dream of being heroes, who accept official versions, like Alicia, to allow them to survive in a fragile balance where thoughts are not spoken and where no one thinks of what shouldn't be thought about, and who one day shyly choose the painful road of knowledge being aware that each step draws them further away from safety, from the happiness of those who do not see – or do not know, are valuable ground to tread on for an actor.'

In the beginning of the film, Alicia is a serious woman, very formal in the way she dresses and in all her attitudes, who reproduces the official version of the Argentine history before her class students. But she gradually loses the stiffness with which she is used to expressing herself. We can see a change in her body language (including her loose hair and more casual clothes which show that there is 'something' going on) and how the rigid and structured way in which she conceived Argentine history vanishes at the same time as she begins to understand that both past and present have more faces than the ones she had been able to contemplate. Little by little, suspicion grows within her. She had accepted too many things without questioning, including the true origin of their adopted daughter Gabi. For the grandmother, Sara, things do not prove to be easy either. In a memorable sequence she shows Alicia the picture of her missing daughter and tells her some of the last memories she treasures. For many years she has been looking for her granddaughter with a mixture of patience and despair and now she imagines a gateway full of hope and pain.

But perhaps the most disturbing character in the film is the girl who carries signs of a memory that cannot be erased. Puenzo makes her sing a song written by María Elena Walsh that reads 'in the country of *I-can't-remember* I take three steps forward and I get lost', making the audience both shudder and understand the necessity of recovering memory and reconstructing identity. It is not by chance that Puenzo and his scriptwriter Aida Bortnik chose to start the film with the Argentine anthem, a sign that broadens the film's scope of interest. In the sequences in which we see Alicia at the school teaching Argentine history, it is obvious that she, as a representative of an educational institution, holds an *institutional* or *official* conception of history that clearly expresses the point of view of the 'victors'. But a new universe surfaces and reveals itself when a student talks about the history of the 'defeated', that refers to an underground memory and to the life of ordinary people. This student exposes a non-official version about the probable political murder of the most radical member of the Government in 1810, but the teacher simply decides to punish him for having offended the academic texts.

Through such a strategy, *La historia oficial* tries to show this recent period of Argentine history as just another link that marks the continuity of the political history of the country; political violence and the silence that sheltered those who instigated it or played its main part. In this regard, it is important to emphasise the relevance of the sequence in which Roberto's father reproaches his son for his complicity with the military regime by saying that 'while the whole country was going downwards, only bastards, thieves, accomplices, and my eldest son went upwards'. The scene has multiple connotations for Argentine audiences since Roberto is presented as the member of a network of complicity at political and economic levels, necessary to build up the 'Proceso'. But he is far from being the only character involved in this network. It also includes, for example, the representative of the Church, Alicia's confessor, who urges her to put all her doubts aside and obey as her only alternative. Or one of Alicia's friends, always repeating a terrible sentence, strongly paradigmatic of those times: 'If they come for him, he surely must have done something wrong.'

According to Puenzo, *La historia oficial* 'tries not only to reflect on the *desaparecidos* and their children but also on what happened to us and on what we allowed to happen to us in the recent years'. Consequently he decided to shoot an 'ordinary' film that could be seen at the movie theatres by as many people as possible: 'I deliberately used the format of intimate, not political cinema, because I believe that usually traditional political cinema – from *La hora de los hornos* to the films by Costa-Gavras, Pontecorvo or others – only catches the attention of people who are previously convinced.' Accordingly, the film narration rejects all kind of transgression to the hegemonic discourse and mode of representation. The achievements of *La historia oficial* are neither in line with aesthetic innovations nor with narrative patterns that break with the classical models, the narration sticks to the story continuity of time and space. The achievements can rather be found in the implementation of techniques that make the emotional identification of the viewer with the female characters possible. In order to do that, most of the scenes take place in unthreatening locations and depend strongly on the performance of the actors, usually emphasised by close-ups that let us appreciate every detail of the contradictory emotions that overpower their characters.

The film thus lacks a radical voice. It does not make a social denunciation because it is not directly focussed on the victims. Instead *La historia oficial* wants to reconstruct the process by which part of the society (represented by Alicia) becomes conscious of what had been happening in the country in spite of its efforts to deny reality. It is necessary to underline once again that the film is contemporary to the disclosure of the crimes committed by State terrorism, thanks both to the publication of the CONADEP report, *Nunca más*, and the hearings of the trials of the Military Juntas. So one might think that Argentine society was seized with horror in parallel with the characters of the film and also tried to get rid of the nightmare. The political function of *La historia oficial* is closely related to this simultaneity of experiences. The film does not propose itself as a conventional political film, appealing instead to a kind of 'unveiling'. Neither does it contain proposals for the future. What will happen to Gabi or to the grandmother looking for her granddaughter remains undefined, as does the punishment the repressors and their accomplices deserve.

Both the public and the critics gave a warm welcome to the film. It was the Argentine hit at the box-office in 1985 (899,940 tickets sold, according to the National Film Institute), although it did not reach the levels of popularity of some Hollywood productions such as *Ghostbusters* (1,222,417 tickets sold the same year, according to the same source). A sort of paradox, the real and the cinematic 'Ghostbusters' shared the screens at the same time. But real 'ghosts' were certainly more terrifying, and that is why Abuelas de Plaza de Mayo considered *La historia oficial* as a great contribution: 'The story casts a light on the drama of the children missing for political reasons, whose identity was obliterated while being raised by families that were not their own, taken as war booty, in a sophisticated example of slavery. With a human touching story it contributes to abolish oblivion, stirring people to collaborate, and at the same time aiding us, the Grandmothers of the Plaza, in our search.'

The film reviewers pointed out its quality as a document, as well as a necessary tool for the reconstruction of memory. As stated by Hugo Paradero (in *Humor* magazine), 'Puenzo's film inaugurates a glorious period in the "harmed" cinematography of this "harmed" country. In this new era cinema will eventually help us to complete our history.' Néstor Tirri, film critic of the prestigious newspaper *Clarín* described *La historia oficial* as a 'polyvalent testimony of a crucial period in the life of our country, triggered by one of those hallucinating cases of everyday life that some day the *official story* will take into account'. And Jorge Abel Martín, in *Tiempo Argentino*, considered the film 'a human and moving document that contributes to prevent oblivion … the painful portrait of a piece of life, a gigantic mirror that returns us thousands of faces'.

Critics also emphasised the formal aspects of the film. Thus Daniel López highlighted the work of Puenzo as 'dense in climates, not complacent in its resolutions and, above all, trying to avoid aestheticism'. But the reaction was not unanimous, especially with regard to the somewhat vague and open ending of the film. Some considered the idea as useful and constructive and so Claudio España praisingly wrote in *La Nación*, 'It leaves the viewer with the mission of judging and resolutely stirs a participatory activity … [It raises] an "enigma" that the remarkable script by Aida Bortnik … does not want to disclose and whose solution it truly puts in the hands of God'. But at the same time some other critics and human rights organisations did not agree with the film, since it failed either to make a clear pronouncement against the repressors or to demand a punishment for their actions. In this sense, the well-known film-maker Alejandro Agresti vehemently declared that in the film, 'Nobody speaks about the one who disappeared, nobody speaks about the one who had the problem. It is rather the criminal who has the problem here. He and his criminal wife, a history teacher whose complete ignorance and innocence they are trying to convince me about'. As a matter of fact, the controversy clearly trascended the film itself and revealed the existence of different levels of complicity about what happened. *La historia oficial* burst into a society that, for a number of different and complex reasons, could not give a coherent answer to the imposition of silence. And that is why Puenzo stresses how in her learning of the language Gabi mixes up the words 'solidario' (solidary) with 'solitario' (lonely), showing us the side of the things we do not like to see.

La historia oficial was born as a result of new film policy implemented by Manuel Antín, the director of the Instituto Nacional de Cinematografía (National Film Institute) in the early years of democratisation, as a response to the demands of increasingly large numbers of young film-makers with long delayed projects. Luis Puenzo was one of them and *La historia oficial*, a low-budget film (US $500,000) shot in his own house, soon became the most awarded film in local history. Among many others, it won the Academy Award for the Best Foreign Picture in 1986 and a prize for Norma Aleandro as Best Actress at Cannes. No doubt all these awards confirmed that at least from a formal and stylistical viewpoint Puenzo had reached an outstanding narrative efficiency, quite uncommon in Argentine cinema. It became by its own right the film that was to symbolise the climate of the democratic opening during Alfonsín's government.

Puenzo's domestic and international success anticipated a promising career, but those foresights never came to fruition and he would subsequently make only two more films. The first one, *Gringo viejo* (*Old Gringo*, 1989) set up the rules of the *civilised* American universe of 1913 – as presented by writer Ambrose Bierce – against the *wild* Latin American alternative embodied by the Mexican Revolution and those who expressed radical and brave ideas through their struggle. As for the second, *La peste* (*The Plague*, 1991), Puenzo ambitiously attempted a transposition of the novel by Albert Camus to a Latin American setting. With large budgets, even by international standards, neither *Gringo viejo* nor *La peste* rose to the occasion and left both the public and the critics dissatisfied.

Clara Kriger

REFERENCES

España, C. (ed.) (1994) *Cine argentino en democracia: 1983–1993*. Buenos Aires: Fondo Nacional de las Artes.

García Oliveri, R. (1993) *Luis Puenzo*. Buenos Aires: Centro Editor de América Latina/Instituto Nacional de Cinematografía.

Kriger, C. (1999) '*La historia oficial*', in A. Elena & M. Díaz López (eds) *Tierra en trance: el cine latinoamericano en cien películas*. Madrid: Alianza, 330–4.

LA BOCA DEL LOBO THE LION'S DEN

19

FRANCISCO J. LOMBARDI, PERU, 1988

Vitín Luna is an ambitious young policeman seeking promotion. That explains his request to be transferred to Chuspi, an Andean town isolated by the violence of the Sendero Luminoso (Shining Path). The local police station was recently attacked by the Maoist terrorists, slaughtering the detachment there. Vitín arrives in this dangerous place, where a sudden attack by the omnipresent but invisible enemy could happen at any time. The detachment is commanded by Lieutenant Basulto, who believes that the enemy must be fought by the force of the law, but when he is killed by the Sendero Luminoso he is replaced by the sadistic Lieutenant Roca. A strict authoritarian used to giving orders without question or complaint, Roca introduces a more ruthless campaign to stamp out any subversive activity, demanding order from both his men and the villagers who live within his jurisdiction. The rape of a country girl, committed by one of the members of the detachment highlights Roca's corruption. Rather than punish the offender, he orders the deaths of civilians to cover up the actions of his men. Vitín, sickened by the violence and abuse of power, confronts Roca. He is challenged by the lieutenant to a game of Russian roulette, from which both survive, but remain enemies, on opposite sides of the law.

Francisco J. Lombardi's fifth feature, *La boca del lobo*, appeared in cinemas at a difficult time for Peru. At the end of the 1980s, the country was plagued by economic crises and political violence. Terrorist acts by the Maoist group, Sendero Luminoso, prompted a vicious response by the army and the police and was followed by the introduction of repressive laws. Premiered in December 1988, the film can be seen as a denunciation of the policies adopted by the government and an indictment of the 'inhumanity' that resulted from the 'dirty war' between the Sendero Luminoso and the Peruvian Army. At least, that was what many expected from the controversial director whose previous films tackled all manner of problems affecting Peruvian society, from the indolence of the ruling classes in *Muerte al amanecer* (*Death at Sunrise*, 1977), homophobia and social exclusion in *Los amigos* (*The Friends*), an episode of the anthological film *Cuentos inmorales* (*Immoral Tales*, 1978), or social isolation in *Maruja en el Infierno* (*Maruja in Hell*, 1983). Such expectations were heightened when it became known that the original script opened with the 'slaughter of Soccos', a sinister episode that took place in the Andes during a state of emergency when a military patrol massacred the population of Soccos, defending its actions with the claim that the villagers were colluding with subversive groups.

But *La boca del lobo* was not an exposition of real facts or the reconstruction of what happened in the Andean village. On the contrary, creating a traditional and linear story, Lombardi, with scriptwriters Giovanna Pollarollo and Augusto Cabada, avoided any topics that could lead the film towards polemic, spectacular, militant or 'committed' statements. He dramatised in a moral rather than documentary way, based on the development of the characters within the narrative and not situations. He chose to identify himself with a character's emotional and psychological state, elaborating on the complexities and conflicts within it, rather than express his convictions or postulate a thesis. Therefore, the slaughter of Soccos was secondary to the central issue of *La boca del lobo* which was an assessment of the repercussions of a violent event upon an individual; in this case, the torn loyalties of the central character. The film became the chronicle of a tense situation amongst the police, exacerbated by fear, loneliness, cultural difference and the irrational threat of an invisible enemy. Far from being an overtly political film, *La boca del lobo* was more a variation of an adventure film, of men in extreme circumstances in a hostile and threatening environment.

La boca del lobo portrays a group of men on a mission against a faceless enemy. The group, linked by institutional demands and united by a blind obedience, have the antecedents in the men of *The Lost Patrol* (John Ford, 1934), *Bataan* (Tay Garnett, 1943) or *Men in War* (Anthony Mann, 1957), and the many other westerns where men traverse 'tribal lands', where danger and fear arises out of the awareness of being seen by a crouching and ubiquitous enemy. *La boca del lobo* articulately details this feeling of paranoia amongst the soldiers. Every walk through the town and its surrounding area was like a journey into a minefield. As Chilean writers Ascanio Cavallo and Antonio Martínez wrote about the film, '*La boca del lobo* is the Latin American *Il deserto dei tartari (Desert of the Tartars,* Valerio Zurlini, 1977). Not only due to the obvious similarity of the story – an isolated military contingent waiting for the assault of the invisible enemy – but especially due to its intention of penetrating, from the same dramatic situation, in the psychology of a group of men confronted with themselves, at the edge of death. Its huge advantage is that the metaphor does not require any effort to join with reality … In *La boca del lobo*, like in some of the greatest works of Hawks, Fuller or Mann, tension modulates every image, every transition, the beginnning of every sequence. Lombardi manages to make nights and days equally threatening, to make the beast of terror roar in both. Does the historic circumstance help him? Certainly. Without the extreme violence of the Sendero Luminoso, the film would be hardly possible; but with it, the film becomes exceptional.'

From the opening moments, the film takes place from the point of view of Vitín. The main narrative thread is the search – both psychological and emotional – by Vitín for a reason to justify his faith in the powers of law and order, which under Roca have questioned his belief in the system. From Vitín's initial blind enthusiasm with rules and discipline, the film traces his submission to the loyalties of an insular community and strictly organised life, through to his disenchantment with the system. The stationed detachment is a microcosm of society at large, like the prison island in *Muerte al amanecer*, the bar in *Los amigos*, the country house in *Muerte de un magnate* (*Death of a Tycoon*, 1980) or the washhouse in *Maruja en el Infierno*.

Young policemen from all the regions of Peru arrive at similar stations, ready to progress through the ranks, an official display of commendation for their commitment to the anti-terrorist war. But this enthusiasm soon transforms into apprehension, fear and for some, a sense of outrage at the injustices meted out. With their confidence in military legality and its ability to settle conflicts shattered, they live in the shadow of an aggressive and over-bearing authoritarian regime. In *La boca del lobo*, this 'military discipline' results in the torture of the suspects of terrorism, the rape of a girl and the slaughter of the population of Chuspi.

In its dramatisation of the tension between individuals and an institution, the film highlights the confrontation between the central character and the symbol of patriarchal power: the law. As with all his films, from *La ciudad y los perros* (*The City and the Dogs*, 1985) to *No se lo digas a nadie* (*Don't Tell It to Anybody*, 1998) Lombardi details the loss of 'innocence' of the central character. Indeed, the incidents in the film are organised around the point of view of the two main protagonists, Vitín and Roca, whose conflict arises out of their different perception of the enforcement of order. In the course of the action, the 'good' father (the sheltering institution) becomes a 'bad' father. The main characters, caught by fear and subject to disciplinary pressure, similarly transform from being from being 'good' sons to 'bad' sons in a mutation that leads them to doubt their most deeply entrenched convictions and to change their view of the world around them.

In critical moments, Vitín even questions his own sexual identity. Submitted to the military ideology, doubt becomes, for Vitín, an unequivocal symptom of softness, feminisation, 'queerness'. Trying to clear and define the nature of the conflict, to keep away those possibilities of his own personality, he ends by confronting the experience of pain and death itself, unequivocal forms of flagellation and validation of his virility. Vitín accepts the challenge of playing Russian roulette in the penultimate scene. It was an extreme way of proving who had more 'balls'. For Lieutenant Roca, having 'balls' meant assuming the most authoritarian values of the institution. Rebelling and breaking the patriarchal law, or obeying it and regaining the lost honor, confidence and virility are the only choices available to the men, choices that do not end with the usual Oedipal conclusion. Here, the acceptance of the institutional code does not open the possibility for the reversion of the father's role. The resolution arrives at different terms.

La boca del lobo, like *La ciudad y los perros* before it, ends with the exit of the 'hero' from the concentrated space. No revolt nor acceptance, expulsion and silence about what was seen and heard. Vitín leaves, watched only by a young country girl who appears as an innocent witness to the incomprehensible violence caused by adults. The inscrutable child presence is full of symbolic connotations in an innocent nation caught in the grip of a corrupt power. For many Andean people during the 1980s and 1990s, the often aggressive presence of state forces was as bewildering, threatening and unwelcome as the motivations of the Sendero Luminoso.

When Vitín becomes an army deserter, a 'coward' after abandoning the police, yet still a possible target of an attack by invisible enemies, his future seems as uncertain as it was inside the institution. Such a dramatic conclusion was more evident for Lombardi and his collaborators after working on the script for more than a year. The director explained the successive changes made to the original script in an interview to *Positif* in 1991: 'At the beginning we imagined a flashback structure. It started with Vitín in a military hospital for the treatment of soldiers who came back disturbed from the area of emergency. He knows what happened in Soccos, but he doesn't say a word about it, entering a stage of silence. After his admission in this psychiatric hospital, the story develops in flashbacks. But all that was left behind. We started all over again with Vitín in Lima, a year and a half after the slaughter, turned into a marginal person, in a shelter for delinquents. When he runs into an old friend, he tells him how his life had changed after his experience in Soccos, recalled in flashbacks. Finally, we started all over again and developed the anecdote in the simplest way regarding point of view and external structure.'

The Russian roulette sequence was questioned by some critics, but also by those who demanded from the film a more realistic portrait, that is, a testimony of the abuses and massacres that took place during the 'dirty war' against the Sendero Luminoso. Hence the commentator José Carlos Hauyhuaca wrote, 'But there is an aspect that secretly voices all the architecture, or in any case, that discloses intentions that do not match up with those set out by the film explicitly. That aspect is the fact that, on one hand (the 'thematic') everything seems to be centred around the historical focus made up by the slaughter of the civil population of Soccos, and, on the other hand (the 'dramatic'), the centre gradually moves towards the relationship between the two main characters whose end is the sequence of the duel playing the Russian roulette game – through which the importance of such an event (the slaughter of some innocent people as part of the dynamic of the 'dirty war') becomes relative and the real topic of the film is finally the old motive sought by Lombardi since his first films: the turn from a friendship based on admiration (of manly values) to a breakdown when these reveal as false and covering up.'

Hauyhuaca did not understand that the film was never explicitly intended to deal with the real issue of the slaughter of country people. From the start, it was evident that its dramatic centre was the presentation of the dilemmas that a man has to face when confronted with such violence. The slaughter of the population was a triggering sequence of the major conflicts within the film and the beginning of the end of their resolution. But it never appeared as the focus or the dramatic centre of the film. Cavallo and Martínez explained this dimension of the film: 'To decide their destiny, the soldier and the lieutenant will have to challenge each other in Russian roulette. This mortal game sets clear that Lombardi's film moves through self-challenges of the Hawksian heroes rather than through political and abstract ways. At the end of the crossroads, Vitín Luna will be more a man than when he began, and Lieutenant Iván Roca less a man than he thought he was. One's future and the other's past will find a strange convergence under fear.'

The similarity of the sequence with the Russian roulette scenes in *The Deer Hunter* (Michael Cimino, 1978) was also questioned. However, the idea of expressing the confrontation between Vitín and Roca through the game and death did not arise from that film about the tarnished honor of Americans in Vietnam. Lombardi disclosed the source in an interview by Federico de Cárdenas on the occasion of the film première: 'It was inspired in *La casa verde* by Mario Vargas Llosa, which has a Russian roulette scene I always liked and which takes place in a context of dramatic confrontation between two characters, which does not occur in *The Deer Hunter*.'

But tension is not the only element in *La boca del lobo*. Many of its sequences show the men relaxed, which only adds to the escalating horror. The best scenes in the film are those that show the policemen having to cope with living in a small cold town. The nostalgic conversations about the creole music of Lima, and the capital's mild weather and good food, such as as *cebiche* (pieces of fish marinated in acid lemon juice) offer welcome digressions from the central story. Joking, the soldiers release their irony against the temper of the *serranos* (mountain people), the natives of the Andean area who, according to the slandering racism of the people from Lima, are slow workers and all-too-often lazy. However, with its close-ups, dark tones and the barren design of the station, the threat of the enemy is never far from their thoughts. The death of Lieutenant Basulto breaks the comradeship and put the group to test. Fear takes over and loyalties are questioned, exposing the men's darker side.

The 'good guys' we knew at the beginning of *La boca del lobo* become 'bad guys', incited by Lieutenant Roca, who makes them see a threat in any member of Andean society. The adoption of Roca's rules, which demand from the characters attitudes and decisions contrary to their convictions, dramatised the conflict between a conscience in a state of change – divided between faithfulness to their personal beliefs and the fulfillment of the authoritarian requirements of the institution. The institution itself was a source of desire of power, stability, personal progress (Vitín accepted the mission in Ayacucho to obtain a mention in dispatches), but also unhappiness.

La boca del lobo thus follows a dramatic pattern recurrent in Lombardi's films, where we often see the main characters undertaking enterprises that challenge their values. The characters suffer the damage of terrible events that end in disaster, usually in the death of third parties, leaving them defenseless. The uncertainty imbued the films with a masochistic quality where the main character's tribulations become the dramatic focus of the film, an element shared by films such as *On the Waterfront* (Elia Kazan, 1954), *Looking for Mr. Goodbar* (Richard Brooks, 1977) or *The Last Temptation of Christ* (Martin Scorsese, 1988). *La boca del lobo* examines the dialectics of individual responsibility and collective guilt against the sense of 'duty'; a struggle in which the main characters confront their own antisocial impulses, which could make them accomplices to abuse and torture. In the end, Vitín's gesture (running away from what he did and, or even worse, of what he could be able of doing in the 'dirty war') is headed against himself, showing his confusion, tribulations and despair.

Ricardo Bedoya

REFERENCES

Bedoya, R. (1992) *Cien años de cine en el Perú: una historia crítica*. Lima/Madrid: Universidad de Lima/Instituto de Cooperación Iberoamericana (Expanded edition, Lima: Universidad de Lima/Fondo de Desarrollo Editorial, 1995).

____ (1997) *Entre fauces y colmillos: las películas de Francisco Lombardi*. Huesca: Festival de Cine de Huesca.

Blanco, D. (1987) *Imagen por imagen*. Lima: Universidad de Lima.

Cavallo, A. & Martínez, A. (1995) *Cien (años) claves del cine*. Santiago de Chile: Planeta.

Huayhuaca, J. C. (1989) *El enigma de la pantalla*. Lima: Universidad de Lima.

Paranaguá, P. A. (1995) 'Francisco Lombardi', in J.-L. Passek (ed.) *Dictionnaire du Cinéma*. Paris: Larousse.

LA NACIÓN CLANDESTINA THE CLANDESTINE NATION

20

JORGE SANJINÉS, BOLIVIA, 1989

La nación clandestina, the seventh full-length feature by Jorge Sanjinés, is considered his best film, both by the director himself and numerous film critics. Sanjinés made the film after three decades of a career devoted in great part to reflecting and expressing an unusual cinematic topic: the Indian peasants and workers in Bolivia's mining industry.

Sanjinés was born in Bolivia in 19s37. He studied cinema in Chile, between 1957 and 1960, before returning to Bolivia and forming a partnership with Óscar Soria, with whom he made the short *Sueños y realidades* (*Dreams and Realities*, 1961). Later, together with Soria, Antonio Eguino and Ricardo Rada, he founded the Ukamau production company, whose name is the title of his first feature film, made in 1966. Since then, Ukamau has produced all of Sanjinés' movies.

In addition to directing, Sanjinés was actively involved in promoting cinema in Bolivia. He also explored the theoretical dimensions of the medium, from social, political and aesthetic points of view. This theorisation threw him into a crisis when he became aware that he was producing a classical-style cinema, from a Western perspective. To many, Hollywood – perceived to be the dominant cinema – was necessarily 'different', because its themes and characters were not ones to which the Latin American public was accustomed. This discovery forced Sanjinés to look for new ways of making films from an indigenous perspective, both in theme and form.

From its beginnings, Sanjinés' radically different cinema stood alone, distanced from the cinema that was then in fashion. It even stood apart from the work of his contemporaries of the New Latin American Cinema (Rocha, Littin, Alea, Birri *et al*). His characters and themes were rarely, if ever, represented in films. And in literature, there was only the dubious sub-genre of 'indigenous literature', written by non-Indians. Given the scarce, almost nonexistent film industry in Bolivia, little had been done to represent these characters and their concerns. The only exceptions to this were Jorge Ruiz, Oscar Soria, Hugo Roncal and Augusto Roca, who had set the foundations for a national cinema. Above all, Ruiz and his extraordinary *¡Vuelve, Sebastiana!* (*Come Back, Sebastiana!*, 1953) helped define a starting point for Bolivian film-making. Sanjinés went further than all of them, because his work expressed the hard struggle of a film-maker searching for an authenticity and a balance between what is filmed with what was seen by the spectator.

From his first short, *Cobre* (*Copper*, 1958) up to *La nación clandestina*, the evolution of Sanjinés' style highlights the search for a poetics and aesthetic that would not only overturn previous representations of the Andean world, but that, rather than 'reflecting' it, would originate from it. The subject would transform itself into the constructor of its own images, to the degree that the film-maker would immerse himself in the culture of its protagonists.

Such a task was extremely difficult since the cinema is a medium of great industrial and economic demands, and did not appear to be the most ideal form for the representation of social sectors as poor as the Bolivian peasantry. Some solutions presented themselves as the films were being made. For example, the 'actors' were the Indians themselves. They were peasants and workers who knew first-hand the real histories upon which the films were based. The scripts were discussed and written together with those actors and, during filming, space was created for them to improvise, to express their feelings with their own vocabulary (Quechua or Aymara speakers for the most part).

Although many problems were solved through the experience of filming these people, other barriers existed, due to the presence of a cultural distance between the filming team and its protagonists. In the beginning, Sanjinés' cinema looked for cinematic models that would benefit or bridge that distance. Italian Neorealism, with its use of non-professional actors, the absence of a constructed scenography, and its search for an almost direct realism, appeared to suit Sanjinés' needs. Another model was Soviet cinema, which was geared toward the masses of peasants and workers who had constructed the Revolution.

Sanjinés' cinema was ideologically Marxist. In this sense his was the most politically radical cinema of his generation. Some of his films end up promoting armed struggle as a social and political solution. Others considered the need for peasants and workers to organise and be united in unions and political groups. This oscillation between proposing armed or political struggles is typical of Sanjinés' cinema, and was also typical of prevailing moods in Latin America during the 1970s.

Of his early shorts, one of the most notable is *Revolución* (*Revolution*, 1963), a social commentary whose images conveyed the themes and message of the film to such a degree, Sanjinés saw no need for an accompanying text. It displayed a slant toward social denunciation, against the injustice suffered by the larger popular community, at the hands of an educated white majority, at once racist and full of social prejudices. Moral indignation against social injustice became central to all of Sanjinés' films.

In 1979, Sanjinés published a collection of essays, manifestos, script fragments and interviews under the title *Teoría y práctica de un cine junto al pueblo* (*Theory and Practice of Cinema with the People*) which highlighted his proposal and specific concern. It was the matter of making a social and political cinema whose perspective coincided with that of the 'people'. The most humble strata of the population were understood as 'the people', in opposition to the bourgeois sectors, such as the government and the army, seen by many as the iron fist of the power class. In Bolivian and, to a larger extent, Latin American terms, the 'people' was also a term opposed to the exploitation practices of North American imperialism. In that sense, Sanjinés aligned with other emerging political projects among Latin American intellectuals and artists inspired by the Cuban Revolution as an initial movement toward continental liberation. He was part of the 'militant' cinema of the 1960s and 1970s which found its audience, outside Bolivia, in the festival circuit that promoted politically committed cinema during those years.

In any case, the movie that put Sanjinés' name onto the international circuit had not yet formed part of that conflict. *Ukamau* (1966) was a classically structured film, but its simplicity moved audiences. It dealt with a doubly tragic story of the rape and murder of an Indian woman at the hands of a *mestizo*, and the husband's subsequent acts of vengeance. The film surprised many and was admired for, among other things, its strong dramatic construction, despite its rudimentary production values. The social analysis observed the difference between *mestizos* and Indians, revealing an unjust social and working order. In that order, the *mestizo* was the small capitalist businessman who exploited the Indian, the basic producer. The film drew its strength from a history of injustice and cruelty. Symbolically, it fitted a view of Latin America in which its history has been one of plundering and violation of the humble.

In the following films, *Ukamau's* social concern was substituted by a more political one, as evinced by *Yawar Mallku/Sangre de cóndor* (*Blood of the Condor*, 1969), *El coraje del pueblo* (*The People's Courage*, 1971), *Jatun Auka/El enemigo principal* (*The Main Enemy*,1973), *¡Fuera de aquí!/Llocsi Caimanta* (*Get Out of Here!*, 1977), and the documentary *Las banderas del amanecer* (*The Flags of Dawn*, co-directed by Beatriz Palacios, 1983).

Yawar Mallku/Sangre de cóndor began as an exercise that was to become common in fiction as well as in documentaries, consisting of an authentic re-dramatisation of real events.

On occasion, these films would start with newspaper headlines announcing the events that were filmed. In *Yawar Mallku/Sangre de cóndor* it was the sterilisation of women in Bolivian Indian communities at the hands of the American Peace Corps under the guise of opening maternity clinics. The same theme was used in *¡Fuera de aquí!/Llocsi Caimanta*, filmed in Ecuador. This movie begins with information about the practice, one of which is almost Nazi in tone, thus seeking to link the racist ideology of Nazism with what was happening in Bolivia and other parts of Latin America, which used people as a human laboratory.

Nevertheless, *Yawar Mallku/Sangre de cóndor* is valuable not only because of the authors' political intention. It is a magnificent tale with an effective dramatic construction, excellent performances (the main roles were played by the same people who had acted in *Ukamau*) and splendid cinematography by Antonio Eguino. Some critics have noted the influence of Italian Neorealism that is evident in the natural settings, the use of non-actors and the film's realist style. Yet, if one were looking for points of comparison, *Yawar Mallku/Sangre de cóndor* also belongs to great Soviet cinema to the degree that its cinematography at times achieves an expressionistic feel that takes the film beyond a realist or naturalistic aesthetic.

The use of unusual angles or the magnificent sequences of a character's mythic contact with nature, such as the scene when Ignacio climbs the mountain to imbue himself with light, are exemplary. If there is something unusual in this film, it has to do with Indian beliefs and animism (perfectly exemplified in the erosion of the coca leaves) which Marxism rejected so frequently, judging it as folkloric or superstitious. In any case, *Yawar Mallku/Sangre de cóndor* offers two approaches to the situation: the rational and the irrational. On the one hand it shows how Ignacio discovers the clinic's operations by looking through a hole on the wall, whilst the Indians discover the truth about the clinic's practices, through the reading of coca leaves. The possibility of accessing the truth through paths that differed from any rational route, would occupy the concern aspect of *Para recibir el canto de los pájaros* (*In Order to Hear Birds Sing*, 1995).

In *El coraje del pueblo*, Sanjinés chose to reconstruct the massacre by the Bolivian Army of workers, women and children in the Siglo XX Mine in 1967. Óscar Soria wrote a script based on the events and later collaborated in its reconstruction, with the remaining survivors taking part. It pointed out that 'the events in this movie are true, their reconstruction relies on testimonies and documents' and that 'the main protagonists are the true witnesses who interpret their own stories'. The film possessed great dramatic force, while at the same time merging individual characters and stories into collective ones. Although Sanjinés was never concerned with fathoming the individual psychology of its characters, in *El coraje del pueblo* he changed his style by trying to express a 'collective' character. Increasingly, his films avoided close-ups and medium shots, preferring to work with wider shots, which were more conducive in 'capturing' the 'people' as a collective character.

One of his main aims was to adopt a style of cinema that would be useful to its own characters, who would become its core audience. While in exile, Sanjinés made two films that were didactically inspired, and pamphleteering in style. The first was destined to redefine *El enemigo principal*, the second was to promote that enemy's expulsion from Latin America (*¡Fuera de aquí!/Llocsi Caimanta).* The 'main enemy' was, of course, United States imperialism. *El enemigo principal's* story was similar to *Ukamau*; a landowner abuses a peasant, then murders him by cutting his throat in front of his wife and son. Angry, the peasant community appeals to the justice system, but the judge is corrupt and an ally of the landowners. The subsequent appearance of guerrillas gives some hope to the peasants. The guerrillas capture, condemn and execute the landowner and his foreman, and as a result the peasants state that 'the sun has come out for us'. Afterward the guerrillas explain to the peasants that, just like the landowner had abused them, the United States abuses Latin American countries.

Fuera de aquí!/Llocsi Caimanta denounced the demographic displacement of the Kalakala Indian community from a valley in the Andes. Yet its themes are varied. There is the political demagoguery of those who arrive in the city looking for Indian votes by means of promises, deceptions and threats. It also looks at the 'evangelisation' of the Indians by Americans who try to convince the populace about the 'end of the world', at the same time as they test the land for mineral deposits. Finally, there is the theme of the sterilisation of women. Once the Kalakala peasants are displaced by the government and the army to deserted zones inappropriate for their harvests, other communities give them shelter and aid, including land. This final section of the film introduces the theme of solidarity, a compensation for the negative aspects of exploitation.

La nación clandestina is Sanjinés' finest achievement, because he managed not only to synthetise themes from previous films, but also in the way he articulated the differences between the rational and irrational worlds, that is, 'Western' narratives and more indigenous mythical narratives. In 1981 Sanjinés said that all his previous work had been 'an essay, a preparation' for the filming of *La nación clandestina*. It is a story of guilt and expiation, as well as a tragic example of the relations between the community and the individual. Told in successive flashbacks during the journey undertaken by the main character, Sebastián, from La Paz to Willkani, his Aymara birthplace, the film pieces together the puzzle of a particular story that exceeds the circumstances of the character to submerge itself into the country's social and political history. Many other conflicts are summarised in Sebastián's identity crisis, in particular, the transculturation of national culture in the modern era. Nevertheless, Sanjinés also returns to the construction of a notable individual character, as he had done in *Ukamau*. That character had been lost until then, given the attention paid to the 'collectivity' in his subsequent films.

In 1952, when he was a child, Sebastián had witnessed the humiliating control the white classes had over the Indians. He had also witnessed the ritual dance of the Jacha Tata Danzante, the last vestige of a sacrificial practice that became lost over time. Later, his parents had handed him over to a Creole family in La Paz, to educate him. Hence, the film's opening, with the mother's crying, because Sebastián had changed his name (he is no longer Mamani but Mainsman), embarrassed by the indigenous background and thus betraying his origins. She also accepts her fault in this, when she sent him far from the community and the family.

Sebastián's return home following the death of his father, is his first opportunity to vindicate himself. Shortly after, through his experience with the outside world, the community name him political chief with the intention of having him negotiate with officials in La Paz some measures that would benefit them. His brother Vicente is opposed to the community's accepting a program of food donated by the United States, since experience showed that there are always ulterior motives for such acts of benevolence. Nevertheless, Sebastián gets his way. The film operates through the ideological contrast between the two positions defined by the brothers. With this dramatic turn Sanjinés seeks to express different tendencies and positions within the communities. Later, Sebastián's mistake consists in deciding collective matters without consulting the community. Moreover, he becomes corrupt with the aid of a *mestizo* who convinces him to keep half of the food aid in order to sell it. When Sebastián's deception is discovered the furious community wants to punish him, and they throw him out, threatening him with death. His betrayal this time is not just against his family name, but against an entire community.

By making Sebastián his main protagonist Sanjinés overcomes the stereotypes that are so common in his previous films. Instead of idealising his humble characters he tries to show, with remarkable subtlety, the peasants's capability for corruption and redemption, represented here by Sebastián. Again, he is the most complex and true-to-life character of all of Sanjinés' work, and although he is a 'negative hero' he manages to move the audience when he returns home. He is a Prodigal Son, ready to sacrifice himself for the community in the ritual dance that will lead to his death ('I want to pay for my guilt'). Before this last act, Sebastián's conduct is reprehensible. He makes Basilia his wife pregnant by raping her on a mountain steep, lies to his friends, steals, gets drunk, denies shelter to those in need, and seems indifferent to everything except in his decision to go back home.

If Sanjinés showed the Indian people as a victim of violations (*Ukamau*) and violence (in most of the films following *Ukamau*), in *La nación clandestina* the character becomes responsible for his own destiny, whether through his bad behaviour or through the path of redemption. Although sequences in which the soldiers abuse the peasants also appear here, they are peripheral, almost 'environmental' in the story. The film is more the history of a return, told with images in which Sebastián walks endlessly through deserted and mountainous regions, toward his village, with flashbacks recalling earlier episodes that refer both to the present and the past. These flashbacks are abundant, such as the moment when Sebastián stops by a brook to drink from it, or in other instances when everything he remembers is linked to conflicts he has caused or provoked. The trip undertaken is thus not only physical but spiritual, a journey within his conscience.

At the same time, some of those flashback episodes are present as minor stories in themselves, relating individual or political events. Once again, Sanjinés uses them to reiterate themes and problems that his movies have dealt with before. The lack of verbal and cultural communication is a recurring theme; although that lack is the central conflict of *Para recibir el canto de los pájaros*, in *La nación clandestina* it is exemplified by the story of a university student pursued by the military in the desert. The student first meets Sebastián and offers to buy his hat and poncho. It also seems odd to the skeptical Sebastián that the student tells him that he is fighting for his 'cause'. Later the student finds an Indian couple whom he also asks for clothes, but does not manage to communicate with them because he does not know their language. Frustrated by the lack of communication, he mutters 'fucking Indians!' almost at the same moment when two soldiers identify him and open fire, killing him. The implication is clear. It is not enough to fight for just causes, one must also familiarise oneself with the cultures for which you are struggling. Sanjinés thus alludes to a leftist intelligentsia divorced from 'reality', emasculated by the fascist military. The city student is *nobody* in the desert, only a pathetic figure, a whiner in threadbare clothes, a victim of his ignorance.

Some flashbacks recover moments of conflict from Sebastián's past: his participation in kidnappings, tortures and murders carried out by the military; the seduction and rape of Basilia; his argument with his brother Vicente after he puts on a military uniform and tries to disarm him due to a purported 'peasant-military pact'; the episodes in which his father throws him out of the house; and later how his mother disowns him ('He is not my son anymore'). Moreover, some of these sequences are integrated into the present, with the past and present sharing the same cinematic space, implying redemption through the acknowledgement of past actions. When Sebastián dies there is a funeral entourage carrying his body, and he walks alongside the cortege. The film ends with a close-up of his face, signaling that one Sebastián died and a redeemed one will continue living.

If the preparations for the opening dance are an integral part of the movie, the final dance itself is of a great tragic beauty. With the viewer's knowledge that Sebastián is dressed with the impeccable outfits of the dance, and has put on a mask whose weight would contribute to the exhaustion that leads to his death, the scene itself is an *agony*, aided by the musicians and the community. The long sequence of Sebastián's dance and death reminds one of a literary antecedent, *La agonía de Rasu Niti*. In that short story by the Peruvian author José María Arguedas, a dancer gets dressed, dances in order to communicate with nature, and finally dies, passing on the mythical properties of his dance to a young disciple as an inheritance. In Sanjinés' film, the community is Aymara not Quechua like in Arguedas' story, but the rite of the Jacha Tata Danzante is also employed as an ancient tradition no longer practiced in the present. It is only through the efforts of the community's wise elder and those of Vicente and Basilia that the group becomes convinced that it is an ancient ritual dance, in which Sebastián will sacrifice himself before the gods for the benefit of the community. With this conflict, Sanjinés also asserts that Indian culture is not unique or unchangeable, and that many aspects of its past have been lost, making it more difficult to understand.

The great formal novelty in *La nación clandestina* is the use of sequence shots. For Sanjinés the attempt to avoid as much as possible the usual film collage of wide shots and detailed close-ups is part of an effort to express with a different aesthetic the peculiar mental rythms with which Indians perceive, understand and express their reality. More than using the 'magic' of movies and the possibilities of omnipresence, it offers to tell a story; the cinematography of *La nación clandestina* seeks to adapt itself to its characters, who are also its spectators. In that regard Sanjinés has said: 'We consider that this new type of visual language adapts itself to some internal rythms of our country's mentality.' The dramatic, ideological, poetic and aesthetic result of *La nación clandestina* is synthetised in the filmic treatment with which it expresses, in fading fashion, the complex problems of a country. While social and political, the treatment reaches symbolic, spiritual and mythical levels that very few Latin American films have achieved.

It is really hard to find a great film that does not have great cinematography and an outstanding musical score at the same time. César Pérez's cinematography has splendid moments, above all because since it deals with a trip where the natural geography changes as Sebastián moves along his path, thus expressing different emotional states. From the very vast desert to the deepest mountains, Bolivia's geography allows for masterful shots that express the smallness and solitude of the individual. In one of the final sequences of the dance scene, filmed with a powerful zoom, the camera starts pulling back until it shows the group of people as a miniscule and marginal group of humans within the great panorama. In another sequence Sebastián abandons La Paz and observes the scattered hamlet from a high mountain. The seduction and rape of Basilia takes place in a ravine that is as impressive as the man's violent act. At other times the cinematography tries expressive experimentalism, as when the camera gyrates many times around a group of people. Regarding Cergio Prudencio's music, the use of intonations developed from Indian culture is magnificent, as is its use based exclusively on natural instruments. In that aspect the film also reaches the artistic authenticity for which it longs.

Jorge Ruffinelli

REFERENCES

Gumucio Dagrón, A. (1982) *Historia del cine en Bolivia*. La Paz: Amigos del Libro (Revised edition, *Historia del cine boliviano*, México: Universidad Nacional Autónoma de México, 1983).

Luis, M. (1999) '*La nación clandestina*', in A. Elena & M. Díaz López (eds) *Tierra en trance: el cine latinoamericano en cien películas*. Madrid: Alianza, 370–4.

Pick, Z. M. (1978) *Latin America Film-makers and the Third Cinema*. Ottawa: Carleton University.

Sánchez, J. (1999) *The Art and Politics of Bolivian Cinema*. Lanham, MD: Scarecrow Press.

Sanjinés, J. (1979) *Teoría y práctica de un cine junto al pueblo*. México: Siglo XXI. (English edition, *Theory and Practice of a Cinema with People*, Willimantic, CT.: Curbstone Press, 1989).

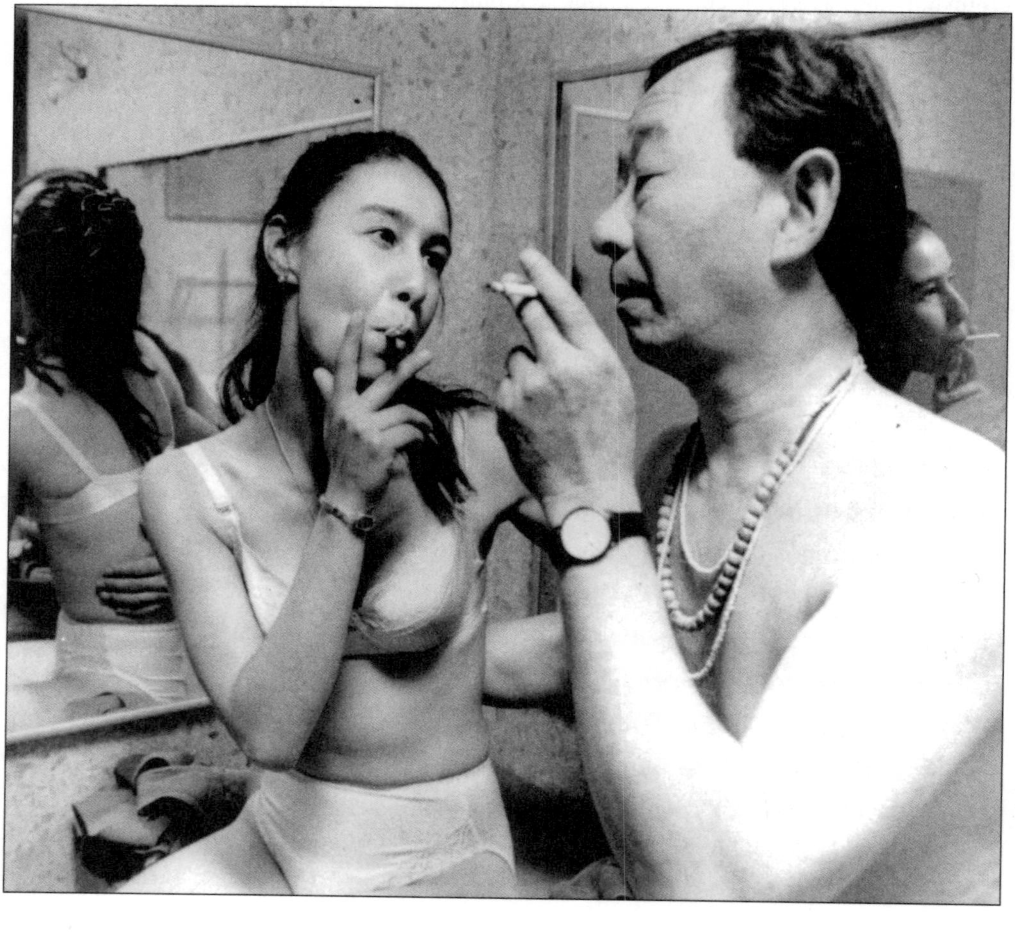

PRINCIPIO Y FIN BEGINNING AND END

21

ARTURO RIPSTEIN, MEXICO, 1993

Principio y fin. The very title of the film clues us into the narrative structure which closes in on itself, forming a circle of suffering and grief. At the beginning of the film a death occurs, or more precisely, we see the reaction of a family upon the sudden death of the father. Then begins the slow, irrevocable decline of each family member ending, finally, with another death – this time a double suicide. Beginning and ending at a similar point seals off the circle. There is no escape. Yet we should not oversimplify the circular narrative as a mere causal chain of events. What we are dealing with here is a complicated process in which we witness, step by step, the inevitable fulfillment of a tragic destiny. The circular form is not only a stylistic device that serves as a narrative structure for the film, it is the essence of the tragic dimension of the characters who cannot escape their destiny.

One day, while Gabriel and Nicolás are at school, they are told that their father has died. They go home to be with the rest of the family, comprised of their mother, their sister Mireya and their older brother Guama, all grief-stricken at the unexpected death. With the visit of the Guardiolas, old friends of the deceased father, we see that the family is facing financial ruin, and that Nicolás is in love with the young Natalia Guardiola. With poverty and an uncertain future looming near, each character is faced with the question of his or her own survival as well as the survival of the rest of the family. The instinctual drives of the characters are revealed under the light of this 'family darwinism'. The first one to leave is Guama, uninterested in education, bohemian in his ways and who, as his mother says, is destined to failure. He ends up as a singer and a bouncer at a run-down bar (El Tío Vivo) owned by a paternalistic, mafioso-styled pimp called Polvorón. It is not long before he finds himself living with one of the local prostitutes. For her part, Mireya takes on sewing jobs to keep food on the family table. Alone all day in a small room, accompanied only by the constant hum of the sewing machine, Mireya finally gives herself to the neighbourhood baker, whom she meets secretly in the warm backroom of the bakery.

Mr. Guardiola tries to help the family by hiring Gabriel and Nicolás to tutor Natalia and her brother. To the dismay of Nicolás, Gabriel seduces Natalia and soon after the two families agree to their marriage. Gabriel will gradually become the family's hope for salvation. He convinces his mother to let him study at the university. With his intelligence and good looks – he is repeatedly told he looks like a prince or an angel – it seems that Gabriel will save the family from poverty. Nicolás must give up his dream of becoming a writer and begins to work so that Gabriel can go to the university and socialise with the upper class. Nicolás will be forced to renounce his love for Julia, a woman he meets in Veracruz, to continue to support Gabriel and finally, in yet another act of self-sacrifice, he willingly agrees to marry Natalia when she has been abandoned by Gabriel and is expecting his child. By this time Guama has become a drug dealer to help pay for Gabriel's expenses, and Mireya, destitute in her loneliness and desire after being abandoned by the baker, turns to prostitution. Just when it looks like Gabriel is going to fulfill his ambitions, his embarrassing truth is revealed when Mireya is arrested, one of her clients having died on her in the middle of a session. Ashamed and dishonored in the eyes of his conservative benefactors, Gabriel convinces his sister to kill herself, and she willingly accepts. When Gabriel sees what he has done, he cannot bear the guilt and he kills himself as well.

The film is based on the novel by the Egyptian writer and Nobel Prize winner Naguib Mahfuz. The film's plot remains essentially faithful to Mahfuz's text. However, the novel's action takes place in 1930s Egypt while the film is situated in modern-day Mexico, thus bringing to the fore a series of contextual and formal changes. In the novel, the Muslim setting focuses on the familial and social dictates of honor and dishonor. Loss of status and dishonor are contextualised within a social framework. This is carried through, to a degree, into Ripstein's film, yet it differs in that character motivation is more abstract, more related to deep, instinctual drives, which arise when the survival of each member of the family is threatened. In a sense, the characters are pared down to ambition and desire, whereas in the novel, character motivation is embedded within the reference points of religion and social status. In fact, in the novel, when the characters are at their most desperate, they look to religion, while the film's characters lack this point of support. Thus, in Ripstein and Paz Alicia Garcíadiego's adaptation, even though the social and moral framework is present, it is overriden by the pathos that drags the characters to their fall. There is a particularly revealing example of this in the scene where Guama arrives home in a fright and asks his mother to keep a package for him. The content of the package is not revealed; we only know that his life depends on it. In this brief moment, mother and son recall the idyllic days of Guama's childhood, now lost forever. When Guama leaves, his mother, still lingering on her memories, opens the box and finds it contains drugs. She furiously pours the drugs down the drain. But just as the last of the drugs whirl down, she realises she has condemned her own son to his death. It is this destructive nature of human impulses that drives the characters to act; even though they may repent, they cannot go back and set things right. This is the nature of the pathos underlying character motivation, and the same happens with Mireya. Having become a prostitute because of her family's poverty, destined as well by her lack of physical beauty (as she says, 'We ugly ones are only ugly, we're neither decent nor indecent'), and in part by her own passion ('I don't care about the money. I do it because I'm a whore, because I like it'), eventually brings about her own destruction as well as destroying the one she loves the most – her brother Gabriel.

The 'excess' which characterises the protagonists, the pathos and the primitive drives in their personal relationships, reveal a disturbing subtext systematically present in the film: that of incest. The family members are constantly caressing each other in a distinctly ambiguous manner, such as in the scene where Gabriel helps his mother to dry off after her shower. It is at that moment when he convinces her to choose him as the one to save the family. Gabriel's relationship with his siblings is also marked by explicit bodily contact. In fact, Gabriel is the one who instigates as well as receives incestuous leanings. Incest is never outwardly manifested, yet it undoubtedly underlies the familial relationships; by taking its inspiration from elements of classical tragedy, the narrative discourse is allowed to go beyond the limits of melodrama.

The *mise-en-scene* also creates parallel levels that reflect the dramatic aspects of the film. The music presents an important series of intertextual references that richly enhance the narrative and visual image. Apart from his mediocre life as a civil servant, the only notable characteristic we know about the deceased father, Narciso Botero, is his love of opera. At the beginning of the film, when Guama sees the corpse, he puts on a record of an operatic aria. The music begins at the point where Rigoletto, the main character in Giuseppe Verdi's famous opera, is thinking about his dead wife, and sings '*Ah! non parlare al misero/del suo perduto bene*'. Rigoletto will remain a continual reference in the film, even at the narrative level. Gabriel wins the favour of his future benefactor Luján, as Luján sees they both share a love of opera, and in fact, he tells him that his father had a special aria of Rigoletto for everyone in the family. Gabriel's aria was, naturally, '*Bella figlia dell'amore*', whose melody is heard in several scenes of the film. The insistent presence of the melody reflects Gabriel's role in bringing about the downfall of the entire family. Other references to Rigoletto confirm the important role of the music. At the bar, for example, Guama sings '*Questa o quella per me pari sono*' for the prostitutes and their clients; and in the shower the mother hums '*La donna è mobile*'. This intertextual reference is carried though to the melodramatic structure of the opera. Rigoletto is the story of a father who tries to protect his daughter, yet unwittingly causes her death. An inescapable destiny (a rival curses the family) is fulfilled. The musical reference to the melodrama thus constitutes an important pillar in the narrative structure. Other musical allusions are made at a more popular level as well. The two boleros sung in the film connote a romantic, idealised notion of love, yet they are heard in squalid bars. Therefore, we have a certain distancing effect because of the extreme incongruity between the sentimental tone of the music and the images on the screen. The contrast is brought out, for example, through the use of the romantic bolero that is initially associated to Nicolás' love story with Julia. The same bolero is heard later, with a close-up shot of her dying father's face. The association of the bolero with this image of death reflects the fact that it will be impossible for Nicolás and Julia, as well as any of the characters, to find consolation through love.

The music brings us to another essential aspect of the audiovisual narrative: its melodramatic structure. *Principio y fin* is, like the majority of Ripstein and Garcíadiego works of the 1990s, a study in the limits of melodrama as a film genre. The implications are great, given that the melodrama is traditionally one of the most popular genres with Mexican filmmakers. Inherent in the very nature of melodrama is that music, rhythm and narrative time are basic elements of the plot. Yet this particular melodrama (as mentioned above in reference to pathos) goes further, reaching towards an epic tragedy.

Stretching the limits of melodrama toward tragedy was part of Garcíadiego's plan. In an interview with Manuel Pérez Estremera, she comments on the character of Gabriel, believing 'He gave a tragic bent to the melodramatic story. And meshing the two genres was, frankly, an unavoidable challenge'. We might ask if there is anything in the musical score that adds a tragic dimension to the film; this would highlight the other main musical motif in the film score – the unmistakable rhythm of Franz Schubert's quartet number 14 in D minor, D. 810, also known as *Death and the Maiden*. The title comes from the melody of the second movement, which Schubert takes from his composition *Der Tod und das Mädchen*, based on a poem by Matthias Claudius. In the poem a young maiden meets death, who tells her not to be afraid because death is not cruel and that she should let herself be taken up into his loving arms. In this same sense, death is a solution and a haven for Mireya who, from the very outset, is identified with Schubert's melody. The first time we hear the music is when the baker seduces her. Throughout the film, it marks typically melodramatic moments for Mireya. The musical motif is also associated with Gabriel's first suicide attempt, and is heard again at the end (at the shot of Mireya's red shoes), bringing a deeply tragic meaning to the film.

Aside from music, the conventions of melodrama are also surpassed through two essential elements in the narrative structure. The first is the absence of a final moral, that is, of a clear definition of good and evil. In his insightful analysis of *Principio y fin*, the Brazilian critic Paulo Antonio Paranaguá states that 'the film-makers turn [the melodramatic structure] around 180 degrees, they go beyond mere appearances, as if to reveal the inextricable intermeshing of love and hate, good and evil.' Not clarifying the moral contradicts typical melodramatic structure, where a choice is always made and which is meant to be a lesson for the spectator. In this film, however, the characters have no choice. Once their passions have been unleashed they are driven to fulfill a destiny that is predetermined from the very start. Hence, a moral determination of their actions would be meaningless.

There is another, perhaps even more important, element that carries the film beyond the boundaries of melodrama, and which has to do with the question of style. The *mise-en-scène* is intimately related to the way time is constructed in the film. In a conventional melodrama, temporal pace is an essential element in constructing emotions within the plot. The narrative typically develops diachronically, in which a past is constructed and becomes the place for emotions – normally painful ones – to be manifested. The passing of time is typically related to loss, a loss whose presence is continually felt in the present through symbols, objects or actions that give an added dimension to the nostalgia felt by the characters. This is the nostalgia Mireya feels as she looks at herself in the mirror wearing the wedding veil she will never use. Other characters feel this as well, such as Julia, Nicolás' lover, or the prostitute who lives with Guama. These women are tied to a past that painfully emerges, and Nicolás or Guama are tragically incapable of saving them.

The Botero characters, on the other hand, do not anchor their emotions in the past. They are trapped in another type of temporality, which we will call synchronic, that is, a temporality that is geared to the immediate outlet of their passions, and to a vague hope of a future that will never arrive. Narrative time thus reflects their passion of the moment, and the notion of duration is essential, as time is condensed in every scene. The nature of synchronic time is reflected in the circularity of tragic time. There is no progession, no maturation process in the characters, nor in the plot itself. There is only stagnation. The characters are fossilised, petrified after the death of their father, caught up in a circular time that continually brings them back to where they started, until the inevitable is fulfilled.

This brings us to propose that the most striking element of the *mise-en-scène* in *Principio y fin* is the systematic use of the sequence shot, or *plan séquence*. The most notable characteristic of the film style is that the scenes are not segmented. Nearly every scene is filmed with only one shot. There is no fragmentation, no shot/reverse-shot sequences, nor are there cuts in the vast majority of the scenes. At times, this technique is striking, as in the scene where the mother, Ignacia Botero, visits Mr. Guardiola to ask him for help. During their dialogue, they are in a close-up shot in profile. The camera pans alternatively from one to the other as each one speaks, thus breaking the conventional shot/reverse-shot sequence.

Limiting each scene to just one shot makes the *mise-en-scène*, the lighting, character movement and camera dynamism the true formal buttress of the film. We should note that the sequence shot in *Principio y fin* is not so much a question of creating a dramatic space (as we find, for example, in the films of Kenji Mizoguchi or Theo Angelopoulos), as it is a detailed observation of the characters in terms of the length of the scene. Thus, in the make-up of each sequence shot, freedom of camera movement is absent. What the camera nearly always does is follow the characters as they move along.

For the most part, the complexity of *mise-en-scène* goes unnoticed. Though the characters occupy the central focus, a certain distance is drawn, and this is something that also goes beyond the limits of melodrama. At the beginning of the film, when the members of the family come in to see the deceased father, the scene lasts approximately six minutes. It consists of a meticulously planned 'choreography' in which the characters enter and exit. As they enter we see their individual reactions that give us the first clue toward how they will behave as the narrative unfolds. The long take technique is used to a greater extent at the end of the film. In a shot that lasts over eight minutes, the camera follows Gabriel and Mireya at the public baths where they will both commit suicide. The camera follows them as they climb up several flights of stairs, recording Mireya's suicide, before following Gabriel in his delerious, guilt-ridden state, all the way to the top floor, whereupon he takes his own life. In spite of the enormous complexity of this 'rise to hell', the camera is always subordinate to Gabriel. There is no attempt to endow the scene with emotion by using the typical technique of showing a close-up of the suffering character's face. The camera nearly always follows Gabriel, and so we rarely see his full face. In sum, the feeling of space conveyed, the color and light variations (the contrast of blue and yellow tones in the hallways, the red tones of the top floor), the obsessive beating of the drums and, above all, the elaboration of pace and time, are what transmit an authentic sense of tragedy to Gabriel's feelings of guilt and his final decision to kill himself.

Distancing emotion and eschewing the conventional technique of filming a close-up of the actor's face allows us to contemplate the characters from a privileged position and offers us a clearer understanding of their tragic destiny. In this sense, there is a key object in the *mise-en-scène* which has an essential narrative function: the mirror. Mirrors appear in nearly every scene. On the one hand, it makes the closed, unfragmented spaces more dynamic. It also creates a distancing, self-questioning perspective for the protagonists themselves. Both Gabriel and the prostitute who lives with Guama smash their mirrors because they cannot bear to see their own reflections. For Mireya, the mirror is the only place she can play out her fantasies, yet, or perhaps because of this, the room where she meets her clients is also filled with mirrors. There are many similar examples for other characters as well. For the protagonists the insistent presence of the mirror presents an incomprehensible enigma: the enigma of their own tragic destiny. Trapped in the circularity of their own reflection, blinded by passion, subjugated to the rhythm of circular time, and unable to progress, they inevitably follow the path to their own destruction. Arthur Ripstein himself declared to Pérez Estremera that 'Circularity, formally speaking, is a moving camera with no cuts in the scene, the emphasis being on the camera movement itself. So the way I see it is that editing is no longer the main thrust of the narrative, it doesn't serve our needs. What we are trying to do is film time.'

This circular time, having come fully around, nevertheless brings us to an ending that questions a solely tragic reading of the film. What we have, rather, is an exploration of the place where tragedy and melodrama converge through a rhetorical technique that combines the registers of both genres. On the one hand, we have Schubert's deeply tragic music and, on the other, a typically melodramatic element; an object that condenses emotion into a symbol. The symbol in this case is a close-up of Mireya's red shoes. They are the only things left of a life devoured by passion, yet, in a final gesture, this scrap of a life reclaims an emotional identification from the spectator.

Vicente J. Benet

REFERENCES

Elena, A. (1999) '*Principio y fin*', in A. Elena & M. Díaz López (eds) *Tierra en trance: el cine latinoamericano en cien películas*. Madrid: Alianza, 400–4.

Paranaguá, P. A. (1997) *Arturo Ripstein*. Madrid: Cátedra/Filmoteca Española.

Pérez Estremera, M. (1995) *Correspondencia inacabada con Arturo Ripstein*. Huesca: Festival de Cine de Huesca.

TERRA ESTRANGEIRA FOREIGN LAND

22

WALTER SALLES, JR. AND DANIELA THOMAS, BRAZIL, 1995

> It is, therefore, a great source of virtue for the practiced mind to learn, bit by bit, first to change about invisible and transitory things, so that afterwards it may be able to leave them behind altogether. The man who finds his homeland sweet is still a tender beginner; he to whom every soil is as his native one is already strong; but he is perfect to whom the entire world is as a foreign land.
>
> – Hugo of St. Victor

Although never explicitly evoked by Walter Salles or Daniela Thomas, this well-known quote from Hugo of St. Victor's *Didascalicon* – often quoted in recent times by literary critics such as Auerbach or Said – clearly frames the work of the authors of this seminal film, which synthetises the best efforts of the revival of Brazilian cinema in the last decade. Perhaps echoing the concept of *terra aliena* used by the great Medieval thinker, Salles and Thomas, during a crucial period of social, political as well as cinematic upheaval, question their country's identity and the effects of distanciation, exile and utopia. Hugo of St. Victor continued in his thesis with the claim that, 'The tender soul has fixed his love on one spot in the world; the strong man has extended his love to all places; the perfect man has extinguished his.' But for Alex and Paco, the two main characters of *Terra estrangeira*, distance and strangeness fail to offer solutions to their confusion and rootlessness. Far from assuming the ascetic, albeit optimistic, creed expressed by Hugo, the film's discourse critically questions the place in the world of a whole generation and the country they come from.

With credits that feature a visa stamp of the República Federativa do Brasil, *Terra estrangeira* opens in March 1990, a historic moment in Brasil's recent history. Fernando Collor de Mello, the first democratically elected President, following many years of military dictatorship, had announced a series of traumatic economic measures that would have a profound impact on Brazilian society. Among these measures, the freezing of bank deposits in order to reduce stock circulation and fight inflation would have the most widespread impact. However, that very same day, as part of the extensive set of measures aimed at turning the *Brasil Grande* so often invoked by the military dictatorship into another *Brasil Grande* as envisaged under the aegis of a neo-liberal government, the new president also shut down Embrafilme (Brazilian Film Enterprise), the state agency in charge of the production, distribution and promotion of Brazilian cinema. Overnight, the country's film industry would become completely paralysed, and its production would decrease to negligible proportions over the next few years. Walter Salles was one of the few film-makers able to shoot a film in these confused times. The film was *A grande arte* (*Exposure*, 1991), an English language thriller with an international cast, which probably accounted for Salles' ability to secure the funding to make the film.

Only two years later, with Collor's presidency accused of corruption, vice-president Itamar Franco came to power. With him came hope that Brazillian cinema may be reborn. This time it counted on the strong support of regional and municipal governments for production and distribution, specially RioFilme, an office dependent on the Rio de Janeiro city council. Another key element in that process was the enactment in 1994 of the so-called Audiovisual Law and its successful policy of tax exemption for film investments. The first fruits of such initiatives would be seen in 1995, when 12 films were shot, among them *Terra estrangeira* and *Carlota Joaquina, princesa do Brasil* (*Carlota Joaquina, Princess of Brazil*), a demythologising historical vision shot by Carla Camurati, a young actress turned film-maker. This film achieved, against all odds, extraordinary success and again drew audiences back to cinemas to see a home-grown product. Movies such as *Yndio do Brasil* (*Our Indians*, Silvio Back, 1995), *Um ceu de estrelas* (*A Starry Sky*, Tata Amaral, 1996), *Como nascem os anjos* (*How Angels are Born*, Murilo Salles, 1996), *Pequeno diccionário amoroso* (*Little Book of Love*, Sandra Werneck, 1996), *O sertão das memórias* (*Landscape of Memories*, José Araújo, 1996), and *Baile Perfumado* (*Perfumed Dance*, Paulo Caldas and Lírio Ferreira, 1997), not to mention the local blockbusters that had an eye on the international market, such as *O quatrilho* (*The Quartet*, Fábio Barreto, 1995), *Tieta do Agreste* (Carlos Diegues, 1996), and *O que é isso, companheiro?* (*Four Days in September*; Bruno Barreto, 1997), would herald the beginning of a new *cinema novo*. Of these, the greatest contribution to the revaluation and revitalisation of Brazilian cinema being Salles' *Central do Brasil* (*Central Station*, 1998), which was awarded the Golden Bear at the Berlin International Film Festival.

Terra estrangeira, considered by some the most successful and interesting of Salles' work, was made between his more conventional debut, *A grande arte*, and his international success, *Central do Brasil*. Co-directed with the playwright and set-designer Daniela Thomas, it is one of the most emblematic films from this new generation of Brazilian film-makers. In analysing the style governing the revitalised cinema, Salles pointed to some clues as to the construction of *Terra estrangeira*'s narrative, 'The unity of this new cinema is rooted in the desire to reflect the reality of the country. There is also the will to share something: although we don't look like a unified group from an aesthetic point of view, we do constitute a movement of young directors in search, through parallel paths but by using different ways, of an essentially Brazilian way of cinematographic expression that reflects our country. And that idea already put forward by *cinema novo* could be the vehicle we need: to put the real face of Brazil in front of the camera, to frame reality again, that reality from which cinema and, above all, television, have been escaping from; to show who we are and where we come from.' An authentic declaration of intent, this statement allows us to clearly identify the worries and concerns that feed *Terra estrangeira* and that vigorously thrive beneath the misleading look of a conventional *film noir*.

The story of *Terra estrangeira* starts simultaneously in São Paulo and Lisbon, at the very moment of Collor de Mello's electoral success. Alex barely makes ends meet working as a waitress in Portugal, and is involved in a troubled relationship with Miguel, another young Brazilian man who is enmeshed in a smuggling operation to support his drug habit. Meanwhile, in Brazil, Paco, a young student of physics who actually wants to become an actor, will be one of the numerous victims of the economic policy of the new government. Son of a Basque woman who dreams of going back to San Sebastián before she dies, Paco will acknowledge the impossibility of such a dream just as Collor enacts the freezing of bank deposits. Unable to overcome the shock, his mother dies. Paco finds escape from the failing economy by smuggling diamonds, an operation that will take him to Lisbon, which he hopes will enable him to visit San Sebastián, in homage to his mother and perhaps to secure a future outside of Brazil. While the smuggling becomes a tangled web of deceit and betrayal, Paco meets Alex and – following Miguel's death – together they begin their journey to San Sebastián leaving behind the lives they are desperate to escape from.

The film traces the collapse of Paco's world – his mother, his fondness for theatre, the Paulist district around the Minhocão traffic overpass and its female underwear advertisements whose brand, *Hope*, acquires a deeply ironic connotation in the film's sombre overture – though the economic crisis will force him, as well as many other Brazilians during the Collor years (400,000 according to official statistics) to emigrate abroad to seek new fortunes. Brazil, a land of immigration for centuries, became for the first time, a departure point for a disaffected nation. Entering Europe, Paco throws himself into an '*estranha forma de vida*' ('a strange lifestyle'), as conveyed by the title of an old *fado* by Amália Rodrigues, which is performed by an enigmatic singer in a Lisbon club where he first joins the smugglers and realises that others before him have tried that blind escape forward, but without apparent success. It is also where he meets Alex.

'Sometimes I am scared of being alone in this place I've not chosen. The more time that passes, the more foreign I feel', confesses Alex in one of the opening sequences, before meeting Paco and walking with him to Cabo Espichel in one of the film's most beautiful scenes. 'They had to be courageous to cross this sea five hundred years ago!' Alex says, sitting on the edge of the great cliffs. 'They thought that paradise was over there. Poor Portuguese! It was Brazil that they discovered!' An initial reading could see the film as being both a *film noir* and road movie, but as it increases in complexity, *Terra estrangeira* is a portrait of a generation in its efforts to find its own identity in an inclement world that disturbs them, and a metaphor of a whole country under crisis, traumatically facing its past and present and uncertain future. Salles' and Thomas' wise move, and the one that confers on the film its extraordinary strength, is to resist a symbolic or overtly discursive tone. The film is a story of exile and hopeless love in which, finally, everything revolves around the relationship conceived by both youngsters as the only possibility of overcoming their circumstances. As will happen later in the second collaboration between Salles and Thomas, *Meia noite* (*Midnight*, 1999), a fortuitous meeting in the middle of a crisis will open a hopeful path for its protagonists. But the possibility of a brighter future, as in *Meia noite,* is ultimately doomed.

Terra estrangeira is less discursive than it is emotional. Even those images that allow an allegorical reading, especially the flooding of Paco's apartment after his mother's death and the abandoned boat he and Alex find on the seashore as they escape towards the Spanish border, work primarily as visual impressions. Walter Carvalho accentuates the expressionistic tones of these scenes through his black and white photography, which depicts the uncertainty of the characters. Jorge Ruffinelli is thus right in stressing the physical dimension of the more symbolic elements in the film: 'The image of the boat stranded offshore and the embracing of the lovers – these two "orphans" of a fatherland – in such a lonely landscape, affords Salles a superb metaphor of economic stagnation and personal distress.' But there are other emblematic sequences in the film. When Alex and Paco make their break for the Spanish border in the middle of the night, the camera shows their conversation from the outside of the windscreen of the car. The mist covering the windows emphasises their difficulty in coping with an uncertain future. Above all it creates an aura of mystery around their relationship; in a scene which builds up to an intense sexual encounter in the close confines of the car, the characters' movements are punctuated by fades to black.

Salles has talked about the twilight look oozed by *Terra estrangeira*, following on from the economic depression both he and Thomas were victims of during Collor's term in power: 'Plunged in despair, we wanted to talk about it in black and white, as if it was archival footage of other times. *Terra estrangeira* is thus the reflection of a generation going through an identity crisis, and of a country uncertain about itself, in the middle of a crisis of self-esteem.' Putting aside initial references to the economic measures adopted by Collor's government – deliberately depicted by the authors through television images – the film avoids becoming a chronicle of events. Instead, it seeks to rebuild the atmosphere of confusion, bitterness and suffering that so deeply marked the Brazilian people at that time and a young generation forced to face a *journey*, both outside and inside their homeland, in search of self-knowledge. As Jean-Claude Bernardet remarked, Alex and Paco are drifters 'pushed by an impulse or chance without any projection in the future (except perhaps for an immediate future), without plans, and without any understanding of the events that surround them'. They are mere instruments in the plans of others; tragic heroes who, like the characters of classic noir thrillers, have no way out.

From their introduction in the film, Alex and Paco live a non-stop, breathless existence, always dreaming of moving to a new foreign land where they will find that inner peace that eludes them. But in the last section of the film, pursued by thugs, this escape becomes a desperate getaway that makes the distant Portuguese-Spanish border an illusory door to happiness; where San Sebastián or central Europe will put an end to their rootlessness. Thus, *Terra estrangeira* becomes a peculiar road movie. The genre, beloved by Salles, which he returns to in *Central do Brasil*, also gave shape to the narrative of the earlier *A grande arte*. He points out that 'It is true that somehow all my films are about wandering, and this involves two evident consequences: firstly, the idea of loss, for all running forward necessarily involves some loss; and secondly, the possibility of finding people, the possibility of change.' It is not surprising that some of the director's favourite films are road movies: *Alice in den Städten* (*Alice in the Cities*, Wim Wenders, 1973), *Professione: Reporter* (*The Passenger*, Michelangelo Antonioni, 1975), and, never completely abandoning the Brazilian context, *Vidas secas* (*Barren Lives*, Nelson Pereira dos Santos, 1963).

Salles' gladly acknowledged debt to *cinema novo* receives various references in his films. *Central do Brasil* makes it explicit by means of its tribute to Glauber Rocha. But it is the realistic and humanistic orientation of Pereira dos Santos that seems to guide Salles' steps: 'Nelson Pereira dos Santos' cinema owns a clear look, a unique ability to translate what Brazil was, to make poetry rise from very particular conditions'. Attributing to himself the role of heir of 'Neorealism revised by *cinema novo*' as opposed to '*Neon-realism* of 1990s' cinema', Salles assumes the heritage of the Brazilian road movie as a means for discovering Brazil; an interior Brazil, deep and secret in *Central do Brasil* and a search for identity in exiled youngsters in *Terra estrangeira*. Unlike *Iracema* (Jorge Bodanzky and Orlando Senna, 1974, but kept censored until 1980) or *Bye Bye Brasil* (*Bye Bye Brazil*, Carlos Diegues, 1979), in which the notion of a journey was used to expose audiences from urban and developed centres to the little known reality of the interior of the country and in this way express a very critical attitude to the megalomaniac plans of a military dictatorship determined at all costs to give birth to its particular *milagre economico* (economic miracle), Salles' characters travel mostly in search of themselves. Their trips, like the films of Wenders and Antonioni, have an existential component.

In its conditions of production and texture, *Terra estrangeira* also reminds us of some of the features of *cinema novo*. Produced by Salles' own company, Videofilmes, together with a Portuguese co-producer and the support of RioFilme, the film had a relatively low budget and was shot over a short period. It also had a high percentage of inexperienced crew members as many professionals had moved into television and advertising after the collapse of the film industry in 1990. Two names stand out among those contributorss: composer José Miguel Wisnik and Fernando Alves Pinto, a young actor who held his own against the more experienced Fernanda Torres. Walter Carvalho, the veteran director of photography – who had just completed work on Salles' celebrated short film *Socorro Nobre* (1995) – embraced the director's decision to shoot in black and white. Deliberately working against the use of vivid colours, a staple of Brazilian cinema and television, the darker tones convey the mood of this deeply sad and unsettling story. But, as José Carlos Avellar emphasised, one of the most illuminating aspects of the film is that 'its visual quality of image somehow comes from the peculiar way of the shooting of Brazilian cinema of the 1960s, the age of *cinema novo*: hand-held camera, natural light, shooting on location, setting the operator in the middle of the scene as any other character in the film, action that seems to be improvised or created in that moment – without previous preparation or rehearsal – as if the camera would have recorded it by chance. On the other hand, the choice of black and white is a way of depicting the colourless universe of the characters, as well as a reference to those films produced in a moment in which Brazilian film-makers (and, with them, most of the youth) wanted to invent, not just a new cinema, but a new country.'

One of the unique features of *Terra estrangeira* is that it was not actually filmed in Brazil. Salles, the son of a notable Brazilian diplomat and banker, had lived abroad for many years, studying in Switzerland and in the United States. Thomas had also spent some years in Great Britain and the United States, studying cinema and performing arts. Although neither of them may be considered a victim of forced exile in Collor's times, the experience of filming in Portugal – the preferred destination of many young people that left the country during those years – would force them not only to face the feeling of remoteness already known to both, but also to confront it with a new experience: the awareness of marginality, racism and North-South inequality. 'Cabaret of colonies', as Miguel would sarcastically describe Portugal at the beginning of the film, remains a destination for many exiles, from Latin America and Africa. Alex, a waitress in a modest restaurant-bar, increasingly feels the pressure of the racist attitudes provoked by her accent ('it is as if the sound of my voice offends them'), and verifies that the value of Brazilian passports in the black market is substantially lower. On the other hand, Brazilians are an elite next to the African immigrants crowding Lisbon's streets. Thus, when Paco complains about his situation to Loli, an Angolan immigrant he meets – played by José Laplaine, who went on to direct *Macadam Tribu* (1996) – Loli angrily reminds him that his problems are minor compared to the situation in his own country, torn apart by war. When Salles became aware of the situation of African immigrants living on the edge, shortly before he began filming in Lisbon, he incorporated their plight into the script.

The dream of Europe affects most of the characters. For Miguel, it offers him the false hope of escape from his troubles. For Paco, San Sebastián is good enough, while Alex seems to have lost all ambition. Nevertheless, when Alex meets the younger Paco, she recovers some of the dreams of her youth, athough the only way she can realise them is by escaping from Spain. Their meeting represents a ray of hope. 'I think the film oscilates between despair and possible redemption', Salles explained, 'a redemption that is born from the discovery of the neighbour, the otherness, and the fact that, at a certain moment, Paco discovers Alex and Alex discovers Paco.' Only a few hundred metres from the Spanish border, and recovering her strength at a roadside diner, Alex starts humming an old song, *Vapor barato* (Cheap Boat), which seems to shake her recovered confidence:

Oh, yes, I'm so tired
But not so much that I can't tell you I'm leaving
I run through every street
To take that old boat
Honey, baby
I don't need much money, thank God
And I don't care

Alex mixes several lines of that popular song written by Waly Salomão – a well-known *baiano* poet close to the Tropicalist movement and a collaborator of Caetano Veloso and Maria Bethânia – and Jards Macalé, author of some film scores for Glauber Rocha, Joaquim Pedro de Andrade and Nelson Pereira dos Santos. Immortalised by Gal Costa in a 1972 recording, *Vapor barato* became the anthem for a whole generation who fought against the military dictatorship and who were forced to choose between despair or exile. In this way, *Vapor barato* assumes an important function in *Terra estrangeira*'s dénouement and creates a bridge between two different generations of Brazilian youngsters searching for a personal and a national plan.

But *Vapor barato* also gives the film an extraordinary emotional dimension. When Paco, seriously wounded and laying on Alex's lap after she has demolished the border barrier and is driving at high speed on Spanish land, seems to be dying, she tries to offer him encouragement so that he may have the chance of seeing his little utopia at last. When she no longer finds any words, she again sings the song and gradually her voice fades into Gal Costa's voice while an aerial shot isolates the car in the middle of a lonely landscape, once again moving forward towards an uncertain future. Although Salles insists on an open ending for the film and, by demolishing the barrier, giving the couple a glimpse of the future – no matter how uncertain it may be – it remains a beautifully enigmatic end, combining a lyrical romanticism with a bitter, even nihilistic, taint. Recalling similar shots from the memorable *They Live By Night* (Nicholas Ray, 1948), a film Salles' feature resembles in both tone and its closing moments, the shot once more isolates the characters, as they escape again, this time leaving them to their uncertain future. Unlike that other famous aerial shot that closed the masterly *Deus e o diabo na terra do sol* (*Black God, White Devil*, 1964) and to which Salles and Thomas could be paying homage, not even the omniscient narrator – the film-maker – seems to predict a better future than the one known to the characters. Contrary to the fulfilment of the prophecy in Glauber's film, due to the film-maker's visionary optimism, here the *sertão* will never become the sea. Alex and Paco may never arrive in San Sebastián. 'Nothing is definitive, not even pain', Alex had been told by a Portuguese friend. Perhaps that is the only comfort she can hold on to after so many broken dreams.

Alberto Elena

REFERENCES

Avellar, J. C. (1997) 'Brasil: para un espectador desatento/Brésil: à l'attention d'un spectateur inattentif', in *Cinémas d'Amérique latine*, 5, 5–16.

Debs, S. (1999) 'Un entretien avec Walter Salles/Una entrevista con Walter Salles', in *Cinémas d'Amérique latine*, 7, 91–7.

Filgueiras Steinberg, S. (ed.) (1997) *Terra estrangeira*. Rio de Janeiro: Relume Dumará/RioFilme.

Ruffinelli, J. (2000) 'Brasil 2001 and Walter Salles: Cinema for the Global Villlage?', in J. C. de Castro Rocha (ed.) *Brasil 2001*, special issue of *Portuguese Literary and Cultural Studies*, 4/5, 681–96.

Thomas, D., M. Bernstein & W. Salles (1996) *Terra estrangeira*. Rio de Janeiro: Rocco.

23

AMORES PERROS LOVE'S A BITCH

ALEJANDRO GONZÁLEZ IÑÁRRITU, MEXICO, 2000

At a time when most Latin American films struggle to attract audiences within their home markets, Alejandro González Iñárritu's *Amores perros* has become a resounding hit both in Mexico and abroad. In its storyline and characters, even in its fast-paced narrative style, *Amores perros* seems tailored to appeal to both a Mexican audience as well as to audiences across national borders. Nor is it surprising that the film does not hide its debt to a slick kind of Hollywood pop cinema. These are elements that have enabled it to circulate in global markets, but they are also features that help audiences focus on the central theme of *Amores perros*: the contradictions of cultural modernity in contemporary Latin American society.

One would need to go back nearly a decade, to Alfonso Arau's *Como agua para chocolate* (*Like Water for Chocolate*, 1992) to find a Mexican film that has done so well both commercially and critically internationally. But unlike Arau's film, *Amores perros* does not present a clichéd Mexico for tourists. This is a modern Mexico of cell phones, boom boxes and fast cars. And yet, beneath the façade of modern technology, the film reinforces certain impressions that the outside world has of a violent Mexican culture, particularly within the urban environment of Mexico City.

Having won the Ariel, the main national film award in Mexico, *Amores perros* was nominated for an Academy Award for best non-English-language film, a rare distinction for a Mexican motion picture. It has also received important awards at festivals in Cannes, Tokyo, Los Angeles, Havana, Chicago, São Paulo and Edinburgh. The critical and commercial success of González Iñárritu's film comes at a time when the Mexican film industry appeared to be going through its worst period since the early 1930s. In 1998, only eleven feature-films were produced; in 1999 the figure hit twenty-eight, but still the industry seemed anemic. Domestic audiences, however, began rallying to support a number of local films, such as the big box-office hit, *Sexo, pudor y lágrimas* (*Sex, Shame and Tears*, Antonio Serrano, 1999). So, from a local point of view, *Amores perros* suggested to many a rebirth of Mexican cinema if not the entire Mexican film industry.

Much of the critical notoriety surrounding the film comes from the impact of its depiction of violence embodied by the omnipresent dogs of the title. They are stark visual reminders of the violence that lurks beneath the façade of contemporary Latin American urban culture. Clearly playing on the popular perception of contemporary Mexico City as a place of danger, the film gradually moves us away from such facile cultural stereotypes and toward a more subtle interrogation of the illusion of modernity. Precisely because of its clever balance between the cultural specificity of its Mexican subject-matter and what might be termed as its transnational texture, *Amores perros* needs to be read not simply as a product of a revived Mexican cinema, but as a pointed interrogation of the position of Latin America's increasingly urbanised culture situated as it is in the slipzone between communities on the margins and mass-mediatised, global culture. That balance may readily be noted in the deftly-constructed script by Guillermo Arriaga Jordán which, as it captures the violence of contemporary Mexico City, also foregrounds an eccentric style of storytelling and editing, and a soundtrack easily recognizable as derived from certain foreign visual models (most notably, MTV and Quentin Tarantino's *Pulp Fiction*, 1994).

Other Latin American films before *Amores perros* have explored the conflicts and contradictions of rapid cultural change in a tradition-bound society. One thinks of Glauber Rocha's *O Draão da Maldade contra o Santo Guerreiro* (*Antonio das Mortes*, 1969) or Sara Gómez's *De cierta manera* (*One Way or Another*, 1974) or, a work that is closer to home for Mexican audiences, Luis Buñuel's *Los olvidados* (*The Young and the Damned*, 1950). Each of those films was set at a precise historical moment and addressed its theme from within the specificity of that society. For a Mexico reeling from decades of corrupt politicians, a demographic explosion, and the not unrelated increase of urban violence, González Iñárritu's film speaks in similarly culturally-specific ways of the contradictions of contemporary urban life at the end of the century. Importantly, it manages to do this in ways that also engage non-Mexican audiences.

The film opens with a stunning pre-credit sequence that establishes the tempo of speed and violence. A car races through the streets of Mexico City carrying two youths. Pursued by a truck that is fast closing in, the frantic car driver makes a series of sharp turns to throw off his pursuers. In the back seat of the car we see the bloodied, injured dog. The chase ends with the car crash and the first intertitle: 'Octavio and Susana.' The pre-credit sequence anchors the first story as a flashback, eventually returning to this very moment at its conclusion to underscore through repetition the centrality of the car crash in what will eventually be recognised as the film's three interlocking stories.

Octavio's story, set in a drab working-class neighborhood, involves two interconnected subplots: his sexual attraction toward his brother's wife, Susana, and his adoption of his brother's dog, Cofi, to use in illegal dogfights. Octavio hopes the money from these fights will enable him to run away with Susana. Though presented as two separate narrative threads, these situations mirror each other in their emphasis on the images of masculine rivalry: Octavio hires goons to beat up his brother; his long-time rival in the dogfights, whose dogs always lose to Cofi, winds up shooting Cofi, leading to the climax in which Octavio responds to this treachery by knifing the rival and escaping in his car, with the fallen leader's gang in hot pursuit.

At one point near the end of this story, as Octavio is preparing to go to his final dog fight, we see him in his room with his partner watching a television talk show, *Gente de Hoy* (*Today's People*), which features an attractive Spanish model, Valeria, and her dog Ricci. The omnipresent audio-visual technology becomes a virtual *mise-en-scène* that links Octavio's world with that of the characters of the second story, 'Daniel and Valeria.' Daniel is a magazine editor, and Valeria, a model, is his mistress. Their pairing, in fact, had been introduced earlier in Octavio's story when, driving his wife and children home, Daniel stops at a traffic light and looks up at a billboard announcing a French perfume. The larger-than-life model on the billboard is Valeria.

Having left his wife and children, Daniel sets up house with Valeria in a modern apartment. She goes off to buy champagne to celebrate their new living arrangement and is driving along the street when her car is hit by Octavio's car at an intersection. Removed from the vehicle, she undergoes painful leg surgery that leaves her wheelchair ridden. Her romantic idyll ends when she becomes obsessed with rescuing Ricci from a hole in the floorboards in which the dog has become lodged. When Daniel returns home from work a few days later, he finds Valeria lying unconscious on her bedroom floor, apparently having taken an overdose of medicines. The complications from her new fall necessitate the amputation of her leg. While she is recovering in hospital, Daniel finally manages to release Ricci from the floorboards. The story ends with the return of the couple and the dog to the apartment. From her wheelchair, Valeria looks out the window to discover the empty billboard across the street where earlier her perfume advertisement had stood, a final confirmation of the end of her career and the dream of an idyllic life with Daniel.

The third story involves Martín, *El Chivo*, a one-time revolutionary turned hired assassin who prowls the streets pushing a cart and surrounded by a pack of mangy dogs. He is offered the job of gunning down the partner of a young businessman, Gustavo. As it turns out, Luis, the intended victim, is also Gustavo's half-brother, thus mirroring in an upper-class setting the fratricidal rivalry of Octavio's story. Instead of killing Luis, as planned, and as he has been partially paid to do, Martín kidnaps the man, brings him home and ties him up. When Gustavo arrives to pay up the remaining amount for the murder, Martín ties up Gustavo and then prepares to depart for his own new life. That new life is symbolised by his shaving off his beard and cutting his hair. Martín leaves the two half-brothers to fight it out as he goes off to leave money and a message with his estranged daughter, Maru. In the final image of the film we see Martín walk down a road across an empty field toward the Mexico City high-rise silhouette accompanied by his trusted companion, Cofi, Octavio's dog, whom he rescued from the accident.

On the surface, the three stories seem to confirm the commonplace of the atomised world of the city with its rigid social stratification and isolation among the various social classes. Even though there is no single scene in which the three section's characters all meet, a careful reading of the film points to the interweaving of lives and itineraries in ways that belie the cliché of urban fragmentation. More than offering a sociological view of Mexico City, however, as some critics have suggested, González Iñárritu is depicting the circumstances that bind his characters together in a new moral and cultural landscape of spiritual desolation rooted in the modern megalopolis.

The city that the film describes is characterised by the continuous juxtapositions between the modern and primitive, between a glamorous world of televisual images and the leitmotifs of animalistic violence. That tension is perhaps best crystallised in a single image: prior to the last dog fight, we see Cofi in Octavio's room, transfixed by the television monitor as he looks at the staged image of Valeria and her dog, Ricci, on the television talk show. The moment underscores the way the television screen and the technologies of modern consumer culture characteristically feed the fantasy lives of those less fortunate. Each character has been nurtured on a series of mass-produced fictions that shape their desires and motivate their actions. Each of those fictions, in turn, seems tied to the dream of family that life in the city has somehow thwarted for them. Octavio's idyll is perhaps the most conspicuous of these fictions. He fantasises running off with Susana to set up house in the North. The dream contrasts sharply with the grim domestic world these characters find themselves in from the very first post-credit sequence: one of absented fathers, neglected children and a continual barrage of verbal violence. Daniel and Valeria seem also to have bought into that same kind of fiction but for them the dream is shattered not by a lack of money, but by the presence of a dog.

Martín is the only character who suggests a more nuanced version of that consumption of domestic fiction. The photo album he covets, showing pictures of the life he left behind as husband and father, includes snapshots of the young daughter he has been forced to abandon. She is now a grown woman, and Martín spies on her from afar. Unlike Octavio and Valeria, however, he no longer sees domestic bliss as the ultimate goal for which to strive. If he shows any signs of sentimentality, as when he saves the bloodied dog or leaves money for the daughter with whom he can only communicate through a telephone answering machine, there remains no doubt that he is still guided by the cold calculations of the hired assassin.

The film's title, *Amores perros*, is inadequately translated as *Love's a Bitch*, which fails to render the underlying meaning of the title as it underscores the condition of the three protagonists. In Spanish, using *perro*, a noun, as an adjective, suggests the instinctual, animal nature of their obsessions. Emphasising the power of instinctual desires rather than the characters themselves, the title thus reminds us that these are not unique, individuated characters, but rather psychological and, perhaps, social types. Octavio is locked at first in simple sibling rivalry. His desire for forbidden love quickly leads him to another obsession for his brother's dog, Cofi, a domesticated animal that Octavio has trained to fight to the death in the staged fights. In this way, the dog becomes an extension of the violent personality of his trainer.

Valeria, played by Spanish model and television actress, Goya Toledo, is the focal point of the tension between the commercially-constructed, superficial beauty of the publicity model and the obsessive self-centered spoiled child. When she appears in the television interview, she jokingly refers to her dog Ricci as her love child, an off-handed comment that underscores the visceral instinctual obsession for Ricci who indeed becomes the lost child whom she must save from beneath the floorboards. Though her fixation on rescuing the dog seems a frivolous plot motivation, it clearly leads to the debunking of her external beauty as she becomes as emotionally violent as Octavio in the previous story. Underscoring Valeria's vanity and her beauty as camouflage, we see her in the moment before the crash stop her car at a red light and take out her lipstick to color her lips, as if to refresh her mask.

Octavio and Valeria bear a certain emotional likeness to one other in their inability to see their lives after the crash as anything but tragic. Each is emotionally and physically immobilised by the accident, as though the loss of beauty and a career, in one case, and thwarted attempts at adultery in the other, were the essence of tragedy. Seen from the distanced perspective of Martín, whose narrative is continually juxtaposed against their would-be tragedies, Valeria and Octavio appear increasingly more like characters from one of the soap operas that has become a staple for Mexican audiences, than tragic hero and heroine they believe themselves to be.

Martín *El Chivo* is the opposite of these characters. A bourgeois turned revolutionary, turned vagrant and hired assassin, Martín is also revealed to be a caring father (the only patriarch present in the film) who nurtures his daughter with money and feeds the abandoned dogs he sees around him. In contrast to Octavio and Valeria, who, because of their obsessive desires, are unable to change, Martín is noteworthy precisely because he is a character who willingly seeks to transform himself in order to survive. He is also an all-seeing character and yet ironically invisible to most of the people around him. He is, in this regard, notable as the only character in the film with a past as well as the hint of a future. In the opening dialogue of the third episode, when the corrupt detective who is bringing Gustavo to meet Martín recounts the gunman's life as a revolutionary and terrorist fighting against the government, Gustavo laughs, 'like sub-comandante Marcos'. Without forcing a political reading of the film, the line helps the audience recognise Martín as the saboteur of bourgeois illusions of social normalcy to which the other characters in one way or another aspire.

The script imbues Martín with additional symbolic meaning through his narrative pairing with Cofi. In a telling cinematic gesture, González Iñárritu frames all of the stories through the silent presence of the dog who appears in both the pre-credit sequence and in the final images of the film as a potent reminder of the duality between the modern and the primitive that is at the heart of the film. When we see him at the beginning of Octavio's story he is simply a domesticated dog, almost invisible amidst the emotional clashes of the human characters. This omnipresent transparency is identical to Martín's situation as he roams with his pushcart and band of stray dogs through the streets of Mexico City, observing and sizing up his prey. When Martín retrieves Cofi after the car wreck, a critical bonding between the dog and his new master occurs that reveals them to be doubles of each other. The once domesticated Cofi, like Martín, has now turned professional killer. Tellingly, at the film's end, they walk together into the distance toward the smog-encrusted city. This final image pays homage to the ending of Vittorio De Sica's classic tale of an old man and a dog, *Umberto D* (1952), but, significantly, suppresses all possibilities of melodrama and sentimentality that framed Octavio and Valeria's images of their own fate.

While the characters and plotline of *Amores perros* are rooted in the topicality of contemporary Mexican urban culture, González Iñárritu's cinematic strategies are decidedly not. He conspicuously borrows from a variety of international cinematic sources, which, far from detracting from the film's power, lend force to its theme of the contradictions of Latin American modernity. As in Tom Tykwer's *Lola rennt* (*Run, Lola Run*, 1998), the fast-paced editing style is often made self-conscious, such as the extreme close-ups that emphasise a particular character's mental agitation. Editing is further emphasised through the careful use of soundtrack music, especially during the tense car chase sequence leading up to the crash, with music accentuating the chaos in the moments leading up to the crash. Yet, more than mere borrowed devices from other cultures, the soundtrack affirms a substantive transnational context for the film, one in which Mexico is not simply an isolated, exotic, 'other place', but a familiar urban *mise-en-scène* that is legible for audiences beyond Mexico. Combined with the frequent images of middle-class Mexico City, the music does much to undercut the potential exoticism of this world. It shatters the impression that this one more exotic Third World narrative by suggesting a more universal urban experience.

Along with the striking editing and soundtrack, the sense of the transnational is clearly evoked through a series of cinematic intertexts, the most of prominent of which is Quentin Tarantino's *Pulp Fiction*, a film from which *Amores perros* borrows freely for some of its stories as well as its narrative structure. Like Tarantino's film, this is an intricate set of interlocking stories and characters set in a violent urban space. The vast panorama of Tarantino's Los Angeles has been replaced by the less glittering cityscape of Mexico City. Despite the presumed cultural differences between the two locales, both are characterised cinematically by the similar intersecting of the lives of self-absorbed characters held together by an omnipresent car culture. González Iñárritu even has his hired killer, Martín, the Samuel L. Jackson character from *Pulp Fiction,* as the source of a distanced knowledge of the world otherwise denied the other characters.

While these and other situations appear to mirror Tarantino's cleverly constructed plots, the most substantive link between the two films is their emphasis on the 'pulp fictions' that help sustain the lives of characters in the city. In *Amores perros* the decisive fiction is one of an easy modernity to which nearly all of the characters seem to subscribe. In a Mexico City with its veneer of first-world urban culture, the protagonists are quickly stripped of that mask of modernity and reduced to their instincts. This is a space readily understood by audiences through the images of violence, a *mise-en-scène* that is both exotic and familiar to the non-Mexican audience by virtue of the global stylistics of violence in the media. The repeated return to the scene of the car crash underscores the perils of contemporary urban space. At any moment things may change and become menace and violence. It is not only the potential violence of the omnipresent dogs that follow Martín through the street. This is a world in which a businessman sitting in a restaurant for lunch with a colleague can be gunned down, where it seems almost natural to plot the disposal of one's brother or business partner, where even the police help you locate the appropriate assassin for the job.

The aura of urban violence, particularly in combination with the images of a youth gang in the first episode, has evoked for many critics and audiences outside of Mexico another cinematic intertext, Luis Buñuel's landmark film, *Los olvidados*. Though the Mexico City of González Iñárritu's film is far different from that depicted by Buñuel, the image of the violent city, especially the connection between violent youth and the mongrel motif, suggest an unavoidable cinematic genealogy for *Amores perros*. Indeed, both films share a commonality in the metaphoric links between animals and humans. As in *Los olvidados*, the insistent disruption of urban life by unexpected violence works as a reminder of the ever-present world of instincts that the modern city seeks to mask. This tension between the images of violence and order is pointedly used to underscore the contradictions of modernity at the foundation of this society. A more pointed Buñuelian homage is also quite apparent in the second story, in which Valeria is transformed into a Tristana type with the amputation of her leg and her tormenting of her lover.

Perhaps as strong as the Buñuelian trace is that of Buñuel's presumed Mexican heir, Arturo Ripstein. The desolation that marks the spaces of action of *Amores perros*, the fatalism of the characters, their often rapid descent from stoicism to violence, all seem to mirror the Mexico depicted in Ripstein's films of the last decade and a half. Ripstein's cinematic rendering of Mexico in *El imperio de la fortuna* (*Empire of Fortune*, 1985), is one within which the traditional forms of life are seen in the process of being contaminated and displaced by the superficial elements of modernity. For Ripstein, the outward trappings of modernity have transformed the folkloric, albeit false, images of traditional Mexican culture into a more universal space of personal disillusionment, fatalism and the postmodern sense of experience itself as having been recycled from bad movies. Characters like Martín and Octavio, who are beyond simple categories of good and evil, evoke the kind of morose world view that has become the hallmark of Ripstein's films in collaboration with Paz Alicia Garcíadiego: *El imperio de la fortuna*, *La mujer del puerto* (*The Woman from the Port*, 1991), *Principio y fin* (*Beginning and End*, 1993) and *Profundo carmesí* (*Deep Crimson*, 1996).

Such treatments of Mexico on screen have played extremely well with European audiences who have discovered in Ripstein's films an aestheticised vision of Latin American society that comfortably fits into their own view of an exotic Third World art cinema. Like Buñuel before him, Ripstein has learned to use Mexico for his international audiences as a symbolic landscape within which the baser, more instinctual reality of characters was laid bare. Like Buñuel's Mexican films, Ripstein's cinema is less caught up with depicting social reality than with developing a brutal, even nihilistic but ultimately cinematic vision of Mexico. It is an approach that has shown strong appeal to European and North American audiences. This has been perhaps the most critical lesson González Iñárritu has learned from his masters as, once again, the devastating portrait of visceral violence and fatalism becomes the privileged image of Mexico that most successfully travels abroad.

Marvin D'Lugo

REFERENCES

Chang, C. (2001) '*Amores perros*', *Film Comment*, 37, 2, 72.
García, G. (2000) 'Toda la carne al asador', *Letras libres*, July, 107—8.
Wood, M. (2001) 'Dog Days', *New York Review of Books*, September 20, 57–8.

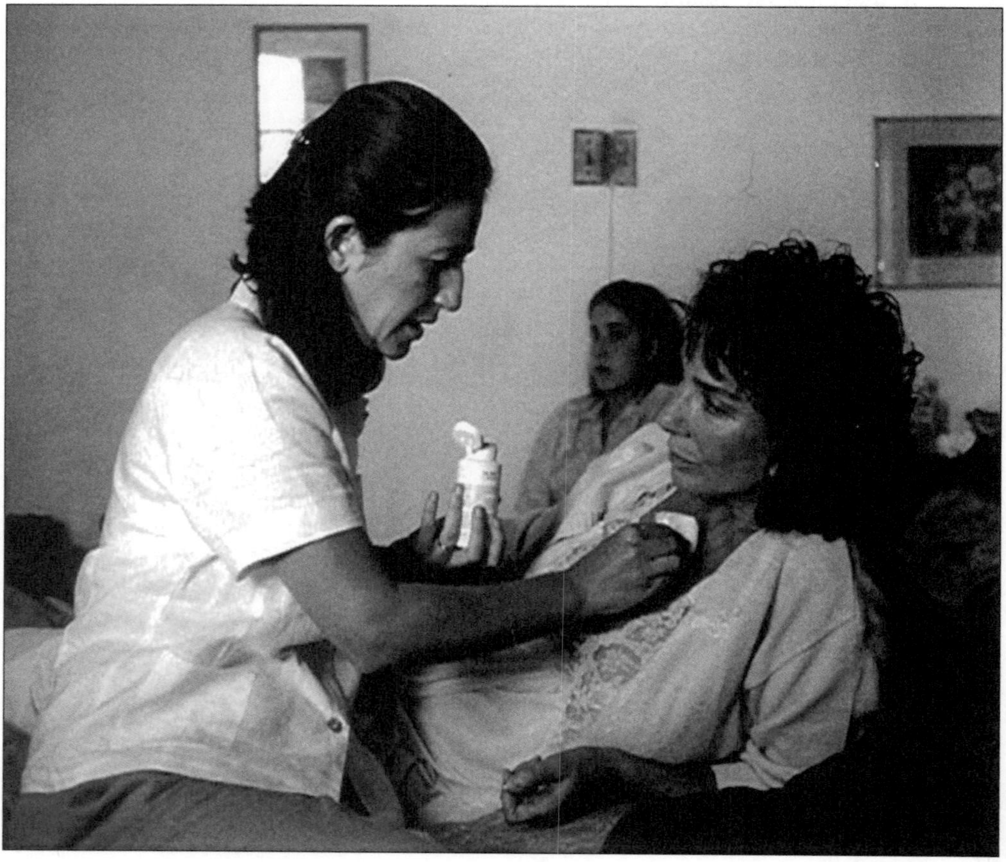

LA CIÉNAGA THE SWAMP

24

LUCRECIA MARTEL, ARGENTINA, 2001

La Ciénaga is a remarkably sensitive and affecting film that goes some way to extending beyond the nature of the medium within which it was made. It lodges itself in a hazy sphere of our perception and, starting from the mental reconstruction of the story, leads us to a strange place, as if it were caught in the mire of memories, between the unconscious and waking world. The remarkable skill of its director, Lucrecia Martel, to achieve such a precise appearance is even more striking if we consider that this was her first feature. It is a rare work that defies comparison with the current Latin American cinema scene.

La Ciénaga, a town situated in the province of Salta, in northwestern Argentina very close to the Bolivian border, not only describes the geographical and climactic environment of the farm, where most of the action takes place. On a basic level, *ciénaga* describes the mud in which animals are trapped and die. It also offers an apt description of how life is paralysed there, of the people resigned to eking out an existence in a foul and putrid atmosphere. In this sylvan landscape, crushed by February's oppressive humid heat (the height of summer in the southern hemisphere) and surrounded by mountains, exists La Mandrágora, a property whose name refers to a plant (the mandrake) formerly used as a sedative. The decadence of this world reveals itself from the opening sequence, in which a group of middle-aged characters are scrutinised by the camera, showing with almost clinical attention, the signs of time on their worn out bodies, while they unwillingly drag deckchairs along the paved edge of the swimming pool. At the same time, we see an ox trapped in the muddy ground, whose agony is contemplated by a group of unemotional children.

It is in La Mandrágora where two families reunite after two accidents result in a chance encounter between the main characters. At first, we see Mecha, owner of a farm growing the red peppers nobody in her family cares for. The mother of four children and married to Gregorio, a moderately wealthy man in his fifties whose ennui and addiction to alcohol equals his wife's, Mecha is taken to hospital after she drunkenly falls on broken glass. It is there she meets Tali, her cousin, with her younger son, Luciano, who has hurt his leg. The children's holidays are the perfect excuse to convince Tali, also a mother of four children, to accept her cousin's invitation to spent a few days at the farm. From this moment on, the plot develops less by linear storytelling than through a minutiae of incidents, comments, actions and the gradual development of each character. It is more rewarding to analyse the film in terms of the presentation of the family portrait, paying attention to the most relevant elements and motifs.

Representative of a certain social class, the Argentine provincial bourgeoisie, the family is portrayed with the intention of exploring a complex structure; a self-governing system ruled by non-explicit laws, which, by their very elliptical nature, are impossible to modify. The sense of 'fatality' that runs through the film, rather than reflecting the imminence of a tragedy, is founded upon the impossibility of introducing changes, of provoking a crisis that might free the characters from their stagnation. The leisure time of the holidays and the sultry climate multiply that effect and function as metonymical of the protagonists' situation. Their relationships bear the imprint of kinship, of daily life in common, in which each of them knows their natural place and where intimacy is only to be found within the boundary of their own bodies. As the director herself explains it, 'this is perhaps the most interesting aspect in *La Ciénaga*, as far as the family is concerned: it is a living and self-sufficient organism where the bodies, apart from their ties of blood, are linked in time, weariness, lunch time, bathrooms, in situations where the body is less exposed to social conventions'.

Mecha has given up on herself. She has surrendered to her fate as a middle-aged woman, and unhappy wife and mother. In turn, her life is marked by fits of rage, alcoholism or her despotic attitude towards the domestic service. Gregorio, her husband, is reluctant to accept the loss of his youth. He dyes his hair but he does not seem to have the strength to struggle against the emptiness pervading his role of head of the family. On the contrary, Tali and Rafael appear to be satisfied with the sense of stability they offer each other. They raise their children in a loving environment and judge Mecha and Roberto both with mistrust and disapproval. Nevertheless, this will not spare Tali a feeling of profound frustration as she is obsessed with the idea of travelling to Bolivia, not to go touring, but to buy the school material for their children at a lower price. Thus, through a few domestic scenes, the film outlines the turbulent and disturbing life of the family unit, avoiding outright conflict, instead weaving a web of relationships that show, little by little, a hidden and almost sinister mood at the heart of the family space.

The other main group of characters, the children of these two families, function as counterbalance to the apathy of the parents, not to infer that their experiences are not tinged with suffering, fear or loneliness. However, their reactions tend, by nature, to be more curious. Almost all children have some kind of wound or scar. Joaquín has gone blind in one eye from a hunting accident and his brother José arrives home with bruises all over his face after a fight. This recurrent motif in the film serves as a sign of pain, but also as a metaphor of growth and the stigma of the learning process. Nothing seems to be easy. Every experience will leave its mark, not only in the mind of these human beings, but also in their own flesh. Sex is another constant presence in the story. Momi experiences an intense dependency on Isabel, the native maid. Her sister Verónica finds shelter in the presence of her brother José, and feels jealous about a relationship that is never outspoken but can be guessed – the one he is having with Mercedes, her mother's friend and her father's former lover, with whom he lived in Buenos Aires. Crouching under suggestive images, sex is never shown in an explicit way but it works as a motive that, like every desire, provokes tension, implying a hidden but all-too-present sign of vitality within this seemingly static family arrangement. Martel underlined this tension: 'I do not encourage incest, but I think that human sexuality goes beyond all taboos. Those are imposed by men, but human existence does not rest on them. Life always ends up escaping from all our attempts of organisation, classification … The only healthy thing I find in the family is eroticism. I think it is an absurd prejudice, a proscription and a sort of intimidation, to deny sexual desire inside the family, which has always been there. It is absurd to deny it, because it is a very strong link, an element that keeps the family together. It is coldness what pulls it apart.'

Otherwise, the marked feminine nature of the narration presents different sides of the male characters (at one time, men are seen as objects of desire; at another time, they are considered turbulent agents), but they are always placed far from the core of the story, seen from the perspective of women who rule the realm of home life where the film rests. Thus, José is viewed by the camera with a morbid curiosity, but this disturbing tension has no conclusion; the situation, like almost everything in the film, remains steady in its suspense. Likewise, Rafael exudes an unconvincing air of calmness, even though he is responsible, caring and affectionate with his children. There is something aggressive beneath the veneer of his daily behaviour that keeps him apart, voluntarily absent, as if his presence could set in motion the machinery of conflict. It explains why he abruptly solves his disagreement with Tali's idea of travelling to Bolivia by buying the school material for the children without telling his wife, thus avoiding a fight.

That family works as a mirror against a broader social group well known to the director, whose background is firmly steeped in the routines of this bourgeois community. 'If there is a key element to be found in *La Ciénaga*', Martel observed, 'it is the sensation of malaise. *La Ciénaga* portraits a social class lacking any kind of tradition to lean on, as well as the necessary means to buy the security provided by tradition. This social class wants things to remain unchanged but, at the same time, it fears terribly that history might repeat itself.' There is a motif in the film that conveys Martel's diagnosis perfectly. In several scenes we witness the members of the family watching the same broadcast on a television permanently turned on which offers the latest news about an event happening in town. A neighbour claims that the Holy Virgin has repeatedly appeared on top of a water tank next to her house. No doubt is cast on these mystic visions. The family hardly show signs of belief in what they see, but also fail to look astonished; such claims are accepted as commonplace. Religion, omnipresent in this conservative society, is just one more element of the popular culture, and is shown in the film as a form of superstition rather than as a way to achieving a sense of spirituality. Another relevant aspect of this portrait of Argentine society is the presence of the large native community living in the north of the country which has been completely ignored in the national identity-building discourses and generally excluded from cinematic representation. The despotic way in which Mecha treats the domestic service, particularly Isabel, whom she derides as a '*colla de mierda*' (fucking Indian), reveals the profound racism of a society that continues to be determined by racial differences and where the opposition superiority/inferiority rules over the conventions. Such pejorative manners constitute signs that reveal a real problem impossible to eradicate. Its denunciation, as the director herself explains, was perceived as the most offensive element of the film by some sectors of Salta's population, who, after the première, accused her of showing the worst side of people. Shortly after that, in the region of Salta, Indians and peasants revolted and took over a refinery, which resulted in a violent confrontation with the army.

The narrative organisation of the film does not correspond with a classical dramatic structure in which the characters and actions provoke a series of situations that in turn lead to a certain dénouement. There is no causal relation between the different events; the sequences are presented as being almost independent from each other. The dense and intricate framework of daily life, which offers no dramatic crescendo and abounds with suspended and static moments, invokes disorientation in spectators and compels them to work in order to clarify the ties between characters as well as the confusing reasons for their actions. Notwithstanding, throughout the film there is a feeling of imminent fall, of permanent threat, a lurking tension that implies a tragic dénouement. Thus, the ending, resolved by means of an intentional anti-climax, does not even leave room for this faux melodrama to conclude. The ending does not solve anything. It is rather one more element to explain the absurd existence that *La Ciénaga* tries to represent, always avoiding any conventional idea of 'drama'.

The second of seven children, Martel admits she wrote *La Ciénaga*'s script making use of an extensive compilation of dialogues and family scenes, taken from her family and from those of parents and friends: 'I have written *La Ciénaga* following the thread of many women's conversations, with my mother, my grandmother and other women in my family. Their words are irrational, literary, still foreign to psychoanalysis … People living in the province tend to relate long, elaborated and often absurd anecdotes fishing for compassion. Their way of telling stories implies a great effort, often crowned with success, that allows them to overcome their worries by expressing them with words.'

Nature is a central element in *La Ciénaga*, whose treatment represents one of the best resorts of the film-maker when it comes to imprint a physical quality on the film: 'Characters have a slightly disturbing relation with nature, and this becomes specially clear in the exterior scenes. I did not want to show landscapes that might seem picturesque at all. On the contrary, nature is neither pleasant nor hospitable. I disagree with the point of view that relates closeness to nature and harmony.' The sensation of 'being there' that takes over the spectator and plunges them into the film, has a great deal to do with a premeditated method that favours spatial description (not only natural, but also urban and domestic) and confers on the physical environment a very strong dramatic influence. The sensuality of the film also owes much to its soundtrack: the almost constant sound of thunder in La Mandrágora, announcing a storm that arrives in intermittent bursts; the harvest bugs and undefined noises from the mountain; and other sounds more subtle and disturbing, like the explosion in Tali's house, the strange distortion of her daughters' voices when they play with the ventilator, or the squeaking of deckchairs and the clinking of ice cubes. The combination of all these sound effects, the mingling of low and high frequencies give shape, according to the director, 'to a sound display which, if one takes the trouble to think about it, defines a very profound thing of the film. Because, in the cinema, you might close your eyes, but you can't stop listening.'

The planning, which combines long sequence shots with almost motionless portraits and hand-held camera shots, shows once again the extraordinary importance attached to the vision of the human body, an essential means of communication within the family framework, which is normally sterilised in films on account of a prejudicial and false idealisation. The sequences in the mountains where the children play at being hunters, covered with dust, sweat and scratches; the siesta scenes in which brothers and sisters lay down close to each other for a long while; or the slow passage of hot days while sitting by a stagnant pool, in which we see the teenagers plunge, but never emerge, are remarkable images because of their corporeal quality and the rare carnality they transmit. But, just like every swampy ground, *La Ciénaga* does not show what lies beneath the surface. At least, not directly. To this effect, there is good use of the space off-screen. What is not shown becomes decisive. At the end of the film, little Luciano, obsessed by the legend of the African rat, told to him by his cousin, tries to verify if the barks he hears beyond the garden wall belong to the legendary animal. He climbs a rotten ladder and falls to the ground. We do not see the fall, just sunlight shimmering on the patio. The presentiment of death materialises here, in a bare and empty image. Not by chance, the last sentence we hear in *La Ciénaga*, uttered by Momi after she returns from the house the Holy Virgin is rumoured to have appeared, is 'I didn't see anything'.

Martel's first feature film was deservedly awarded the Alfred Bauer Prize for the best first film at the Berlin Festival, a long 13 years since an Argentine film had previously been selected for the festival. It was also another overseas award, 1998's Sundance Best Script Award, which made the making of the film possible. The backing provided by Lita Stantic (a director and producer of enormous prestige, who produced María Luisa Bemberg's films, and recently those of Pablo Trapero and Adrián Caetano) and the important support of Cuatro Cabezas (the successful production company founded by the journalist Mario Pergolini, whose television shows topped the ratings for the last five years), as well as the financial aid granted by the INCAA (Argentine National Institute of Cinema), contributed decisively to the budget of the film, the first from a new generation of film-makers that has been shot under really professional conditions.

Indeed, the circumstances under which a group of young directors have struggled and succeeded in proving, both at home and abroad, that something was happening in Argentine cinema, were not easy. In the context of a close-minded industrial cinema, following television investors' prescriptions and increasingly ignored by the audience, the controversial Cinema Act, passed in 1994 (that imposed a tax on audiovisual reproduction and established a public aid system, shadily managed by the INCAA as a clientele system throughout President Menem's term of office), contributed in part to the appearance of new film-makers. The commercial release of *Historias breves* (*Short Stories*, 1995), a series of short films awarded at the script contest sponsored by the Institute, and realised, among others, by Adrián Caetano, Bruno Stagnaro, Daniel Burman and Lucrecia Martel herself (*Rey Muerto* (*Dead King*) was her entry), is usually identified with the appearance of this new trend in Argentine cinema.

The acknowledgement of audiences and reviews proved not only the existence of a new generation of talented film-makers, but also that of a young audience eager to identify itself with a cinema that, until that moment, had ignored it. Thus, *Pizza, birra, faso* (*Pizza, Booze, Smokes*, 1998), directed by Adrián Caetano and Bruno Stagnaro, became the first box-office success of the new cinema, though it was far from the usual fare normally associated with commercial cinema. It is necessary to also mention other examples of this renewal that went unnoticed because they could not reach the commercial screens. *Rapado* (*Skinhead*, 1991), the first feature-film of Martin Rejtman, one of the spiritual leaders of this generation, or *Picado fino* (*Fine Powder*, 1993–96), Esteban Sapir's first film, were two works that, though different from each other, showed a clear rupture with the preceding cinema and proposed, with uncharacteristic zeal, a change of direction towards new cinematic formulas, regarding both themes and narrative structure.

But the appearance of a new generation on the Argentine cinematic scene cannot be exclusively considered as the spontaneous occurrence of a group of young film-makers in the 1990s. Besides the fact that they hardly constitue a school or movement based on explicit and common premises, several elements have greatly contributed to this renewal. On one hand, the proliferation of private and public film schools, among which the Universidad del Cine in Buenos Aires has played a remarkable role. Founded in 1991, it has produced over 400 short films and four features, including the fascinating *Mala época* (*Bad Times*, 1998), co-directed by a group of students. It has also enabled the training of numerous professionals, from directors and producers to technicians, who previously experienced trouble in making films. On the other hand, there has also been a renewal in specialised criticism, thanks to the appearance of reviews like *El Amante*, *Film*, *Haciendo Cine* or *La Cosa*. Last, but not least, the attention paid to these new film-makers' works in international festivals abroad has been decisive in providing a platform from which to distribute the films. And with awards and acclaim, the films are more visible in their home country. In 1999, *Silvia Prieto*, Martín Rejtman's second film, was presented in Venice and San Francisco. In 1999 and 2000, Pablo Trapero's *Mundo grúa* (*Crane World*) was screened in Venice, Rotterdam, Edinburgh, Buenos Aires and Havana. And in 2001, beside the success of *La Ciénaga*, Cannes recognised the Argentine verve by selecting Lisandro Alonso's *La Libertad* (*Freedom*) and Adrián Caetano's *Bolivia*. In 1999, the Buenos Aires Independent Cinema Festival was created, which not only competes with the Mar del Plata Festival as far as international cinema is concerned, but it also prides itself on hosting the world premières of many of these Argentine films.

One of the most important unifying elements of this generation is its will to produce work despite the scarcity of means by which to do it. The wide variety of proposals ranges from a renewed realism, sometimes fluctuating between fiction and documentary, such as *Mundo grúa* and *Pizza, birra, faso*, or narratives with an emphasis on experimentation, like *Picado fino*, Daniel Burman's *Un crisantemo estalla en Cincoesquinas* (*A Chrysanthemum Explodes in Cincoesquinas*, 1996) and Fernán Rudnik's *El nadador inmóvil* (*The Motionless Swimmer*, 1998). Another important trend is represented by those films that re-evalute genre films, while registering the daily heart beat of an exhausted Argentina, sunk in a social and economical failure. Comedies like *Rapado* and *Silvia Prieto*, filmed in a minimalist tone, or urban chronicles mixing irony with humour and melancholy, like Burman's second film, *Esperando al Mesías* (*Waiting for the Messiah*, 2000), Ariel Rotter's *Sólo por hoy* (*Just for today*, 2000) and *Sábado* (*Saturday*, 2001) by Juan Villegas, deal with one of the most explored subjects by the new Argentine cinema; the disenfranchisement of the country's youth. In that sense, this new generation can be distinguished by a vigorous treatment of the problems affecting a new generation, and by the search for new ways of expressing its worries.

There is an unquestionable disappointment in all these films, but they do not criticise, directly or indirectly, the situation they describe. They do not try to offer solutions, or to defend any cause. They just present facts, enclosing them in personal narratives and poetic structures not inclined to over-dramatisation. They stand aside of conventional cinema and offer new representations of their country, paying attention to different aspects of life. These everyday ethics can be found in the gratitude expressed by Lucrecia Martel to the critic Daniel Link for defining *La Ciénaga* as an 'exquisite political' film. This director, both model of and exception to, a new generation of Argentine film-makers, is currently working, thanks to a scholarship granted by the Cannes Film Festival, on the script of her second long film, *La niña santa* (*The Saint Girl*). Her colleagues have managed to overcome financial difficulties and have even turned them into a matter of inspiration. Nevertheless, the box-office remains dominated by commercial cinema, and few distributors are interested in the first works of these film-makers. In order to consolidate a far-reaching transformation of Argentine cinema, the enthusiasm shown by its protagonists is not enough, though it is certainly an essential part of the long road they will hopefully have ahead of them.

Ana Martín Morán

REFERENCES

Cipollini, M. & G. L. De Rosa (2002) *Tanghi feroci e ceneri di paradiso: il cinema argentino degli anni '90*. Salerno/Turin: Paguro/Museo Nazionale del Cinema.

Martín Peña, F., P. Félix-Didier & L. Ezequiel (2001) 'Una cierta mirada. Entrevista con Lucrecia Martel', at www.filmonline.com.ar/nuevo/actualidad/2001/martel. htm

Ricagno, A. (2001) 'Cine argentino. Imágenes al borde del nuevo siglo', in T. Toledo (ed.) *Utopías y realidades: el cine latinoamericano de los noventa*. San Sebastián: Festival Internacional de Cine de San Sebastián, 70–83.

Saad, N. & T. Toledo (eds) (2000) *Miradas: el cine argentino de los noventa*. Madrid: Agencia Española de Cooperación Internacional/Casa de América.

Valens, G. (2001) 'Cinéma argentin: une nouvelle garde', in *Positif*, 487, 55–60.

FILMOGRAPHY

LIMITE LIMIT 1931
Director: Mário Peixoto
Production: Mário Peixoto (Brasil)
Screenplay: Mário Peixoto
Photography: Edgar Brazil (b&w)
Editing: Mário Peixoto
Music: Alexander Borodin, Claude Debussy, César Franck, Sergei Prokofiev, Maurice Ravel, Erik Satie and Igor Stravinski (selection by Brutus Pedreira)
Assistant Director: Rui Costa
Cast: Olga Breno (First Woman), Taciana Rei (Second Woman), Raul Schnoor (First Man), Brutus Pedreira (Cinema Accompanist), Mário Peixoto (Man in the Cemetery), Carmen Santos (Woman on the Quay).
Running Time: 120' (at 16 frames per second)

ALLÁ EN EL RANCHO GRANDE OVER THERE ON THE BIG RANCH 1936
Director: Fernando de Fuentes
Production: Alfonso Rivas Bustamante and Fernando de Fuentes (Mexico)
Screenplay: Fernando de Fuentes and Guz Águila [Antonio Guzmán Aguilera], based on an original story by Guz Águila and Luz Guzmán de Arellano
Photography: Gabriel Figueroa (b&w)
Editing: Fernando de Fuentes
Music: Lorenzo Barcelata
Art Direction: Jorge Fernández
Sound: B.J. Kröger
Cast: Tito Guízar (José Francisco Ruelas), René Cardona (Felipe), Esther Fernández (Cruz), Lorenzo Barcelata (Martín), Emma Roldán (Ángela), Carlos López 'Chaflán' (Florentino), Margarita Cortés (Eulalia), Dolores Camarillo (Marcelina), Manuel Noriega (Don Rosendo), Hernán Vera (Don Venancio), Alfonso Sánchez Tello (Nabor Peña), David Valle González (Don Nicho), Carlos L. Cabello (Emeterio), Juan García (Gabino), Armando Alemán (Little José Francisco), Gaspar Núñez (Little Felipe), Lucha María Ávila (Little Cruz), Clifford Carr (Pete).
Running Time: 100'

BESOS BRUJOS ENCHANTING KISSES 1937
Director: José Agustín Ferreyra
Production: Alfredo Murúa for Estudios Argentinos SIDE (Argentina)
Screenplay: José Agustín Ferreyra based on a novel by Enrique García Velloso
Photography: Gumer Barreiros (b&w)
Editing: Emilio Murúa and Daniel Spósito

Music: Alfredo Malerba and Rodolfo Sciammarella
Art Direction: Juan Manuel Concado
Sound: Alfredo Murúa and Fernando Murúa
Cast: Libertad Lamarque (Marga Lucena), Floren Delbene (Alberto), Carlos Perelli (Sebastián), Sara Olmos (Laura), Antonio Daglio (Eusebio), Satanela (Satanela), Morena Chiolo (Alberto's mother), Salvador Arcella (Zenón)
Running Time: 78'

MARÍA CANDELARIA 1943
Director: Emilio Fernández
Production: Agustín J. Fink for Films Mundiales (Mexico)
Screenplay: Emilio Fernández and Mauricio Magdaleno based on an original story by Emilio Fernández
Photography: Emilio Figueroa (b&w)
Editing: Gloria Schoemann
Music: Francisco Domínguez
Art Direction: Jorge Fernández
Sound: Howard Randall, Jesús González Gancy and Manuel Esperón
Cast: Dolores del Río (María Candelaria), Pedro Armendáriz (Lorenzo Rafael), Alberto Galán (the painter), Margarita Cortés (Lupe), Miguel Inclán (Don Damián), Beatriz Ramos (the journalist), Rafael Icardo (the priest), Arturo Soto Rangel (the doctor), Guadalupe del Castillo (the healer), Lupe Inclán (the gossip), Julio Ahuet (José Alonso)
Running Time: 101'

LOS OLVIDADOS THE YOUNG AND THE DAMNED 1950
Director: Luis Buñuel
Production: Oscar Dancigers for Ultramar Films (Mexico)
Screenplay: Luis Buñuel and Luis Alcoriza
Photography: Gabriel Figueroa (b&w)
Editing: Carlos Savage
Music: Rodolfo Halffter
Art Direction: Edward Fitzgerald
Sound: José B. Carles and Jesús González Gancy
Cast: Alfonso Mejía (Pedro), Roberto Cobo ('El Jaibo'), Stella Inda (Pedro's mother), Miguel Inclán (Don Carmelo), Alma Delia Fuentes (Meche), Francisco Jambrina (the school's director), Jesús García Navarro (Julián's father), Efraín Arauz ('Cacarizo'), Jorge Pérez ('Pelón'), Javier Amézcua (Julián), Mario Ramírez ('El Ojitos'), Juan Villegas (Cacarizo's grandfather), Héctor López Portillo (the judge), Ángel Merino (Carlos).
Running Time: 88'

O CANGACEIRO 1953
Director: Lima Barreto
Production: Cid Leite da Silva for Companhia Cinematográfica Vera Cruz (Brasil)
Screenplay: Lima Barreto and Rachel de Queiroz
Photography: Chick Fowle (b&w)
Editing: Oswald Hafenrichter
Music: Gabriel Migliori
Art Direction: Carybé and Pierino Massenzi
Sound: Erik Rasmussen and Ernst Hack
Cast: Alberto Ruschel (Teodoro), Marisa Prado (Olívia), Milton Ribeiro (Galdino), Vanja Orico (María Clódia), Ricardo Campos, Adoniram Barbosa, Neusa Veras, Zé do Norte, Lima Barreto, Felicidade, Joao Batista Giotto, Manuel Pinto, Galileu Garcia, Nieta Junquiera, Pedro Bisgo.
Running Time: 105'

RIO, 40 GRAUS RIO, 40 DEGREES 1955
Director: Nelson Pereira dos Santos
Production: Nelson Pereira dos Santos, Cyro Freire Cúri, Mário Barros, Luiz Jardim, Louis Henri Guitton and Pedro Kosinski for Equipe Moacyr Fenelon (Brasil)
Screenplay: Nelson Pereira dos Santos based on an original story by Arnaldo Farias
Photography: Hélio Silva (b&w)
Editing: Rafael Valverde
Music: Radamés Gnatalli
Art Direction: Júlio Romito and Adrian Samailoff
Sound: Amedeo Riva
Cast: Modesto de Souza, Roberto Batalin, Jece Valadão, Ana Beatriz, Glauce Rocha, Cláudia Sagrera, Walter Sequeira, Zé Keti, Vargas Junior, Paulo Matosinho, Hilda Mena, Arinda Serafin, Ivone Miranda, Ary Cahet, Pedro Cavalcanti, Jorge Faura, Cleo Tereza.
Running Time: 97'

LA CASA DEL ÁNGEL THE HOUSE OF THE ANGEL 1956
Director: Leopoldo Torre Nilsson
Production: Argentina Sono Film SACI (Argentina)
Screenplay: Beatriz Guido, Leopoldo Torre Nilsson, and Martín Rodríguez Mentasti based on the novel of the same title by Beatriz Guido
Photography: Aníbal González Paz (b&w)
Editing: Jorge Gárate
Music: Juan Carlos Paz
Art Direction: Emilio Rodríguez Mentasti
Sound: Mario Fezia
Cast: Elsa Daniel (Ana Castro), Lautaro Múrua (Pablo Aguirre), Berta Ortegosa (Ana's mother), Bárbara Mújica (Vicenta), Yordana Fain (Naná), Guillermo Battaglia (Dr. Castro), Alejandro Rey, Eduardo Naveda, Lily Gacel, Alicia Bellán, Paquita Vehil, Elvira Moreno, Domingo Manía, Miguel Caiazzo, Roberto Bordoni, Flarian Mitchell, Rosita Zucker, Onofre Sansac Lovero, Eva Pisardo, Alberto Rudoy, Beto Gianola, Alberto Barcel.
Running Time: 78'

DEUS E O DIABO NA TERRA DO SOL BLACK GOD, WHITE DEVIL 1964
Director: Glauber Rocha
Production: Luiz Augusto Mendes, Jarbas Barbosa and Glauber Rocha for Copacabana Filmes (Brasil)
Screenplay: Glauber Rocha
Photography: Waldemar Lima (b&w)
Editing: Rafael Valverde
Music: Heitor Villa-Lobos and songs by Sérgio Ricardo and Glauber Rocha
Art Direction: Paulo Gil Soares
Sound: Geraldo José
Cast: Geraldo del Rey (Manuel), Yoná Magalhães (Rosa), Othon Bastos (Corisco), Maurício do Valle (Antônio das Mortes), Lídio Silva (Sebastiao), Sônia dos Humildes (Dadá), João Gama (the Priest), Marrom (Júlio), Antonio Pinto (the 'Colonel'), Milton Roda ('Colonel' Moraes), Roque Santos (Sabiá).
Running Time: 125'

MEMORIAS DEL SUBDESARROLLO MEMORIES OF UNDERDEVELOPMENT 1968
Director: Tomás Gutiérrez Alea
Production: Miguel Mendoza for the Instituto Cubano del Arte e Industria Cinematográficos (Cuba).
Screenplay: Tomás Gutiérrez Alea and Edmundo Desnoes based on the novel by Edmundo Desnoes.

Photography: Ramón F. Suárez (b&w)
Editing: Nelson Rodríguez
Music: Leo Brouwer
Art Direction: Julio Matilla
Sound: Carlos Fernández, Germinal Hernández and Eugenio Vesa
Cast: Sergio Corrieri (Sergio), Daisy Granados (Elena), Eslinda Núñez (Laura), Beatriz Ponchora (Noemi), Gilda Hernández, Omar Valdés, René de la Cruz, Yolanda Farr, Ofelia González, José Gil Abad, Daniel Jordán, Luis López, Rafael Sosa, Tomás Gutiérrez Alea.
Running Time: 97'

LUCÍA 1968
Director: Humberto Solás
Production: Raúl Canosa and Camilo Vives for the Instituto Cubano del Arte e Industria Cinematográficos (Cuba)
Screenplay: Humberto Solás, Julio García Espinosa and Nelson Rodríguez based on a story by Humberto Solás
Photography: Jorge Herrera (b&w)
Editing: Nelson Rodríguez
Music: Leo Brouwer
Art Direction: Pedro García Espinosa y Roberto Miqueli
Sound: Eugenio Vesa, Carlos Fernández and Ricardo Istueta
Cast: Raquel Revuelta, Eslinda Núñez, Adela Legrá, Eduardo Moure, Ramón Brito, Adolfo Llauradó, Idalia Anreus, Herminia Sánchez, Silvia Planas, Flora Lauten, María Elena Molinet, Rogelio Blain, Tete Vergara, Flavio Calderín, Aramis Delgado, Sergio Corrieri, Yolanda Farr, Gilda Hernández, Omar Valdés
Running Time: 160'

LA HORA DE LOS HORNOS THE HOUR OF THE FURNACES 1968
Director: Fernando E. Solanas
Production: Edgardo Pallero and Fernando E. Solanas (Argentina)
Screenplay: Fernando E. Solanas and Octavio Getino
Photography: Juan Carlos Desanzo (b&w)
Editing: Antonio Ripoll, Juan Carlos Macías and Fernando E. Solanas
Music: Roberto Lar and Fernando E. Solanas
Sound: Aníbal Libenson and Octavio Getino
Running Time: 255' [Three parts: Neocolonialismo y violencia, 90'; Acto para la liberación: notas, testimonios y debate sobre las recientes luchas de liberación del pueblo argentino, 120'; Violencia y liberación, 45']

REED: MÉXICO INSURGENTE REED: INSURGENT MEXICO 1971
Director: Paul Leduc
Production: Luis Barranco and Bertha Navarro for Salvador López Ollín y Asociados (México)
Screenplay: Juan Tovar, Paul Leduc and Emilio Carballido based on the book 'Insurgent Mexico' by John Reed
Photography: Alexis Grivas (b&w, toned to sepia)
Editing: Giovanni Korporaal and Rafael Castanedo
Art Direction: Luis Jaso and Yolanda Melo
Sound: Ernesto Higuera, Max López, Miguel Ramírez and Antonio Bermúdez
Cast: Claudio Obregón (John Reed), Ernesto Gómez Cruz (Captain Pablo Seáñez), Eduardo López Rojas (General Tomás Urbina), Juan Ángel Martínez (Lieutenant Julián Reyes), Carlos Castañón (Fidencio Soto), Hugo Velázquez (Longino Guereca), Eraclio Zepeda (Pancho Villa), Enrique Alatorre (Venustiano Carranza), Carlos Fernández del Real (Felipe Ángeles), Víctor Fosado (Isidro Maya), Héctor García (García), Max Kerlow (Antonio Swafeyta), Lynn Tillet (Isabel).
Running Time: 105'

DE CIERTA MANERA ONE WAY OR ANOTHER 1974
Director: Sara Gómez
Production: Camilo Vives for the Instituto Cubano del Arte e Industria Cinematográficos (Cuba)
Screenplay: Sara Gómez Yera and Tomás González Pérez
Photography: Luis García (b&w)
Editing: Iván Arocha (and Tomás Gutiérrez Alea)
Music: Sergio Vitier
Art Direction: Roberto Larrambure
Sound: Germinal Hernández
Cast: Yolanda Cuéllar (Yolanda), Mario Balmaseda (Mario), Mario Limonta (Humberto), Isaura Mendoza, Bobby Carcasés, Sarita Reyes, Guillermo Díaz, Berta Hernández, Lazarito González, Cándido López Rosal, Ámparo Calderín, Regla Padrón, Eloy Machado, Luis Sánchez, Rubén Cedrón, Rafael Idarte, Angelita Valdés
Running Time: 79'

LA BATALLA DE CHILE THE BATTLE OF CHILE 1975–79
Director: Patricio Guzmán
Production: Federico Elton for Equipo Tercer Año (Chile) [and Instituto Cubano del Arte e Industria Cinematográficos (Cuba) in Part III]
Screenplay: Patricio Guzmán
Photography: Jorge Müller Silva (b&w)
Editing: Pedro Chaskel
Sound: Bernardo Menz
Voice Over: Pedro Luis Fernández Vila
Running Time: 265' (Part I: 97'; Part II: 89'; Part III: 79')

BYE BYE BRASIL BYE BYE BRAZIL 1979
Director: Carlos Diegures
Production: Lucy Barreto for Carnaval Films (Brasil)
Screenplay: Carlos Diegues and Leopoldo Serran
Photography: Lauro Escorel Filho (c)
Editing: Mair Tavares
Music: Roberto Menescal and songs by Dominguinhos and Chico Buarque
Art Direction: Anísio Medeiros
Sound: Jean-Claude Laureux and Victor Raposeiro
Cast: José Wilker (Lorde Cigano), Betty Faria (Salomé), Fábio Junior (Ciço), Zaira Zambelli (Dasdô), Príncipe Nabor (Andorinha), Jofre Soares (Zé da Luz), Emanoel Calvacanti (the prefect), José Márcio Pasos (the adviser), Carlos Kroeber (the truck driver), Catalina Bonaky (the widow), Rinaldo Genes (the headman), Marcus Vinícius (the businessman), Oscar Reis (Leão de Chácara), Cleodon Gondin (Fregues), José Carlos Lacerda (Radomaço), Marieta Severo (the social worker).
Running Time: 100'

TIEMPO DE REVANCHA TIME OF REVENGE 1981
Director: Adolfo Aristarain
Production: Héctor Olivera and Luis Osvaldo Repetto for Aries Cinematográfica (Argentina).
Screenplay: Adolfo Aristarain.
Photography: Horacio Maira (c)
Editing: Eduardo López
Music: Emilio Kauderer
Art Direction: Abel Facello

Sound: Daniel Castronuovo
Cast: Federico Luppi (Pedro Bengoa), Haydée Padilla (Amanda Bengoa), Julio De Grazia (Larsen), Ulises Dumont (Bruno Di Toro), José Jofre Soares (Aitor), Aldo Barbero (Rossi), Enrique Liporace (Basile), Arturo Maly (Dr. García Brown),Rodolfo Ranni (Torrens), Jorge Hacker (Guido Ventura), Alberto Benegas (Golo), Ingrid Pellicori (Lea).
Running Time: 112'

LA HISTORIA OFICIAL **THE OFFICIAL STORY** 1984
Director: Luis Puenzo
Production: Marcelo Piñeyro for Cinemanía/Historias Cinematográficas (Argentina)
Screenplay: Aida Bortnik and Luis Puenzo
Photography: Félix Monti (c)
Editing: Juan Carlos Macías
Music: Atilio Stampone
Art Direction: Abel Facello
Sound: Abelardo Kuschnir
Cast: Héctor Alterio (Roberto), Norma Aleandro (Alicia), Chunchuna Villafañe (Ana), Analía Castro (Gabi), Hugo Arana (Enrique), Chela Ruiz (Sara), Guillermo Battaglia (José), Patricio Contreras (Benítez), María Luisa Robledo (Nata), Jorge Petraglia (Macci), Augusto Larreta (the General), Leal Rey (Padre Ismael)
Running Time: 115'

LA BOCA DEL LOBO **THE LION'S DEN** 1988
Director: Francisco J. Lombardi
Production: Francisco J. Lombardi and Gerardo Herrero for Inca Films (Peru) and Tornasol Films (Spain).
Screenplay: Giovanna Pollarollo, Augusto Cabada and Gerardo Herrero
Photography: José Luis López Linares (c)
Editing: Juan San Mateo
Music: Bernardo Bonezzi
Art Direction: Marta Méndez
Sound: Daniel Padilla
Cast: Gustavo Bueno (Lieutenant Iván Roca), Toño Vega (Vitín Luna), José Tejada (Gallardo), Gilberto Torres (Sergeant Moncada), Berta Pagaza (Julia), Antero Sánchez (Sergeant Basulto), Aristóteles Picho ('Chino'), Fernando Vásquez (Bacigalupo), Luis Saavedra (Escalante), Jorge Quiñe (Perico), Carlos Herrera (Martínez), Walter Florian (Polanco), Dionisio Tovar (Rogelio)
Running Time: 123'

LA NACIÓN CLANDESTINA **THE CLANDESTINE NATION** 1989
Director: Jorge Sanjinés
Production: Beatriz Palacios for Grupo Ukamau (Bolivia) / Channel Four (United Kingdom) / Televisión Española (Spain) / AZF (Germany) / OTA Masakuni (Japan).
Screenplay: Jorge Sanjinés
Photography: César Pérez (c)
Editing: Jorge Sanjinés
Music: Cergio Prudencio
Sound: Juan Guaraní
Cast: Reynaldo Yujra (Sebastián Mamani), Delfina Mamani (Basilia), Orlando Huanca (Vicente), Roque Salgado, Willy Pérez, Luis Severich, Percy Brum, Macario Zurco, Juan Carlos Calcina, Zulema Bustamante, Víctor Condori, Tatiana Mancilla, Julia Baltazar, Félix Quisbert, Jaime Gonzáles, José Flores, Grover Loredo, Isabel Melazini, Elenita Apaza, Eduardo Martínez, Rubén Portugal, Arminda Mérida.
Running Time: 124'

PRINCIPIO Y FIN BEGINNING AND END 1993
Director: Arturo Ripstein
Production: Alfredo Ripstein, Jr. for Alameda Films / Consejo Nacional para la Cultura y las Artes / Instituto Mexicano de Cinematografía / Universidad de Guadalajara (Mexico)
Screenplay: Paz Alicia Garciadiego based on the novel by Naguib Mahfuz
Photography: Claudio Rocha (c)
Editing: Rafael Castanedo
Music: Lucía Álvarez
Art Direction: Marisa Pecanins
Sound: Antonio Diego
Cast: Ernesto Laguardia (Gabriel Botero), Julieta Egurrola (Ignacia), Bruno Bichir (Nicolás), Alberto Estrella (Guama), Lucía Muñoz (Mireya), Blanca Guerra (Julia), Verónica Merchant (Natalia), Luis Felipe Tovar (César), Ernesto Yáñez (Polvorón), Alfonso Echánove (Cariñoso), Luisa Huertas (Isabel), Julian Pastor (Luján), Alejando Parodi (the President of the University), Darío Pie (Maurer), Luis Rábago (Guardiola), Jorge Fegan (Absalón), Gastón Melo (the Prefect), Alejandra Montoya (Tamara).
Running Time: 188'

TERRA ESTRANGEIRA FOREIGN LAND 1995
Directors: Walter Salles, Jr. and Daniela Thomas
Production: Flávio Tambellini, Paulo Dantas and Antonio da Cunha Telles for Videofilmes (Brasil)/Animatógrafo (Portugal).
Screenplay: Daniela Thomas, Marcos Bernstein and Walter Salles, Jr.
Photography: Walter Carvalho (b&w)
Editing: Walter Salles Jr. and Felipe Lacerda
Music: José Miguel Wisnik
Art Direction: Daniela Thomas
Sound: Geraldo Ribeiro and Carlos Alberto Lopes
Cast: Fernanda Torres (Alex), Fernando Alves Pinto (Paco Eizaguirre), Luis Melo (Igor Bentes), Alexandre Borges (Miguel de Moraes), Laura Cardoso (Manuela), João Lagarto (Pedro), Tchéky Karyo (Kraft), José Laplaine (Loli), João Grosso (Carlos), Miguel Guilherme (André).
Running Time: 100'

AMORES PERROS LOVE'S A BITCH 2000
Director: Alejandro González Iñárritu
Production: Alejandro González Iñárritu for Zeta Films and Altavista Films (Mexico)
Screenplay: Guillermo Arriaga Jordán
Photography: Rodrigo Prieto (c)
Editing: Alejandro González Iñárritu, Luis Carballar and Fernando Pérez Unda
Music: Gustavo Santaolalla
Art Direction: Brigitte Broch
Sound: Martín Hernández
Cast: Emilio Echevarría (Martín, El Chivo), Gael García Bernal (Octavio), Goya Toledo (Valeria), Álvaro Guerrero (Daniel), Vanessa Bauche (Susana), Jorge Salinas (Luis), Marco Pérez (Ramiro), Rodrigo Murray (Gustavo), Humberto Busto (Jorge), Gerardo Campbell (Mauricio), Rosa María Bianchi (Aunt Luisa), Dunia Saldívar (Susana's mother), Adriana Barraza (Octavio's mother), José Sefami (Leonardo), Lourdes Echevarría (Maru), Laura Almela (Julieta).
Running Time: 147'

LA CIÉNAGA **THE SWAMP** 2001
Director: Lucrecia Martel
Production: Lita Stantic and José María Morales for Producciones Cuatro Cabezas (Argentina) / Wanda Visión (España)
Screenplay: Lucrecia Martel
Photography: Hugo Colace (c)
Editing: Santiago Ricci
Art Direction: Graciela Oderigo
Sound: Hervé Guyader, Emmanuel Croset, Guido Beremblum y Adrián de Michele
Cast: Graciela Borges (Mecha), Mercedes Morán (Tali), Martín Adjemián (Gregorio), Sofía Bertolotto (Momi), Leonora Balcarce (Verónica), Juan Cruz Bordeu (José), Silvia Bayle (Mercedes), Daniel Valenzuela (Rafael), Andrea López (Isabel), Sebastián Montagna (Luciano), Diego Baenas (Joaquín), Fabio Villafañe ('Perro'), Noelia Bravo Herrera (Agustina), María Nicol Ellero (Mariana), Franco Veneranda (Martín).
Running Time: 100'

BIBLIOGRAPHY

GENERAL WORKS

Aprà, A. (ed.) (1981) *America Latina: lo schermo conteso*. Venice/Pesaro: Marsilio/Mostra del Nuovo Cinema.

Aufderheide, P. (1989) *Latin American Visions: A Half Century of Latin American Cinema, 1930–1989*. Philadelphia: International House.

Avellar, J. C. (1995) *A ponte clandestina: Teorías de cinema en América Latina*. Rio deJaneiro/São Paulo: 34 Letras/ EDUSP.

Avellar, J. C., P. Fernández Jurado, E. García Riera, R. Izaguirre, I. León Frías, M. Martínez Carril and T. Toledo (1991) *Antología del cine latinoamericano*. Valladolid: Semana Internacional de Cine de Valladolid.

Barnard, T. & P. Rist (eds) (1996) *South American Cinema: A Critical Filmography, 1915–1994*. New York: Garland (Reprinted: Austin, University of Texas Press, 1998).

Birri, F. (1996) *Por un nuevo nuevo nuevo cine latinoamericano, 1956–1991*. Madrid: Cátedra/Filmoteca Española.

Blaquière-Roumette, M. & B. Gille (2001) *Films des Amériques latines*. Paris: Editions du Temps.

Bremme B. (2000) *Movie-mientos. Der lateinamerikanische Film: Streiflichter von Unterwegs*. Stuttgart: Schmetterling Verlag.

Burns, E. B. (1975) *Latin American Cinema: Film and History*. Los Angeles: University of California Press.

Burton, J. (1983) *The New Latin American Cinema: An Annotated Bibliography of Sources in English, Spanish and Portuguese, 1960–1980*. New York: Smyrna Press.

Burton, J. (ed.) (1986) *Cinema and Social Change in Latin America. Conversations with Filmmakers*. Austin: University of Texas Press (Spanish translation, *Cine y cambio social en América Latina: imágenes de un continente*, México: Diana, 1991).

Burton, J. (ed.) (1990) *The Social Documentary in Latin America*. Pittsburgh: The University of Pittsburgh Press.

Burton-Carvajal, J. (ed.) (1998) *Revisión del cine de los cincuenta/Revisioning Film in the Fifties*, special issue of *Nuevo Texto Crítico*, 21–2.

Burton-Carvajal, J., P. Torres & A. Miquel (eds) (1998) *Horizontes del segundo siglo: Investigación y pedagogía del cine mexicano, latinoamericano y chicano*. Guadalajara/México: Universidad de Guadalajara/Instituto Mexicano de Cinematografía.

Cham, M. (ed.) (1992) *Ex-iles: Essays on Caribbean Cinema*. Trenton, N.J.: Africa World Press.

Chanan, M. (ed.) (1983) *Twenty-five Years of the New Latin American Cinema*. London: British Film Institute.

Ciompi, V. & T. Toledo (eds) (1999) *La memoria compartida: ccoperación para la preservación fílmica en Iberoamérica*. Madrid: Filmoteca Española.

Cortés, M. L. (1999) *Amor y traición: cine y literatura en América Latina*. San José de Costa Rica: Universidad de Costa Rica.

D'Agostini, P. (1991) *Il nuovo cinema latinoamericano*. Rome: Edizioni Associate.

Díaz López, M. (ed.) (1999) *Cine y política en América Latina*, special issue of *Secuencias: Revista de Historia del Cine*, 10.

Elena, A. (1993) *El cine del Tercer Mundo: diccionario de realizadores*. Madrid: Turfán.

Elena, A. & M. Díaz López (eds) (1999) *Tierra en trance: el cine latinoamericano en cien películas*. Madrid: Alianza.

Elena, A. & P. A. Paranaguá (eds) (1999) *Mitologías latinoamericanas*, special issue of *Archivos de la Filmoteca*, 31.

Fregoso, R. L. (1993) *The Bronze Screen: Chicana and Chicano Film Culture*. Minneapolis/London: University of Minnesota Press.

Fundación Mexicana de Cineastas (1988) *Hojas de cine: Testimonios y documentos del nuevo cine latinoamericano*. México: Secretaría de Educación Pública/Universidad Autónoma Metropolitana.

Fusco, C. (ed.) *Reviewing Histories: Selections from New Latin American Cinema*. Buffalo, N.Y.: Hallwalls Contemporary Art Center.

García Espinosa, J. (1973) *Por un cine imperfecto*. Caracas: Salvador de la Plaza.

____ (1982) *Una imagen recorre el mundo*. México: Universidad Nacional Autónoma de México.

García Mesa, H. (1992) *Cine latinoamericano (1896–1930)*. Caracas: Fundación del Nuevo Cine Latinoamericano/Consejo Nacional de la Cultura/Foncine/Fundacine UC.

Getino, O. (1981) *A diez años de 'Hacia un Tercer Cine'*. México: Universidad Nacional Autónoma de México.

____ (1987) *Cine latinoamericano: economía y nuevas tecnologías audiovisuales*. Havana/Mérida: Fundación del Nuevo Cine Latinoamericano/Universidad de los Andes. (Reprinted in Buenos Aires: Legasa, 1988).

Gumucio Dagrón, A. (1979) *Cine, censura y exilio en América Latina*. La Paz: Film Historia.

Gutiérrez Alea, T. (1982) *Dialéctica del espectador*. Havana: Unión (Portuguese translation, *Dialética do espectador*, São Paulo: Summus, 1984; English translation, *The Viewer's Dialectic*, Havana: José Martí, 1988).

Hennebelle, G. & A. Gumucio-Dagrón (eds) (1983) *Les cinémas de l'Amérique latine*. Paris: L'herminier.

Híjar, A. (ed.) (1972) *Hacia un Tercer Cine (Antología)*. México: Universidad Nacional Autónoma de México.

Irazábal, C. (2002) *La otra América: directoras de cine de América Latina y el Caribe*. Madrid: Horas y Horas.

Jahnke, E., Schmidt, M. & Krautz, A. (eds) (1972) *Film im Freiheitskampf der Völker: Lateinamerika, 2 vols*. Berlin: Hochschule für Film und Fernsehen der DDR.

Keller, G. (1985) *Chicano Cinema: Research, Reviews and Resources*. Binghampton, N.Y.: Bilingual Press/State University of New York (Spanish translation, *Cine chicano*. México: Cineteca Nacional, 1988).

King, J. (1990) *Magical Reels. A History of Cinema in Latin America*. London/New York: Verso (Spanish translation, *El carrete mágico: Una historia del cine latinoamericano*. Bogotá, Tercer Mundo, 1994).

King, J., A. M. López & M. Alvarado (eds) (1993) *Mediating Two Worlds: Cinematic Encounters in the Americas*. London: British Film Institute.

Kriger, C. & A. Portela (eds) (1997) *Cine latinoamericano: diccionario de realizadores*. Buenos Aires: Jilguero.

León Frías, I. (1979) *Los años de la conmoción (1967–1973): entrevistas con realizadores sudamericanos*. México: Universidad Nacional Autónoma de México.

Mahieu, J. A. (1990) *Panorama del cine iberoamericano*. Madrid: Cultura Hispánica/Instituto de Cooperación Iberoamericana.

Martin, M. T. (ed.) (1997) *The New Latin American Cinema, 2 vols*. Detroit: Wayne State University Press.

Martínez Torres, A. & Pérez Estremera, M. (1973) *Nuevo cine latinoamericano*. Barcelona: Anagrama.

Millán, F. J. (1990) *Un cine para el mañana: políticas cinematográficas en América Latina*. Zaragoza: Gandaya.

____ (1999) *La mirada de las dos orillas: Panorama del cine iberoamericano*. Teruel: Maravillas.

____ (2001) *La memoria agitada: cine y represión en Chile y Argentina*. Huelva/Madrid: Festival de Cine Iberoamericano de Huelva/Ocho y Medio.

Newman, K. (1991) *Latin American Cinema*, special issue of *Iris*, 13.

Noriega, C. A. (ed.) (1992) *Chicanos and Film: Representation and Resistance*. New York: Garland.

Noriega, C. A. & A. M. López (eds) (1996) *The Ethnic Eye: Latino Media Arts*. Minneapolis/London: University of Minnesota Press.

Noriega, C. A. (ed.) (2000) *Visible Nations: Latin American Cinema and Video*. Minneapolis/London: University of Minnesota Press.

Oroz, S. (1992) *Melodrama: o cinema de lágrimas da América Latina*. Rio de Janeiro: Rio Fundo Editora (Expanded edition, Rio de Janeiro: Funarte, 1999; Spanish translation, *Melodrama: el cine de lágrimas de América Latina*. México: Universidad Nacional Autónoma de México, 1995).

Paranaguá, P. A. (1985) *Cinema na América Latina: longe de Deus e perto de Hollywood*. Porto Alegre: L&PM.

____ (1992) *A la découverte de l'Amérique Latine: petite anthologie d'une 'ecole documentaire méconnue*. Paris: Centre Georges Pompidou.

____ (2000) *Le cinéma en Amérique Latine: le miroir éclaté (historiographie et comparatisme)*. Paris: L'Harmattan.

____ (2003) *Tradición y modernidad en el cine de América Latina*. Madrid/México: Fondo de Cultura Económica.

____ (ed.) (2003) *Cine documental en América Latina*. Madrid/Málaga: Cátedra/Festival de Cine de Málaga.

Pick, Z. M. (ed.) (1978) *Latin American Filmmakers and the Third Cinema*. Ottawa: Carleton University.

____ (1993) *The New Latin American Cinema: A Continental Project*. Austin, University of Texas Press.

Ranucci, K. & J. Feldman (eds) *Guide to Latin American, Caribbean and U.S. Latino Made Film and Video*. Lanham. MD.: Scarecrow Press.

Sanjinés, J. (1979) *Teoría y práctica de un cine junto al pueblo*. México: Siglo XXI. (English edition, *Theory and Practice of a Cinema with People*. Willimantic, CT.,: Curbstone Press, 1989).

Schnitman, J. A. (1984) *Film Industries in Latin America: Dependency and Development*. Norwood, N.J.: Ablex.

Schumann, P. B. (1971) *Film und Revolution in Lateinamerika*. Oberhausen: Karl Maria Laufen.

____ (1976) *Kino und Kampf in Lateinamerika (Zur Theorie uns Praxis des politischen Kino)*. Munich/Viennna: Carl Hanser.

____ (1982) *Handbuch des lateinamerikanischen Films*. Frankfurt/Berlin: Klaus Dieter Vervuert/Freunde der Deutschen Kinemathek.

____ (1987) *Historia del cine latinoamericano*. Buenos Aires: Legasa.

Schwartz, R. (1997) *Latin American Films, 1932–1994*. Jefferson, N.C./London: McFarland.

Solanas, F. E. & O. Getino (1973) *Cine, cultura y descolonización*. Buenos Aires/México: Siglo XXI.

Stock, A. M. (ed.) (1997) *Framing Latin American Cinema: Contemporary Critical Perspectives*. Minneapolis/London: University of Minnesota Press.

Tamásné, P. & P. Sándor (1983) *A latin-amerikai filmművészet antológiája*. Budapest: Magyar Filmtudományi Intézet és Filmarchívum.

Toledo, T. (1997) *Bibliography of Latin American Cinema, 1931–1997* [CD-Rom]. London: FIAF.

____ (ed.) (2000) *Directores de América Latina*. San Sebastián: Festival Internacional de Cine de San Sebastián.

____ (ed.) (2001) *Utopías y realidades: el cine latinoamericano de los noventa*. San Sebastián: Festival Internacional de Cine de San Sebastián.

Trelles Plazaola, L. (1986) *Cine sudamericano (Diccionario de directores)*. Río Piedras: Universidad de Puerto Rico (English translation, *South American Cinema: Dictionary of Filmmakers*. Río Piedras: Universidad de Puerto Rico, 1989).

____ (1991) *Cine y mujer en América Latina: directoras de largo metraje de ficción*. Río Piedras: Universidad de Puerto Rico.

Usabel, G. S. de (1982) *The High Noon of American Films in Latin America*. Ann Arbor, Michigan: UMI Research Press.

Vaillant, F. (1980) *Der Film Lateinamerikas: eine Dokumentation*. Mannheim: Internationale Filmwoche Mannheim.

ARGENTINA

Barnard, T. (ed.) (1986) *Argentine Cinema*. Toronto: Nightwood/The Ontario Film Institute.

Birri, F. (1964) *La escuela documental de Santa Fe*. Santa Fe: Universidad Nacional del Litoral.

Brenner, F. (1993) *Adolfo Aristarain*. Buenos Aires: Centro Editor de América Latina/Instituto Nacional de Cinematografía.

Calistro, M., O. Centrángolo, C. España, A. Insaurralde and C. Landini (1978) *Reportaje al cine argentino: los pioneros del sonoro*. Buenos Aires: Anesa/Crea.

Caneto, G., M. Cassinelli, H. González Bergerot, C. Maranghello, E. Navarro, A. Portela and S. Strugo (1996) *Historia de los primeros años del cine en la Argentina, 1895–1910*. Buenos Aires: Fundación Cinemateca Argentina.

Cipollini, N. & G. L. De Rosa (eds) *Tanghi feroci e ceneri di paradiso: il cinema argentino degli anni '90*. Salerno/Turin:

Paguro/Museo Nazionale del Cinema.
Couselo, J. M. (1969) *El Negro Ferreyra: un cine por instinto*. Buenos Aires: Freeland.
Couselo, J. M., M. Calisto, C. España, R. García Oliveri, A. Insaurralde, C. Landini, C. Maranghello and M. A. Rosado (1984) *Historia del cine argentino*. Buenos Aires: Centro Editor de América Latina (Expanded edition, 1992).
Couselo, J. M. (1985) *Torre Nilsson por Torre Nilsson*. Buenos Aires: Fraterna.
Di Núbila, D. (1959–60) *Historia del cine argentino, 2 vols*. Buenos Aires: Cruz de Malta (Expanded edition [only vol. 1], Buenos Aires: Jilguero, 1998).
España, C. (ed.) (1994) *Cine argentino en democracia, 1983–1993*. Buenos Aires: Fondo Nacional de las Artes.
____ (ed.) (2000) *Cine argentino: industria y clasicismo, 1933–1956, 2 vols*. Buenos Aires: Fondo Nacional de las Artes.
España, C. & M. A. Rosado (1984) *Medio siglo de cine: Argentina Sono Films*. Buenos Aires: Abril/Heraldo del Cine.
Fernández Jurado, G. & M. Cassinelli (eds) (1995) *El cine argentino, 1933–1995* [CD-Rom]. Buenos Aires: Fundación Cinemateca Argentina.
Foster, D. W. (1992) *Contemporary Argentine Cinema*. Columbia: University of Missouri Press.
García Oliveri, R. (1993) *Luis Puenzo*. Buenos Aires: Centro Editor de América Latina/Instituto Nacional de Cinematografía.
____ (1997) *Cine argentino: crónica de cien años*. Buenos Aires: Manrique Zago.
Getino, O. (1988) *Cine y dependencia: el cine en la Argentina*. Buenos Aires: Puntosur.
____ (1998) *Cine argentino: entre lo posible y lo deseable*. Buenos Aires: Ciccus.
King, J. & N. Torrents (eds) (1991) *The Garden of Forking Paths: Argentine Cinema*. London: British Film Institute.
Labaki, A. & M. Cereghino (1993) *Solanas por Solanas: um cineasta na América Latina*. São Paulo: Iluminuras/Fundação Memorial da América Latina.
Mahieu, J. A. (1961) *Historia del cortometraje argentino*. Santa Fe: Universidad Nacional del Litoral.
____ (1966) *Breve historia del cine argentino*. Buenos Aires: EUDEBA.
____ (1974) *Breve historia del cine nacional*. Buenos Aires: Alzamor.
Manrupe, R. & M. A. Portela (1995) *Un diccionario de films argentinos*. Buenos Aires: Corregidor.
Maranghello, C. & A. Insaurralde (1997) *Fanny Navarro, o un melodrama argentino*. Buenos Aires: Jilguero.
Martín, J. A. (1980) *Los films de Leopoldo Torre Nilsson*. Buenos Aires: Corregidor.
____ (1987) *Diccionario de realizadores contemporáneos*. Buenos Aires: Instituto Nacional de Cinematografía.
Monteagudo, L. (1993) *Fernando Solanas*. Buenos Aires: Centro Editor de América Latina/Instituto Nacional de Cinematografía.
Oms, M. (1962) *Leopoldo Torre Nilsson*. Lyon: Premier Plan.
Oubiña, D. & G. M. Aguilar (1993) *El cine de Leonardo Favio*. Buenos Aires: Nuevo Extremo.
Saad, N. & T. Toledo (eds) (2000) *Miradas: el cine argentino de los noventa*. Madrid: Agencia Española de Cooperación Internacional/Casa de América.
Solanas, F. E. (1989) *La mirada: reflexiones sobre cine y cultura: Entrevista de Horacio González*. Buenos Aires: Puntosur.
Vieites, M. C. (ed.) (2002) *Leopoldo Torre Nilsson: una estética de la decadencia*. Buenos Aires: Altamira/Museo del Cine/INCAA.
Wolf, S. (ed.) (1993) *Cine argentino: la otra historia*. Buenos Aires: Letra Buena.

BOLIVIA

Gamboa, A. (1999) *El cine de Jorge Sanjinés*. Santa Cruz: Festival Iberoamericano de Cine de Santa Cruz.
Gumucio Dagrón, A. (1982) *Historia del cine en Bolivia*. La Paz: Amigos del Libro. (Revised edition, *Historia del cine boliviano*. México, Universidad Nacional Autónoma de México, 1983).
Mesa Gisbert, C. D. (ed.) (1979) *Cine boliviano: del realizador al crítico*. La Paz: Gisbert.
____ (1985) *La aventura del cine boliviano, 1952–1985*. La Paz: Gisbert.
Sánchez, J. (1999) *The Art and Politics of Bolivian Cinema*. Lanham, MD.: Scarecrow Press.
Susz Kohl, P. (1991) *Filmo-videografía boliviana básica (1904–1990)*. La Paz: Cinemateca Boliviana.
____ (1997) *Cronología del cine boliviano, 1897–1997*. La Paz: Cinemateca Boliviana.

BRAZIL

Amâncio, T. (1998) *Estudos sobre 'Limite' de Mário Peixoto* [CD-Rom]. Niterói/Rio de Janeiro: Universidade Federal Fluminense/RioFilme.

Amico, G. (ed.) (1964) *Il cinema brasiliano*. Genoa: Silva.

Aprà, A. (ed.) (1981) *Brasile: 'Cinema Novo' e dopo*. Venice/Pesaro: Marsilio/Mostra Internazionale del Nuovo Cinema.

Araújo, V. de P. (1976) *A bela época do cinema braileiro (1898–1912)*. São Paulo: Perspectiva.

Avellar, J. C. (1995) *Deus e o diabo na terra do sol: a linha reta, o melaço de cana e o retrato do artista quando jovem*. Rio de Janeiro: Rocco.

____ (2002) *Glauber Rocha*. Madrid: Cátedra / Filmoteca Española.

Avellar, J. C. & J. Bodanzky (eds) (1997) *Cinema brasileiro anos 60: uma câmera na mao, uma idéia na cabeça* [CD-Rom]. Rio de Janeiro: RioFilme.

Bentes, I. (ed.) (1997) *Cartas ao mundo: Glauber Rocha*. São Paulo: Companhia das Letras.

Bernardet, J. C. (1967) *Brasil em tempo de cinema (Ensaio sôbre o cinema brasileiro de 1958 a 1966)*. Rio de Janeiro: Civilização Brasileira.

____ (1979) *Cinema brasileiro: propostas para uma história*. Rio de Janeiro: Paz e Terra.

____ (1985) *Cinema e imagens do povo*. São Paulo: Brasiliense.

Bernardet, J. C. & M. R. Galvao (eds) (1983) *Cinema: repercussôes em caixa de eco ideológica (As idéias de 'nacional' e 'popular' no pensamento cinematográfico brasileiro)*. São Paulo: Brasiliense.

Costa, J. B. da (ed.) (1987) *Cinema brasileiro*. Lisbon: Fundação Calouste Gulbenkian/Cinemateca Portuguesa.

Debs, S. (2002) *Cinéma et littérature au Brésil. Les mythes du sertão: émergence d'une identité nationale*. Paris: L'Harmattan.

Dias, R. de O. (1993) *O mundo como chanchada: cinema e imaginário das classes populares na década de 50*. Rio de Janeiro: Relume Dumará.

Fabris, M. (1994) *Nelson Pererira dos Santos: um olhar neo-realista?* São Paulo: EDUSP.

Foster, D. W. (1999) *Gender and Society in Contemporary Brazilian Cinema*. Austin. University of Texas Press.

Galvão, M. R. (1975) *Cronica do cinema paulistano*. São Paulo: Atica.

____ (1981) *Burguesia e cinema: o caso Vera Cruz*. São Paulo: Civilização Brasileira/Embrafilme.

Gerber, R. (1982) *O cinema brasileiro e o processo político e cultural (de 1950 a 1978)*. Rio de Janeiro: Embrafilme/DAC.

____ (1982) *O mito da civilização atlântica: Glauber Rocha, cinema, política e a estética do insconsciente*. Petrópolis: Vozes.

Giusti, M. & M. Melani (eds) (1995) *Prima e dopo la rivoluzione: Brasile, anni '60, dal cinema novo al cinema marginal*. Turin: Lindau/Festival Internazionale Cinema Giovane.

Johnson, R. (1984) *Cinema Novo x 5: Masters of Contemporary Brazilian Film*. Austin: University of Texas Press.

____ (1987) *The Film Industry in Brazil: Culture and the State*. Pittsburgh: The University of Pittsburgh Press.

Johnson, R. & R. Stam (eds) (1982) *Brazilian Cinema*. New Brunswick: Associated University Presses (Expanded edition, New York: Columbia University Press, 1995).

Mendonça, A. R. (1999) *Carmen Miranda foi a Washington*. Rio de Janeiro: Record.

Mello, S. P. de (1978) *Limite, filme de Mário Peixoto*. Rio de Janeiro: Funarte/Inelivro.

____ (1996) *Limite*. Rio de Janeiro: Rocco.

Micciché, L. (ed.) (1975) *Il cinema novo brasiliano, 2 vols*. Rome/Pesaro: Mostra Internazionale del Nuovo Cinema.

Miranda, L. F. (1990) *Dicionário de cineastas brasileiros*. São Paulo: Art/Secretaría de Estado da Cultura.

Moreno, A. (1994) *Cinema brasileiro: história e relações com o Estado*. Niterói/Goiânia: Universidade Federal Fluminense/Universidade Federal de Goiás.

Noronha, J. (ed.) (1997) *Pioneiros do cinema brasileiro (1896 a 1936)* [CD-Rom]. São Paulo: EMC/Melhoramentos.

O'Grady, G. (ed.) (1994) *Nelson Pereira dos Santos: Cinema Novo's 'Spirit of Light'*. New York/Cambridge, Mass.: Film Society of Lincoln Center/Harvard University.

Paranaguá, P. A. (ed.) (1987) *Le cinéma brésilien*. Paris: Centre Georges Pompidou.

____ (ed.) (2000) *Brasil, entre modernismo y modernidad*, special issue of *Archivos de la Filmoteca*, 36.
Pierre, S. (1987) *Glauber Rocha*. Paris: Cahiers du Cinéma.
Ramos, F. (ed.) (1987) *História do cinema brasileiro*. São Paulo: Art.
Ramos, F. & L. F. Miranda (eds) (2000) *Enciclopédia do cinema brasileiro*. São Paulo: SENAC.
Rocha, G. (1963) *Revisão crítica do cinema brasileiro*. Rio de Janeiro: Civilização Brasileira (Spanish translations, *Revisión crítica del cine brasilero*. Havana: ICAIC, 1965, and *Revisión crítica del cine brasileño*. Madrid: Fundamentos, 1971).
____ (1981) *Revolução do Cinema Novo*. Rio de Janeiro: Alhambra/Embrafilme.
____ (1983) *O século do cinema*. Rio de Janeiro: Alhambra/Embrafilme.
Salem, H. (1996) *Nelson Pereira dos Santos: o sonho posível do cinema brasileiro*. Rio de Janeiro: Nova Fronteira (Expanded edition, Rio de Janeiro: Record, 1996; Spanish translation, *Nelson Pereira dos Santos: el sueño posible del cine brasileño*. Madrid, Cátedra/Filmoteca Española, 1997).
Salles Gomes, P. E. (1974) *Humberto Mauro, Cataguases e Cinearte*. São Paulo: Perspectiva/EDUSP.
____ (1980) *Cinema: trajetória no subdesenvolvimento*. Rio de Janeiro: Paz e Terra/Embrafilme.
Simis, A. (1996) *Estado e cinema no Brasil*. São Paulo: Annablume/FAPESP.
Stam, R. (1997) *Tropical Multiculturalism: A Comparative History of Race in Brazilian Cinema and Culture*. Durham, N.C./London: Duke University Press.
Viany, A. (1959) *Introdução ao cinema brasileiro*. Rio de Janeiro: Instituto Nacional do Livro.
____ (1978) *Humberto Mauro: su vida, sua arte, sua trajetória no cinema*. Rio de Janeiro: Artenova/Embrafilme.
____ (1999) *O processo do Cinema Novo*. Rio de Janeiro: Aeroplano.
Vieira, J. L. (ed.) (1998) *Cinema Novo and Beyond*. New York: Museum of Modern Art.
Xavier, I. (1983) *Sertão/Mar: Glauber Rocha e a estética da fome*. São Paulo: Brasiliense/Embrafilme.
____ (1993) *Alegorias do subdesenvolvimento: cinema novo, tropicalismo, cinema marginal*. São Paulo: Brasiliense (English translation, *Allegories of Underdevelopment: Aesthetics and Politics in Modern Brazilian Cinema*. Minneapolis/London: University of Minnesota Press, 1997).
Xavier, I. (2001) *O cinema brasileiro moderno*. Rio de Janeiro: Paz e Terra.

CHILE

Bolzoni, F. (1974) *Il cinema di Allende*. Venice: Marsilio Editori (Spanish translation, *El cine de Allende*. Valencia: Fernando Torres, 1974).
Cavallo, A., P. Douzet & C. Rodríguez (1999) *Huérfanos y perdidos: el cine chileno de la transición*. Santiago de Chile: Grijalbo.
Chanan, M. (ed.) (1976) *Chilean Cinema*. London: British Film Institute.
Francia, A. (1990) *Nuevo Cine Latinoamericano en Viña del Mar*. Santiago de Chile: CESOC ChileAmérica.
Guzmán, P. (1977) *La batalla de Chile: la lucha de un pueblo sin armas*. Pamplona/Madrid: Peralta/Ayuso.
Guzmán, P. & P. Sempere (1977) *Chile: el cine contra el fascismo*. Valencia: Fernando Torres.
Jara Donoso, E. (1994) *Cine mudo chileno*. Santiago de Chile: Ministerio de Educación.
Lichtenstein, M. & G. Meier (eds) (1983) *Film im Freiheitskampf der Völker: Chile*. Berlin: Staatsliche Filmarchiv der DDR.
López Navarro, J. (1997) *Películas chilenas*. Santiago de Chile: La Noria.
Mouesca, J. (1988) *Plano secuencia de la memoria de Chile: veinticinco años de cine chileno (1960–1985)*. Santiago de Chile/Madrid: Litoral/Michay.
Mouesca, J. (1992) *Cine chileno, veinte años (1970–1990)*. Santiago de Chile: Ministerio de Educación.
Ossa Coo. C. (1971) *Historia del cine chileno*. Santiago de Chile: Quimantú.
Ruffinelli, J. (2001) *Patricio Guzmán*. Madrid: Cátedra/Filmoteca Española.
Vega, A. (ed.) (1979) *Re-visión del cine chileno*. Santiago de Chile: Aconcagua/CENECA.

COLOMBIA

Alvarez, C. (1983) *Una década de cortometraje colombiano (1970–1980)*. Bogotá: Arcadia va al cine.

Alvarez, C. (1989) *Sobre cine colombiano y latinoamericano*. Bogotá: Universidad Nacional de Colombia.

Duque, E. P. (1992) *La aventura del cine en Medellín*. Bogotá: Universidad Nacional de Colombia/El Ancora.

Martínez Pardo, H. (1978) *Historia del cine colombiano*. Bogotá: América Latina.

Nieto, J. & D. Rojas (1992) *Tiempos del Olympia*. Bogotá. Fundación Patrimonio Fílmico Colombiano.

Salcedo Silva, H. (1981) *Crónicas del cine colombiano, 1897–1950*. Bogotá: Carlos Valencia.

COSTA RICA

Cortés, M. L. (2002) *El espejo imposible: un siglo de cine en Costa Rica*. San José de Costa Rica: Farben.

Marranghello, D. (1988) *El cine en Costa Rica, 1903–1920*. San José de Costa Rica: Cultura Cinematográfica.

____ (1989) *Cine y censura en Costa Rica*. San José de Costa Rica: Cultura Cinematográfica.

CUBA

Adelman, A. (ed.) *A Guide to Cuban Cinema*. Pittsburgh: University of Pittsburgh.

Agramonte, A. (1966) *Cronología del cine cubano*. Havana: ICAIC.

Aprà, A. (ed.) (1981) *Teorie e pratiche del cinema cubano*. Venice/Pesaro: Marsilio Editori/Mostra Internazionale del Nuovo Cinema.

Aray, E. (1983) *Santiago Alvarez, cronista del Tercer Mundo*. Caracas: Cinemateca Nacional.

Chanan, M. (1985) *The Cuban Image: Cinema and Cultural Politics in Cuba*. London/Bloomington: British Film Institute/Indiana University Press.

Douglas, M. E. (1989) *Diccionario de cineastas cubanos, 1959–1987*. Havana/Mérida: Cinemateca de Cuba/Universidad de los Andes.

____ (1996) *La tienda negra: el cine en Cuba (1897–1990)*. Havana: Cinemateca Cubana.

Evora, J. A. (1994) *Tomás Gutiérrez Alea*. Huesca: Festival de Huesca/Agencia Española de Cooperación Internacional/Gobierno de Aragón (Expanded edition, Madrid: Cátedra/Filmoteca Española, 1996).

García Borrero, J. A. (2001) *Guía crítica del cine cubano de ficción*. Havana: Arte y Literatura.

____ (ed.) (2001) *Julio García Espinosa: las estrategias de un provocador*. Madrid/Huelva: Casa de América/Festival de Cine Iberoamericano de Huelva.

____ (2002) *La edad de la herejía: Ensayos sobre el cine cubano, su crítica y su público*. Santiago de Cuba: Oriente.

González, R. (2002) *Cine cubano: ese ojo que nos ve*. Havana: Plaza Mayor.

Jahnke, E. & M. Lichtenstein (1994) *Kubanischer Dokumentarfilm*. Berlin: Staatliches Filmarchiv der DDR.

Labaki, A. (1994) *O olho da revoluçao: o cinema-urgente de Santiago Alvarez*. São Paulo: Iluminuras (Spanish translation, *El ojo de la revolución: el cine urgente de Santiago Alvarez*. São Paulo: Iluminuras, 1994).

Larraz, E. (ed.) (2002) *Voir et lire Tomás Gutiérrez Alea*. Dijon: Hispanistica XX/Université de Bourgogne.

Myerson, M. (ed.) (1973) *Memories of Underdevelopment: The Revolutionary Films of Cuba*. New York: Grossman.

Oroz, S. (1985) *Tomás Gutiérrez Alea: os filmes que nao filmei*. Rio de Janeiro: Anima (Spanish translation, *Tomás Gutiérrez Alea: los filmes que no filmé*. Havana: Unión, 1989).

Paranaguá, P. A. (ed.) (1990) *Le cinéma cubain*. Paris: Centre Georges Pompidou.

Rodríguez, R. (1992) *El cine silente en Cuba*. Havana: Letras Cubanas.

Schumann, P. B. (1980) *Kino im Cuba, 1959–1979*. Frankfurt/Oberhausen: Klaus Dieter Vervuert/Westdeutsche Kurzfilmtage.

DOMINICAN REPUBLIC

Sáez, J. L. (1983) *Historia de un sueño importado: Ensayos sobre el cine en Santo Domingo*. Santo Domingo: Siboney.

ECUADOR

Granda Noboa, W. (1995) *El cine silente en Ecuador (1895–1935)*. Quito: Casa de la Cultura Ecuatoriana.

Serrano, J. L. (2001) *El nacimiento de una noción: apuntes sobre el cine ecuatoriano*. Quito: Acuario.

Villacres Moscoso, J. W. (1973) *Historia del cine ecuatoriano*. Guayaquil: Instituto de la Cinemateca Ecuatoriana.

FRENCH ANTILLES

Silou, O. (1991) *Le cinéma dans les Antilles Françaises*. Brussels: OCIC.

HAITI

Antonin, A. (1987) *Material para una prehistoria del cine haitiano/Matériel pour une prehistorire du cinéma haïtien*. Caracas: Foncine.

MEXICO

Almoina, H. (1980) *Notas para la historia del cine en México (1896–1925), 2 vols*. México: Universidad Nacional Autónoma de México.

Arredondo, I. (ed.) (2001) *Palabra de mujer: Historia oral de las directoras de cine mexicanas (1988–1994)*. México: Iberoamericana/Universidad Autónoma de Aguascalientes.

Aub, M. (1984) *Conversaciones con Buñuel*. Madrid: Aguilar (French translation, *Luis Buñuel, Entretiens avec Max Aub*. Paris: Pierre Belfond, 1991).

Avila Dueñas, I. H. (1994) *El cine mexicano de Luis Buñuel: estudio analítico de los argumentos y personajes*. México: Instituto Mexicano de Cinematografía.

Ayala Blanco, J. (1968) *La aventura del cine mexicano (1931–1967)*. México: Era.

____ (1974) *La búsqueda del cine mexicano (1968–1972)*. México: Universidad Nacional Autónoma de México.

____ (1986) *La condición del cine mexicano (1973-1985)*. México: Posada.

Berg, C. R. (1992) *Cinema of Solitude: A Critical Study of Mexican Film, 1967–1983*. Austin: University of Texas Press.

Ciuk, P. (2000) *Diccionario de directores del cine mexicano*. México: Consejo Nacional para la Cultura y las Artes/Cineteca Nacional.

Colina, J. de la (1984) *Emilio 'Indio' Fernández*. Huelva: Festival de Cine Iberoamericano.

Colina, J. de la & T. Pérez Turrent (1986) *Luis Buñuel: prohibido asomarse al interior*. México: Joaquín Mortiz/Planeta (French translation, *Conversations avec Luis Buñuel: il est dangereux de se pencher au-dehors*. Paris: Cahiers du Cinéma, 1993; English translation, *Objects of Desire: Conversations with Luis Buñuel*. New York: Marsilio, 1993).

Fuentes, V. (1993) *Buñuel en México*. Teruel: Instituto de Estudios Turolenses.

García, G. & D. R. Maciel (2001) *El cine mexicano a través de la crítica*. México/Ciudad Juárez: Universidad Nacional Autónoma de México/Instituto Mexicano de Cinematografía/Universidad Autónoma de Ciudad Juárez.

García Canclini, N. (ed.) (1994) *Los nuevos espectadores: cine, televisión y video en México*. México: Instituto Mexicano de Cinematografía.

García Riera, E. (1969–78) *Historia documental del cine mexicano, 9 vols*. México: Era (Revised and expanded edition, 18 vols., Guadalajara/México: Universidad de Guadalajara/Gobierno de Jalisco/Consejo Nacional para la Cultura y las Artes/Instituto Mexicano de Cinematografía, 1993–97).

____ (1984) *Fernando de Fuentes*. México: Cineteca Nacional.

____ (1987) *Emilio Fernández*. Guadalajara/México: Universidad de Guadalajara/Cineteca Nacional.

____ (1998) *Breve historia del cine mexicano*. México/Guadalajara: Mapa/Instituto Nacional de Cinematografía/Canal 22/Universidad de Guadalajara.

Hershfield, J. (1996) *Mexican Cinema, Mexican Woman, 1940–1950*. Tucson: University of Arizona Press.

Hershfield, J. & D. R. Maciel (eds) (1999) *Mexico's Cinema: A Century of Film and Filmmakers*. Wilmington: SR Books.

Isaac, A. (1993) *Conversaciones con Gabriel Figueroa*. Guadalajara: Universidad de Guadalajara/Universidad de Colima.

Martínez Ruiz, F. & R. Reynoso Serralde (eds) (1999) *Cien años de cine mexicano, 1896–1996* [CD-Rom] México Colima: Consejo Nacional para la Cultura y las Artes/Instituto Mexicano de Cinematografía/Universidad de Colima/Cenedic.

Martini, A. & N. Vidal (eds) (1997) *L'età d'oro del cinema messicano, 1933–1960*. Turin: Festival Internazionale Cinema Giovane/Lindau.

____ (eds) (1997) *Arturo Ripstein*. Turin: Festival Internazionale Cinema Giovane/Lindau.

Millán, M. (1999) *Derivas de un cine en femenino*. México: Universidad Nacional Autónoma de México/Miguel Ángel Porrúa.

Miquel, A. (ed.) (1996) *Cien años de cine en México*, special issues of *El Acordeón: Revista Cultural*, 17 and 18.

____ (1997) *Salvador Toscano*. Guadalajara/Puebla/Veracruz/México: Universidad de Guadalajara/Gobierno del Estado de Puebla/Universidad Veracruzana/Universidad Nacional Autónoma de México.

Monsiváis, C. & C. Bonfil (1994) *A través del espejo: el cine mexicano y su público*. México: El Milagro/Instituto Mexicano de Cinematografía.

Monsiváis, C., G. Figueroa Flores & N. Chalaman (1993) *Gabriel Figueroa: la mirada en el centro*. México: Porrúa.

Mora, C. J. (1982) *Mexican Cinema: Reflection of a Society, 1896–1980*. Berkeley: University of California Press.

Paranaguá, P. A. (ed.) (1992) *Le cinéma mexicain*. Paris: Centre Georges Pompidou (English translation, Mexican Cinema. London: British Film Institute, 1995).

____ (1998) *Arturo Ripstein: la espiral de la identidad*. Madrid: Cátedra/Filmoteca Española.

Pérez Turrent, T. (1985) *La fábrica de sueños: Estudios Churubusco, 1945–1985*. México: Instituo Mexicano de Cinematografía.

Ramírez, G. (1989) *Crónica del cine mudo mexicano*. México: Cineteca Nacional.

Reyes, A. de los (1981–1983) *Cine y sociedad en México, 1896-1930, 2 vols*. México: Universidad Nacional Autónoma de México.

____ (1987) *Medio siglo de cine mexicano*. México: Trillas.

____ (1996) *Dolores del Río*. México: Codumex.

Reyes de la Maza, L. (1973) *El cine sonoro en México*. México: Universidad Nacional Autónoma de México.

Reyes Nevares, B. (1974) *Trece directores del cine mexicano*. México: Secretaría de Educación Pública (English translation, *The Mexican Cinema: Interviews with Thirteen Directors*. Albuquerque: University of New Mexico Press, 1976).

Tuñón, J. (1998) *Mujeres de luz y sombra en el cine mexicano: la construcción de una imagen, 1939–1952*. México: El Colegio de México/Instituto Mexicano de Cinematografía.

Vega Alfaro, E. (ed.) (2000) *Microhistorias del cine en México*. Guadalajara/México: Universidad de Guadalajara/ Universidad Nacional Autónoma de México/Instituto Mexicano de Cinematografía/Cineteca Nacional/ Instituto Mora.

Viñas, M. (1987) *Historia de cine mexicano*. México: Universidad Nacional Autónoma de México/UNESCO.

____ (1992) *Indice cronológico del cine mexicano (1896–1992)*. México: Universidad Nacional Autónoma de México.

NICARAGUA

Cereghino, M. (1988) *'Senza il bacio finale': Cinema e rivoluzione in Nicaragua*. Rome: Edizioni Associate.

PERU

Bedoya, R. (1997) *Entre fauces y colmillos: las películas de Francisco Lombardi*. Huesca: Festival de Cine de Huesca.

____ (1992) *Cien años de cine en el Perú: una historia crítica*. Lima/Madrid: Universidad de Lima/Instituto de Cooperación Iberoamericana (Expanded edition, Lima, Universidad de Lima/Fondo de Desarrollo

Editorial, 1995).
____ (1997) *Un cine reencontrado: Diccionario ilustrado de las películas peruanas*. Lima: Universidad de Lima/Fondo de Desarrollo Editorial.
Benavente García, A. & Gutiérrez Vásquez, C. (1991) *La escuela cusqueña de cine*. Cuzco: Instituto Americano de Arte.
Carbone, G. (1992) *El cine en el Perú, 1897–1950*. Testimonios. Lima: Universidad de Lima.
____ (1993) *El cine en el Perú, 1950–1972*. Testimonios. Lima: Universidad de Lima.
Núñez Gorritti, V. (1990) *Pitas y alambre: la época de oro del cine peruano, 1936–1950*. Lima: Colmillo Blanco.

PUERTO RICA

Almodóvar Ronda, R. (ed.) (1994) *Idilio tropical: la aventura del cine en Puerto Rico*. San Juan de Puerto Rico: Banco Popular de Puerto Rico.

URUGUAY

Alvarez, J. C. (1957) *Breve historia del cine uruguayo*. Montevideo: Cinemateca Uruguaya.
Alvarez, L. (1993) *La casa sin espejos: perspectivas de la industria audiovisual uruguaya*. Montevideo: Fin de Siglo.
Hintz, E. (ed.) (1988) *Historia y filmografía del cine uruguayo*. Montevideo: Plaza.

VENEZUELA

Acosta, J. M. (1998) La década de la producción cinematográfica oficial: Venezuela, 1927–1938. Caracas: Fundación Cinemateca Nacional.
Aguirre, J. M. & M. Bisbal (1980) *El nuevo cine venezolano*. Caracas: Ateneo de Caracas.
Hernández, T. (ed.) (1997) *Panorama histórico del cine en Venezuela*. Caracas: Fundación Cinemateca Nacional.
Izaguirre, R. (1978) *El cine en Venezuela*. Caracas: Fundarte.
____ (1983) *Cine venezolano: largometrajes*. Caracas: Cinemateca Nacional/Fondo de Fomento Cinematográfico.
Marrosu, A. (1985) *Exploraciones en la historiografía del cine en Venezuela: campos, pistas e interrogantes*. Caracas: ININCO.
____ (1997) *'Don Leandro el Inefable': análisis fílmico, crónica y contexto*. Caracas: Fundación Cinemateca Nacional/ININCO.
Miranda, J. E. (1982) *Cine y poder en Venezuela*. Mérida: Universidad de los Andes.
____ (1994) *Palabras sobre imágenes: treinta años de cine venezolano*. Caracas: Monte Avila.
Tirado, R. (1988) *Memoria y notas del cine venezolano, 2 vols*. Caracas: Fundación Neumann.

INDEX